Breadcrumbs

Finding Your Way Home

Wanda Taylor

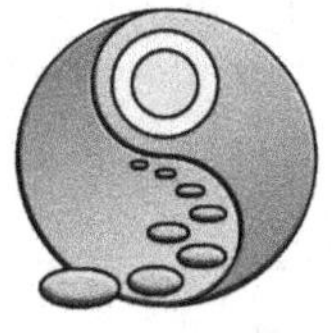

Breadcrumbs Publishing

Breadcrumbs: Finding Your Way Home

A Self-Coaching Journey

Published by Breadcrumbs Publishing, A division of Bay Centre Coaching Group LLC, Pensacola, Florida

First published 2026

ISBN: 979-8-9957547-0-1 (paperback) ISBN: 979-8-9957547-1-8 (ebook)

The information in this book is intended for personal growth and self-coaching purposes only. It is not a substitute for professional mental health treatment, therapy, counseling, or medical advice. If you are experiencing a mental health crisis or require clinical support, please seek the help of a licensed professional.

Free Community Membership: https://www.skool.com/breadcrumbs/about

Website: www.breadcrumbspublishing.com

Preface

Acknowledgements

It is in the release of all things that are drama in nature that I am free to see clearly and to remember what I've always known - I am the hero in my journey. I have tools and weapons to fight myself and the enemy, and I have discovered them to be the same. And now I also know that I came to use the returning home to fulfill my sacred contract. And I am grateful.   Wanda Taylor, May 4, 2026

My first memories were of wanting to "go home". Not that I remembered the place that I came from as much as I had a sense of oneness that I didn't feel any longer. I searched for home in the faces of all who cared for me and some who didn't. I searched for it in books, art, and music. I searched for it in relationships that temporarily felt like home. I searched for it in counselors' offices and at church. No one seemed to know what I meant, and so I continued alone. Slowly, I recognized the difference between being alone and being lonely. I made friends with alone and she invited me to come home to myself. And my journey finally came into sharp relief as I turned toward the sun.

To all of those who have walked with me for a time, I am grateful. Each of you taught me something, regardless of your intent. It is now grist for the mill. To all of those who encouraged me to write my first book, your voices spoke to me until I did. To all of my teachers along the way, thanks for giving me your perspective and also for teaching me about relative truth. To all of you who let me into your lives, thank you for teaching me empathy, restraint, and love in action. To my dearest and oldest friends, David, Scott, Laura, Ron, and Mike, you continue to be my oldest and sweetest foundation. And, to my family, my mother and daddy, and Grandma Martin, I would not be without you. A solo journey is no journey at all. Thank you all for being who you are.

My greatest knowledge that I am loved and that I have loved myself is the 44-year journey that I've taken with Steve Taylor. This journey gave me the gift of music and the interplay of words. It gave me the knowledge of energy management, patience, and searing presence. It taught me stillness in the face of incessant drama and the landmines of emotion. And it taught me it is possible to have an unshakable confidence not built on fear but built on right-principled love-in-action. And it taught me commitment to something larger than myself here on earth, as above. We have persevered through swamps of monsters, and we've felt the pull of angels. We have remained true to our own self-development and service to others. I suspect this fourth quarter will be the ride of our lives. And I'm grateful to be on it with you.

Introduction

My Legacy

For forty years, I've sat across from people who were lost.

Not lost in any way the world could see—many of them were accomplished, admired, successful by every external measure. But inside, they felt like strangers to themselves. Somewhere along the way, they had left pieces of who they were behind—abandoned dreams, silenced voices, needs that went unmet for so long they forgot they had them. They had spent years, sometimes decades, performing a version of themselves that the world approved of, until they could no longer remember who they were beneath the performance.

I've listened. I've witnessed. I've walked alongside thousands of people as they found their way back to themselves. And in doing so, I learned something I now want to share with you: the path home isn't as far as you think. You've been leaving yourself breadcrumbs all along.

Those moments of unexpected tears. The dreams that won't stop visiting you. The quiet ache when you see someone living a life that looks like the one you once wanted. The things that make you come alive, even when you've tried to bury them. These aren't random. They're breadcrumbs—left by the truest part of you, marking the trail back to wholeness.

Over four decades, I've seen this truth confirmed again and again: we don't need to become someone new. We need to remember who we were before the world told us who to be. Home isn't a place we create or earn—it's a place we return to. And it's been waiting for us all along.

This book is my legacy. I don't use that word lightly.

After forty years of coaching, after training hundreds of coaches, after bearing witness to more homecomings than I can count, I felt a pull to gather what I've learned and set it down somewhere it could live beyond me. Not because I have all the answers—I don't. But because I've seen patterns emerge, truths repeat themselves, and pathways reveal themselves so consistently that I couldn't keep them to myself any longer.

Everything in these pages comes from real work with real people. The questions I ask you are questions I've asked thousands of times. The reflections I offer have been refined through countless conversations. The exercises aren't theoretical—they're the same ones that have helped people reconnect with parts of themselves they thought were gone forever.

I wrote this book for the person who has achieved much but feels little. For the caregiver who has poured themselves out until they're empty. For the people-pleaser who has abandoned their own needs so completely they can't even name them anymore. For anyone who looks at their life and thinks, *this is good—so why do I feel so lost?*

I wrote it for you if you're ready.

You don't have to be broken to want to be whole. You don't have to have a dramatic story or a rock-bottom moment. You just have to be willing to follow the breadcrumbs—the ones you've been leaving yourself your entire life, even when you didn't know it.

This book is my attempt to walk beside you on that journey. Not as someone who has arrived, but as someone who has witnessed the path so many times that I can help you trust your own feet.

The way home is yours to walk. But you don't have to walk alone.

Table of Contents

How to Read this Book

The Dual Compass

You're holding a map to yourself.

Not a map I've drawn for you—I couldn't do that even if I wanted to. Your inner landscape is yours alone, shaped by experiences only you have lived, by losses only you have grieved, by dreams only you have quietly tended. No one else has walked where you've walked.

But here's what I've learned after forty years of sitting with people who felt lost: while every journey is unique, the *territory* has patterns. The woods where we wander have landmarks. And the breadcrumbs we leave ourselves—those signals from our authentic self—follow a logic we can learn to read.

This book offers you two compasses to help you find your way. Use one. Use both. Use whichever calls to you in this moment. There is no wrong way to journey home.

The Dual Compass

I've organized this book around two navigation systems that work together—or independently, depending on what you need.

Compass One: The Trail

The Trail is the linear path through transformation. It follows the natural arc of awakening: from realizing you're lost, to learning to see the breadcrumbs, to mapping the territory, to actively walking the path, to finally coming home. Five parts, eighteen chapters, each building on what came before.

Choose The Trail if:

- You want the full journey from beginning to end
- You prefer structured, sequential learning
- You're not sure where to start and want guidance
- You have time to immerse yourself in the complete process

The Trail takes you through:

- **Part One: Realizing You're in the Woods** — Awakening to the journey
- **Part Two: Learning to See the Breadcrumbs** — Developing Your Inner Witness
- **Part Three: Understanding the Territory** — Mapping Your Inner Landscape
- **Part Four: Following the Trail** — The Active Journey Home
- **Part Five: Coming Home** — Integration and Wholeness

Compass Two: The Questions

The Questions are six provocative inquiries that cut straight to what matters. They're the kind of questions a great coach asks—the ones that stop you in your tracks, that challenge your assumptions, that invite you to look at your life with fresh eyes. Each question opens a doorway into specific chapters.

Choose The Questions if:

- You know exactly what's keeping you up at night
- You want to dive into what's most alive for you right now
- You prefer to follow your intuition rather than a sequence
- You're returning to this book and want to focus on a specific area

The Questions and where they lead:

WHO do you think you are? → Chapters 1–3

Start here if you feel like a stranger to yourself, if you've lost touch with who you are beneath the roles you play, or if you sense there's more to you than the life you're currently living.

WHAT do you think you are doing? → Chapters 4–6

Start here if you feel disconnected from your inner wisdom, if you struggle to trust yourself, or if you want to learn how to recognize the signals your authentic self has been sending all along.

WHEN will you ever learn? → Chapters 7–10

Start here if you keep repeating the same patterns, if your boundaries feel eroded or non-existent, or if you suspect there are parts of yourself you've hidden away that need to be reclaimed.

WHERE do you think you are? → Chapters 11–12

Start here if you feel stuck in old programming, if you're ready to rewrite the code that's been running your life, or if you want to understand how to make choices from wholeness rather than wounds.

HOW are you going to make it in life? → Chapters 13–14

Start here if fear is stopping you, if perfectionism has you paralyzed, or if you're ready to move through resistance instead of waiting for it to disappear.

WHY are you here? → Chapters 15–18

Start here if you're searching for purpose and meaning, if you want to understand what wholeness actually looks like in daily life, or if you're ready to consider the legacy you're creating by who you're becoming.

The Coach Approach: You Are the Expert

This is a self-coaching workbook, which means something important: **you are the expert on your own life.**

I'm not here to tell you what's wrong with you or to prescribe solutions. A great coach doesn't do that. A great coach asks questions that help you access your own wisdom, reflects back patterns you might not see, and holds space for you to discover what you already know but haven't yet claimed.

That's what this book does. Through each chapter, I'll offer you frameworks for understanding, questions for reflection, and exercises for integration. But the answers? Those come from you. They've always been in you. My job is simply to help you find them.

This means there's no failing here. There's no "doing it wrong." If a question doesn't resonate, skip it. If an exercise brings up more than you expected, pause. If you need to close the book and come back in a week, do that. This is your journey, at your pace, in your way.

What You'll Find in These Pages

Each chapter follows a rhythm designed to support both understanding and integration:

The Opening Question

Every chapter begins with a provocative coaching question—a variation of one of the six Reporter Questions tailored to that chapter's focus. Sit with it before you read. Let it work on you. Notice what comes up.

The Teaching

I'll share frameworks, research, and insights from forty years of coaching. This isn't theory for theory's sake—it's the understanding that makes self-coaching possible. You can't navigate territory you don't understand.

The Reflection

Questions designed to help you apply the teaching to your own life. These aren't quizzes with right answers. They're invitations to look inward, to notice what's true for you, to begin connecting the dots of your own experience.

The Practice

Exercises and activities that move insight into integration. Reading about wholeness isn't the same as experiencing it. These practices are where the real work happens—where understanding becomes embodied, where breadcrumbs become a path.

The Breadcrumb

Each chapter closes with a single key insight to carry forward—a breadcrumb for your journey. These build on each other, creating a trail of wisdom you're gathering as you go.

Building Your Mindset Mind Map

As you move through this book, you'll be creating something I call your **Mindset Mind Map**—a visual representation of your inner landscape. This isn't a onetime exercise but an evolving document that grows with each chapter.

Think of it as the map you're drawing of yourself: your values, your beliefs, your patterns, your cast of characters, your boundaries, your breadcrumbs. By the end of this journey, you'll have something you've never had before—a clear picture of the operating system that's been running your life, and the tools to rewrite the code that no longer serves you.

Permission to Wander

Here's something important: **you have permission to use this book however it serves you.**

Read it straight through. Flip to the chapter that's calling you. Do the exercises in order. Skip around. Read it once, then return in six months and read it again—you'll be a different person, and different wisdom will emerge.

Some people devour this book in a weekend. Others take a year, sitting with one chapter at a time. Some do every exercise; others read reflectively without writing a word. All of these approaches work. The only wrong way to read this book is to let perfectionism stop you from starting.

Trust yourself. If something resonates deeply, stay with it. If something doesn't land, let it go—it might make sense later, or it might not be for you. You are your own best guide.

A Word About Discomfort

This work will sometimes be uncomfortable. That's not a sign you're doing it wrong—it's often a sign you're doing it right.

When we look at the parts of ourselves we've hidden away, when we examine patterns we've been running on autopilot, when we question beliefs we've never questioned—it can feel unsettling. You might experience sadness, anger, grief, or resistance. You might want to put the book down. You might feel worse before you feel better.

This is normal. This is part of the journey. The breadcrumbs lead not only through sunny clearings—they also lead through shadowy woods. But they always, always lead home.

That said, this book is not a substitute for professional support. If you're dealing with trauma, severe depression, or other mental health challenges, please work with a qualified therapist or counselor. Self-coaching is powerful, but it has its limits. Knowing when you need additional support is itself a form of wisdom.

Continuing the Journey

This book is complete in itself—everything you need for the journey home is in these pages. But if you want to go deeper, additional resources are available:

The Companion Course

A guided experience that walks you through the book with video teachings, extended exercises, and additional support. Ideal if you want more structure or prefer learning through multiple formats.

Coaching Services

For those who want personalized guidance, one-on-one and group coaching options are available. Sometimes the journey home benefits from a fellow traveler who can witness your path and reflect what you might not see.

Community

Connection with others on the same journey. Because while the path home is ultimately one you walk yourself, you don't have to walk it alone.

Details on all resources can be found at the end of this book.

The Journey Begins

You picked up this book for a reason.

Maybe you can name it—a specific ache, a question that won't leave you alone, a longing for something you can't quite articulate. Or maybe you can't name it yet. Maybe you just knew, somehow, that this was meant for you.

Either way, trust that knowing. It's a breadcrumb.

The path home isn't as far as you think. You've been leaving yourself clues all along—in your tears, your dreams, your longings, your moments of unexpected aliveness. Everything you need is already within you. This book is simply a lantern for the journey, a companion for the walk, a reminder that you know more than you think you know.

So, take a breath. Choose your compass. And let's begin.

The breadcrumbs are waiting.

THE DUAL COMPASS

Two Ways to Navigate Your Journey Home

Use one. Use both. There is no wrong way to journey home.

COMPASS ONE *The Trail*	COMPASS TWO *The Questions*	CHAPTERS
Part One *Realizing You're in the Woods*	**WHO do you think you are?** *When you feel like a stranger to yourself*	1-3
Part Two *Learning to See the Breadcrumbs*	**WHAT do you think you are doing?** *When you've lost touch with your inner wisdom*	4-6
Part Three *Understanding the Territory*	**WHEN will you ever learn?** *When the same patterns keep repeating*	7-10
Part Four *Following the Trail*	**WHERE do you think you are? · HOW are you going to make it?** *When you're ready to rewrite the code and move through fear*	11-14
Part Five *Coming Home*	**WHY are you here?** *When you're ready for purpose, wholeness, and*	15-18

Part One: Realizing You're In the Woods

Awakening to the Journey

Chapter One

The Call That Brought You Here

WHO do you think you are...when the achievements stop working?

"Hiraeth: the longing for a home your soul remembers but your mind has forgotten." -Welsh word and concept

There is no direct English translation for the concept of hiraeth. It describes a deep longing for a home that you sense exists, even if you can't quite name it. It's homesickness for yourself. Whether you've heard the word before, I imagine you recognize the feeling. That quiet call beneath the surface of your life. That whisper, wondering if this is really all there is. That's hiraeth. It's not a sign that something is wrong. It's a call, an invitation, guiding you back to what you never truly lost. It's the first breadcrumb that you left for yourself, the one that's been calling you home all along.

Something brought you here.

Maybe you can name it—a specific moment when the life you'd built so carefully stopped fitting quite right. A morning when you caught your reflection and didn't recognize the person looking back. A conversation where you heard yourself say "I'm fine" and felt the lie land heavy in your chest.

Maybe you can't name it at all. Maybe it's a hum beneath everything, a quiet dissonance you've learned to talk over, work around, numb away. You've done what you were supposed to do, checked boxes, met expectations, built something that looks—on the outside—like a life worth envying. And yet, here you are.

There's a word for what you're feeling, though it might not be the word you'd choose. You might say, "I'm functioning, showing up, getting things done. It's not exactly depression or anxiety, though anxiety visits. It's more like displacement—as if you're living in someone else's house, or wearing a coat that almost fits but never feels warm enough. Maybe the house became too small. Or maybe it just feels too big."

You are not alone in this. Not even close.

The Successful and the Searching

In 40 years of coaching and human development work, I've sat across from thousands who, by all measures, seemed to have figured it out.

Executives who commanded boardrooms. Parents who raised remarkable children. Entrepreneurs who were imaginative and committed. Healers who held space for everyone's pain but their own.

They came to me not because their lives were falling apart, but because something essential was missing—and they couldn't name what it was. I call them the successful and the searching. They've achieved. They've accumulated. They've done everything right. And somewhere along the way, they've lost themselves.

Maybe you recognize yourself in this description. Maybe you've felt the uneasy guilt that comes with wanting more when you already have so much. You've asked yourself, "What do I have to complain about? Other people have real problems. I should be grateful."

Gratitude and longing can coexist. You can appreciate your life and still sense that something is misaligned. You can be thankful for what you've built and still feel like a stranger in your own story.

This isn't ingratitude. It's awareness. It's the call.

Fragmented, Not Broken

You are not broken. You are fragmented. There's a profound difference. Fragmented means you came into this world whole, and then life happened. Pieces of you were set aside to meet expectations. Parts of your authentic self were tucked away for safekeeping when it wasn't safe to express them. Dreams were deferred, desires were buried, and truths were swallowed.

You didn't break. You adapted. You fragmented yourself into the pieces that were acceptable, rewarded, and safe, leaving the rest behind.

The good news? Those pieces aren't gone. They're waiting. And the call you're feeling right now? It's coming from them.

Reclaiming, Not Fixing

Coaching work isn't about fixing you. It has never been. This work calls for something different: reclamation.

Reclamation isn't about becoming someone new. It's about remembering who you were before the world convinced you to be someone else. It's not about adding more skills, more knowledge, more self-improvement strategies. It's not about adding more. It's about returning to what's always been there.

I love to tell the story of Michelangelo's sculpture, David. When asked about his process, some say Michelangelo replied that he simply chipped away everything that was not David. The masterpiece wasn't created—it was revealed. It had been waiting inside the marble all along.

This is the work ahead—not building a new self, but revealing the one that's always been there. Chip away at expectations and roles performed for so long, until what remains is unmistakably you.

The Quiet Rebellion of Your Soul

That restlessness you feel. The one you've tried to silence with busyness, with achievement, with the next goal and the next and the next, is not a problem to be solved. It's not a character flaw or a symptom of never being satisfied. It's information.

Something in you has been pushing back for a while, against a life that doesn't quite fit. Every time you feel that twinge of emptiness after accomplishing something you thought would fulfill you—that's information. Every time you watch someone living the life you believe you should be living and feel an unexpected pang of envy—that's information. Every time you're moved to tears by a song or a story and can't explain why—that's information.

These moments are breadcrumbs—signals from the part of you that knows the difference between a life that looks right and one that truly fits. They've been accumulating all your life, even if you didn't notice you were leaving them.

The call that brought you here isn't new. You've been hearing it for years, maybe decades. You just finally stopped long enough to listen.

The Trail You've Already Been Walking

Here's the truth: you've been on this path longer than you know.

Every time you felt restless, you heard the call. Each time you questioned if this was all there was, you paid attention. Each choice to honor something true in yourself rather than something expected, left a breadcrumb.

You didn't start this journey when you picked up this book. It began the first time you noticed the gap between your performance and your true self. It started in quiet moments, wondering how things might've been if you'd made truer choices.

This book isn't the beginning of your journey home. It's a companion for the path you've already been walking. A lantern for the trail you've already been on, even when you couldn't see it. A guide to help you trust the breadcrumbs you've been leaving yourself all along.

What the Breadcrumbs Are

Let me tell you what I mean by breadcrumbs, because this concept is at the very heart of everything we'll explore together, and it's the essence of the work of coaching, growing, and learning.

You may remember the fairy tale of Hansel and Gretel—two children who left a trail of breadcrumbs through the forest so they could find their way back home. The story is usually told as a cautionary tale: the birds ate the crumbs, and the children got lost.

But I've always read it differently.

The children knew, even as they were being led somewhere they didn't want to go, that they would need to find their way back. They had the foresight to mark the trail. They trusted their future selves to find the breadcrumbs and follow them back home.

You've been doing the same thing your entire life.

Every time you felt a flash of joy doing something that had nothing to do with productivity or approval—that was a breadcrumb. Every recurring interest, every persistent curiosity, every moment when you felt most like yourself—breadcrumbs. The career you fantasized about before "practical" took over. The creative pursuit you set aside because it wasn't "serious."

The way certain music moves you. The places that feel familiar even when you've never been there. The values you hold that no one had to teach you.

These aren't random. They're not distractions from your "real life". They're trail markers. Evidence of who you are when you're not trying to be anything for anyone else.

The birds didn't eat your breadcrumbs. They're still there, waiting to be noticed.

Why We Wander

If we come into this world whole, how do we end up so far from home?

It happens slowly. So slowly that you don't notice it is happening at all.

It starts with love. Your parents, your caregivers—most of them loved you the best way they knew how. But their own conditioning, their own limitations, their own unexamined beliefs also shaped them. They passed down what they knew, and these became your filters. They rewarded the parts of you that made sense to them and discouraged the parts that didn't fit, and these became your patterns. Not out of cruelty, but out of habit, out of fear, out of their own unfinished business.

Then came school, where you learned that your worth could be measured, ranked, and compared. Where certain kinds of intelligence were celebrated and others ignored. Where you figured out quickly which parts of yourself earned approval and which parts were better kept hidden.

Then came culture, the vast, invisible life curriculum that taught you what success looks like, what beauty looks like, what a good life looks like. Messages so pervasive you absorbed them without question, never asking whose definition of "good" you were chasing.

Then came religion, perhaps, or its absence. Community, with its expectations. Career, with its demands. Relationships, with their negotiations and compromises. Each one asks you to adapt, to fit, to become a version of yourself that works for the situation at hand.

None of this was necessarily wrong. Adaptation is how we survive. Fitting in is how we belong. But somewhere along the way, the adaptations became the identity. The role became the reality. And the whole, authentic person you came in as got buried so deep you forgot it was there.

You didn't lose yourself in one dramatic moment. You lost yourself one small compromise at a time, each one so reasonable it didn't feel like a loss at all.

Until one day, you looked around and realized you were living a life that didn't feel like yours at all.

The Price We Pay for Wandering

Living disconnected from yourself has a cost. It's a cost you've been paying so long that you may have stopped noticing it.

It shows up as exhaustion that sleep doesn't fix—because it's not physical tiredness; it's the fatigue of performing.

It shows up as relationships that look good on paper but feel hollow in practice—because people are connecting with the version of you that you present, not the one you actually are.

It shows up as success that doesn't satisfy—because you're achieving goals that were never really yours to begin with.

It shows up as a persistent, low-grade tension, the background awareness that something's off, that the life you're living doesn't match who you know yourself to be.

It shows up as the Sunday evening dread, the midlife questioning, the "is this all there is?" that haunts your quieter moments.

And it shows up as that longing—that hiraeth—that brought you to this page.

The cost is real. But here's what I want you to understand: you've been paying it for a reason. The adaptations that took you away from yourself also kept you safe. The roles you played helped you feel you belonged. The fragmentation wasn't a failure—it was a strategy that worked until it didn't.

You did what you had to do.

And now you're ready to do something different.

The Invitation

This book is an invitation, nothing more, nothing less.

It's not a demand. It's not a prescription. It's not someone telling you what's wrong with you and how to fix it.

It's an invitation to get curious about your own life. To look at the patterns you've been running and ask whether they're still serving you. To examine the beliefs you absorbed without questioning and decide which ones you actually agreed with. To reconnect with the parts of yourself that you set aside and see if they still fit.

It's an invitation to follow the breadcrumbs.

I won't pretend this work is easy. Looking honestly at your life takes courage. Questioning long-held beliefs can be unsettling. Reconnecting with parts of yourself you abandoned years ago can bring up grief for the time you lost.

But I can tell you this: the path home is real. I've walked it myself, and I'm still walking it. I've witnessed thousands of others walk it. And it leads somewhere worth going.

Not to a perfect life. Not to a life without challenges or complexity. But to a life that fits. A life where the outside matches the inside. Where you recognize yourself in your own choices. Where you can finally stop performing and just be.

That's what home means. And it's closer than you think.

How to Use This Chapter and This Book

Before we go further, I want to tell you how this book is designed to work.

This is not a book you simply read. It's a book you experience. Each chapter will offer you concepts to consider, but understanding alone doesn't create change. Transformation happens when insight meets action—when you take what you're learning and apply it to the specific territory of your own life.

That's why each chapter includes reflection questions and practices. These aren't optional extras. They're where the real work happens. I encourage you to linger, to resist the urge to rush through to the next chapter before you've sat with the current one. That's why this book comes with a digital companion, a private space where you can journal, reflect, and do the deeper work that each chapter invites through integrative exercises. You won't find lined pages in this book asking you to write in the margins. Instead, you have a free, dedicated place to return to again and again because this isn't a one-time journey. The trail home is one where you'll walk many times, and each time you return, you'll see something new. You can access your digital companion by setting up a free, private account at https://journalengineportal.com/login.

And remember, you are your own expert. I'm not here to tell you what's true for you. I'm here to ask questions that help you discover, rediscover, or uncover it for yourself. Trust your responses. Trust your resistance. Trust your own knowing.

This is your journey. I'm just walking beside you for a while. Thank you for that privilege.

Pause and Reflect

Before moving to the next chapter, take a moment to sit with these questions. You don't need perfect answers. You don't even need to write anything down if that doesn't serve you. Just let the questions work on you.

When did you first sense that something was missing—that the life you were living didn't quite match the life you were meant for?

What breadcrumbs have you been leaving for yourself? What moments, interests, longings, or dreams keep surfacing, no matter how many times you've pushed them aside?

What does the wandering cost you? And what survival purpose did it serve?

What would it mean for you to come home to yourself?

The Breadcrumb

Each chapter will close with a single breadcrumb—a key insight to carry forward on your journey.

Here is the first:

The call you've been feeling isn't a sign that something is wrong with you. It's a sign that something is right, something deep within you that still remembers wholeness and refuses to let you settle for less. Trust it. It's leading you home.

Going Deeper: Your Digital Companion

The questions above are meant to stir something in you—to begin the inner conversation. But real integration happens when you take time to explore your responses more fully. That's why this book comes with a digital companion, a private space where you can journal, reflect, and do the deeper work that each chapter invites. You won't find lined pages in this book asking you to write in the margins. Instead, you'll have a dedicated place to return to again and again—because this isn't a one-time journey. The trail home is one you'll walk many times, and each time you return, you'll see something new.

In your digital companion, you'll find the following exercises for Chapter 1:

The Breadcrumb Inventory — Identifying the trail markers you've been leaving yourself: joys without purpose, recurring themes, and the envy map

The Fragmentation Timeline — Mapping when and how you adapted, fragmented, and left pieces of yourself behind

The Cost and the Purpose — Understanding both what the wandering has cost you and the survival purpose it served

A Letter from Home — Writing to yourself from the place of wholeness you're journeying toward

The First Breadcrumb Ritual — A simple practice to mark the beginning of your journey

Your Mindset Mind Map — Foundation — Beginning the visual map of your inner landscape that you'll build throughout this journey

---

The trail begins here. In Chapter 2, we'll explore how you got lost in the first place—the programming, the conditioning, and the Life Code that was written for you before you could choose for yourself. Understanding how you wandered is the first step to finding your way home.

Chapter Two

How You Got Lost

WHO do you think you are...beneath the programming?

"What lies behind us and what lies before us are tiny matters compared to what lies within us." — Oliver Wendell Holmes

"Be yourself; everyone else is already taken." — Oscar Wilde

You arrived as a miracle of staggering complexity—trillions of cells orchestrating a symphony of life, billions of neurons reaching for connection, a consciousness so vast that science still cannot explain how you became aware that you exist at all. You arrived whole. Complete. Hardwired for love, curiosity, and belonging.

Then something happened.

Not something dramatic, necessarily. Not a single wound or trauma (though for some of us, there was that too). Something quieter. Something so gradual that you didn't notice it happening.

The world began to rewrite you.

In this chapter, we'll explore how you got from there to here—from that original wholeness to the fragmented sense of self that brought you to this book. Not to assign blame or reopen wounds, but to understand. Because when you can see the code that's been running your life, you can finally begin to rewrite it.

The Miracle You Arrived As

Before we talk about what was done to you, let's talk about what you actually are. Because the story you've been told about yourself—that you're limited, flawed, not quite enough—is a story written over something far more magnificent.

The Miraculous Body

You are, right now, hosting approximately 37.2 trillion cells—each one performing thousands of functions every second, communicating with other cells, maintaining the impossible balance that keeps you alive. You didn't have to learn how to do this. Your body simply knows.

Your brain contains roughly 86 billion neurons, connected by an estimated 100 trillion synaptic connections. If you stretched out all the neural pathways in your brain, they would reach to the moon and back. This is the hardware you were born with—a processing system more sophisticated than any computer ever built.

But here's what's even more remarkable: your brain isn't your only intelligence center.

Your heart contains approximately 40,000 neurons—its own neural network, sometimes called the "heart brain." Research from the HeartMath Institute has shown that your heart sends more signals to your brain than your brain sends to your heart. When we talk about "following your heart" or having a "gut feeling," we're not speaking metaphorically. These are actual neurological events.

Speaking of your gut: it contains over 500 million neurons—more than your spinal cord—and produces approximately 95% of your body's serotonin, the neurotransmitter associated with wellbeing and happiness. Your gut literally helps regulate your mood through its own intelligence.

You are not a brain piloting a body. You are an integrated system of multiple intelligences, all working in concert. This is what you arrived as.

The Miraculous Mind

In the first years of your life, your brain was forming more than one million new neural connections every second. By the time you were six years old, you had absorbed approximately 13,000 words and could understand complex social dynamics, recognize faces in a crowd, and navigate spatial environments—all without formal instruction.

Your mind can process an image in as little as 13 milliseconds—faster than the blink of an eye. It can store unlimited information in long-term memory, organize it into patterns, and retrieve it decades later through a single scent, song, or sensation.

Perhaps most remarkably, you came equipped with mirror neurons—brain cells that fire both when you perform an action and when you watch someone else perform it. This is the neurological basis of empathy, of learning through observation, of feeling what others feel. You were literally wired for connection from your first breath.

And then there's your Default Mode Network—the part of your brain that activates when you're not focused on the external world. This is where self-reflection happens, where you integrate experiences into identity, where you construct the ongoing story of who you are. No other species has this capacity for self-narrative to the degree that humans do.

Here's what neuroscience has confirmed, for our purposes: neuroplasticity is real. Your brain continues to change and reorganize throughout your entire life. The patterns laid down in childhood are powerful, yes—but they are not permanent. The code can be rewritten. We'll come back to this.

The Miraculous Spirit

And then there's the part that science cannot fully explain: consciousness itself.

Somehow, you are aware that you exist. You don't just process information—you experience it. You don't just react to stimuli—you make meaning of it. You can think about your own thinking. You can observe your own observing. This capacity for metacognition—for standing outside your own mind and reflecting on it—is perhaps the greatest mystery in the known universe.

Viktor Frankl, the psychiatrist who survived the Nazi concentration camps, discovered something essential about human consciousness: even in the most horrific circumstances, humans can choose their response. "Everything can be taken from a man but one thing," he wrote, "the last of the human freedoms—to choose one's attitude in any given set of circumstances." This capacity for choice, even in the face of suffering, points to something in us that transcends mere biology.

You came with the capacity for awe—for being stopped in your tracks by beauty, by vastness, by the sheer improbability of existence. You came with the capacity to create meaning, to make art, to love beyond reason, to sacrifice for others, to imagine futures that don't yet exist, and then work to create them.

This is you. This is what you are. Not a collection of problems to be fixed, but a miracle that got temporarily buried under programming it didn't choose.

Now let's look at what that programming actually is.

What Conditioning Actually Is

In coaching, we talk about conditioning as the process by which you learned automatic responses to the world. Conditioning isn't inherently bad—it's how you learned to walk, speak, and navigate your environment. Without it, you'd have to consciously think through every action, every decision, every social interaction.

The problem isn't conditioning itself. The problem is unconscious conditioning that no longer serves you—patterns installed without your consent that now run in the background of your life, shaping your choices without your awareness.

Conditioning happens through three primary mechanisms:

Repetition: Messages you heard over and over became embedded as "truth." If you were told repeatedly that you were "too sensitive," or "not athletic," or "the smart one," those messages became part of your identity code.

Emotional Intensity: Experiences charged with strong emotion—positive or negative—create deeper neural pathways than neutral experiences. A single moment of humiliation in fourth grade can create a pattern that runs for forty years.

Modeling: You absorbed how to be in the world by watching the people around you. How your parents handled conflict, expressed (or suppressed) emotion, related to money, treated their bodies—all of this became data your developing mind incorporated.

Conditioning becomes problematic when it's:

Unconscious: running without your awareness

Outdated: appropriate for childhood but limiting in adulthood

Borrowed: someone else's values or beliefs masquerading as your own

Conflicting: at odds with your authentic self

A helpful distinction: adaptive conditioning serves your well-being and helps you navigate life effectively. Limiting conditioning constrains your choices and keeps you smaller than you actually are. Both types are installed through the same mechanisms. The difference is in the outcome.

Our work together is about becoming conscious of your conditioning—seeing it clearly so you can evaluate it objectively. Not to throw it all out, but to keep what serves you and release what doesn't.

The Layered Life Code

I find it helpful to think of conditioning as a Life Code—an operating system that runs beneath your conscious awareness, shaping your perceptions, reactions, and choices. Like any operating system, your Life Code has multiple layers:

The Biological Layer: Your genetic inheritance, your temperament, your body's predispositions. This is your hardware—the platform on which everything else runs. You came with certain tendencies toward introversion or extroversion, sensitivity or resilience, risk-taking or caution. This layer is the least changeable, though even here epigenetics shows the environment and choice can influence that gene expression.

The Neurological Layer: The neural pathways formed by your earliest experiences—patterns laid down before you had language to describe them. Your attachment style, your baseline stress response, your nervous system's defaults. Much of this was installed in the first three years of life, before conscious memory. This is why you sometimes react in ways that surprise you—the code was written before "you" (as you know yourself) existed.

The Psychological Layer: Your beliefs about yourself, others, and the world. Your identity stories. Your cognitive patterns. This layer develops throughout childhood and adolescence as you make meaning of your experiences. It's where statements like "I'm not good enough" or "People always leave" get encoded.

The Cultural Layer: The invisible operating system of your society—definitions of success, beauty, worth. Scripts for how to be a man, a woman, a good person. Rules about what's acceptable to want, feel, or express. This layer is particularly insidious because it masquerades as "just the way things are."

The Relational Layer: Patterns for how you connect (or disconnect) from others. How you define love, how you express needs, and what you expect from intimacy. Strategies for belonging that you developed in your family of origin and carried forward.

The Spiritual/Meaning Layer: Your frameworks for ultimate questions. What you believe about purpose, about consciousness, about what happens after death. Whether the universe is friendly or hostile. Whether you matter.

Each layer influences the others. A belief about yourself (psychological) might originate in a childhood experience (neurological) that confirmed a cultural message (cultural), which now affects how you show up in relationships (relational) and what you believe is possible for your life (spiritual).

This interconnection is why change can feel so hard—and also why a shift in one layer can cascade through all the others. When you update your Life Code, the effects ripple through your entire system.

The Original Self

Beneath all this code—beneath the layers of conditioning, the decades of programming, the stories you've been told about who you are—there exists something that was never touched by any of it.

I call it your Original Self.

This is the you that existed before your parents' anxieties became your own. Before school taught you that your worth was measured in grades and gold stars. Before culture handed you a script for success that may have had nothing to do with what actually makes you come alive.

The Original Self isn't a past version of you that you need to return to chronologically. It's the essence of you that has always been present—watching from beneath the adaptations, the performances, the personas you developed to survive and belong.

Think of it like this: when Michelangelo was asked how he created his statue of David, he reportedly said, "I saw the angel in the marble and carved until I set him free." David was always in the marble—Michelangelo's job was to remove what wasn't David.

Your Original Self is David. The conditioning is the marble. Our work together isn't about adding something you lack. It's about chipping away at what was never really you to begin with.

The World's Rewrites

Now let's look at how the programming actually happened—where these layers came from and how they got installed.

Family Programs

Your first programmers were your family, and they began coding before you could speak.

From your earliest moments, you were absorbing data: Is the world safe or threatening? Will my needs be met? Am I welcome here? The answers to these questions—communicated through touch, tone, presence, and absence—became your baseline programming. This happened at the neurological and psychological layers simultaneously.

By the time you were verbal, the programming became more explicit. Messages about who you were, what was expected of you, what emotions were acceptable, what dreams were realistic, and what kind of person you should become.

Some of this programming was direct: "You're the responsible one." "Don't be so dramatic." "Money doesn't grow on trees." "We don't talk about those things."

But most of it was indirect—absorbed through watching how your family members lived their lives. How did your parents handle conflict? What happened when someone expressed anger, sadness, or joy? What did success look like? What did love require?

None of this was malicious. Your parents were passing along the programming they received, trying to equip you for the world as they understood it. But their code—their beliefs, their limitations, their unresolved wounds—became your inheritance.

As the saying goes, we don't inherit just eye color and temperament from our families. We inherit unfinished emotional business.

Education Programs

Then came school—a system designed, in many ways, to standardize you.

Let me be clear: education itself isn't the problem. Learning is a profound human need. But the way most education systems operate installs some very specific code:

Your worth is measured by external evaluation. Grades, test scores, rankings. Someone else decides if you're good enough.

There's a right answer, and your job is to find it. Creativity and divergent thinking take a back seat to compliance and correct responses.

Sit still, be quiet, and follow instructions. Your body's needs are subordinate to the schedule. Your curiosity is funneled into predetermined channels.

Competition determines your place in the hierarchy. Success means outperforming others. Collaboration is often called cheating.

By the time you finished your formal education, you had spent approximately 15,000 hours in this system. That's a lot of conditioning. And much of it directly contradicted the miracle you arrived as—being wired for curiosity, movement, connection, and intrinsic motivation.

Cultural Programs

Beyond family and school, you swam in the invisible waters of culture—and fish don't notice water.

Culture operates at the most invisible layer of your Life Code because it presents itself as reality rather than perspective. It's "just the way things are." It's "common sense." It's so ubiquitous that questioning it feels almost impossible—like questioning gravity.

But cultural programming is programming, nonetheless. And it shapes everything:

What success looks like. In American culture, success often means wealth, status, productivity, and upward mobility. But these are cultural definitions, not universal truths. Other cultures have very different measures of a life well-lived.

What your body should look like. Beauty standards are cultural inventions that change across time and place. The current standard you're measuring yourself against would be unrecognizable to someone from a different era or culture.

What emotions are acceptable? Cultural scripts dictate which emotions can be expressed and by whom. Men and women receive very different programming about anger, sadness, and vulnerability.

What you should want. The house, the car, the career trajectory, the relationship milestones. These desires feel personal, but are often cultural downloads.

The fish is starting to see the water. That's the first step.

Religious and Spiritual Programs

If you grew up within a religious tradition, you received additional layers of code about the nature of reality, your relationship to the divine, and your fundamental worthiness.

Some of this programming may have been beautiful—a sense of belonging to something larger, rituals that marked life's passages, a framework for meaning and morality. Spirituality itself is a profound human capacity.

But religious programming can also install code that works against your wholeness:

Original sin narratives that teach you to distrust your own nature

Shame-based sexuality that divorces you from your own body

Rigid rules about who's acceptable and who isn't

Fear-based compliance rather than love-based connection

External authority positioned above your own inner knowing.

The spiritual layer of your Life Code deserves careful examination—not to discard spirituality, but to distinguish between programming that connects you to something larger and programming that keeps you small and afraid.

Relationship Programs

Finally, your relationships themselves became sources of programming.

Every significant relationship taught you something about what to expect from connection. Every heartbreak, betrayal, and disappointment became data that shaped your future approach to love and intimacy.

If you learned that love was conditional, you may now perform for affection rather than trusting you're lovable as you are.

If you learned that vulnerability was dangerous, you may now keep parts of yourself hidden—even from those closest to you.

If you learned your needs were "too much," you may now minimize what you require, settling for less than what nourishes you.

Relationship patterns are self-reinforcing: we attract and are attracted to dynamics that confirm our existing programming. This isn't random. It's the code running as designed.

Life Code: The Operating System You Didn't Write

Put all these layers together—biological, neurological, psychological, cultural, relational, spiritual—and you have your Life Code. It's the operating system running beneath your conscious awareness, influencing nearly everything you think, feel, and do.

Here's the thing about your Life Code: you didn't write most of it.

Other people's beliefs became your beliefs. Other people's fears became your fears. Other people's definitions of success, worth, love, and possibility became the invisible boundaries of your life.

This isn't about blame. Your parents did the best they could with the code they inherited. Your teachers were operating within systems they didn't design. Your culture is the water everyone swims in. No one sat down and decided to limit you.

But the result is the same: you've been running on software you never chose, and much of it was written to serve someone else's needs—or no one's needs at all.

Your Life Code contains:

Installed Programs: Beliefs and behaviors that were programmed, like "I have to be perfect to be loved," or "Asking for help is weakness," or "Money is the root of evil."

Default Settings: Automatic responses that run without conscious choice—like people-pleasing, conflict avoidance, or shutting down when emotions get intense.

Background Processes: Patterns running beneath your awareness that consume energy and shape your life—like chronic self-criticism, hypervigilance, or the constant need to prove yourself.

Bugs and Glitches: Code that made sense once but now creates problems—like the self-protection that kept you safe as a child but now keeps you isolated as an adult.

In the digital companion, you'll audit your own Life Code—to identify what's running and evaluate whether it still serves you. For now, just let this framework settle. Start noticing moments when you might be operating from code rather than choice.

The Cost of Living Someone Else's Program

When you remember what you actually are—37 trillion cells working in concert, a consciousness that can contemplate its own existence, a being wired for love and meaning and awe—you begin to see the true cost of living someone else's program.

The cost is that the miracle gets constrained.

The cost is exhaustion.

Running programs that don't align with your authentic self takes enormous energy. It's like running software that wasn't designed for your operating system—everything works harder than it should.

The cost is disconnection.

When you're performing a version of yourself that others programmed, you can't be truly known. Even when you're surrounded by people, you're alone—because the "you" they're relating to isn't really you.

The cost is an unlived life.

Every path not taken because of someone else's fears. Every dream dismissed because it didn't fit the program. Every relationship diminished because you couldn't show up as your whole self. Every unique expression of the miracle you are that never made it into the world.

The cost is the quiet ache you know too well.

The sense that something is missing. The feeling of being a stranger in your own life. The hiraeth—the longing for a home you can't quite name.

This isn't meant to create despair. It's meant to create clarity. When you can see what the old programming has cost you, you can make a clear choice about what you're willing to pay going forward.

The Good News

Here's what I want you to hold on to as we close this chapter:

The code can be changed.

Remember neuroplasticity? Your brain's ability to reorganize itself, to form new neural pathways, to literally rewire itself based on new experiences and practices? It's real. It's documented. And it's available to you.

The patterns laid down in childhood are powerful—but they are not permanent. The beliefs installed by your family, your culture, your experiences feel like truth, but they are just code. And code can be rewritten.

This is what the rest of our journey together is about. Not erasing your past or pretending it didn't shape you. But examining the code, identifying what serves you and what doesn't, and consciously choosing what code you want to run going forward.

You are the programmer now.

The miracle you arrived as? It's still there. It's been there all along, beneath the layers of code that obscured it. Your Original Self has gone nowhere—it's simply been waiting for you to remember the way home.

And now you're beginning to see the trail.

Pause and Reflect

Before moving to the next chapter, take a moment to sit with these questions. You don't need perfect answers. Just let the questions work on you.

When you read about the miracle you arrived as—37 trillion cells, 86 billion neurons, a consciousness that can contemplate itself—what shifts in how you think about yourself?

Which layer of your Life Code (biological, neurological, psychological, cultural, relational, spiritual) do you sense has the strongest hold on you right now?

What messages did you receive from your family about who you were supposed to be?

What did your education teach you about your worth and how it should be measured?

What cultural "water" are you swimming in that you rarely notice?

If you could trace your current patterns back to their source code, what would you find?

What has living according to programming you didn't choose cost you? And what survival purpose did it serve?

The Breadcrumb

Each chapter closes with a single breadcrumb—a key insight to carry forward on your journey.

You arrived as a miracle of staggering complexity—trillions of cells orchestrating life, billions of neurons reaching for connection, a consciousness that science cannot fully explain. Then the world handed you code that wasn't yours: other people's beliefs, fears, and limitations masquerading as truth.

That code has been running your life, but it is not who you are. Beneath the programming, your Original Self remains—the miracle that was never touched by any of it. When you learn to see the code, you can finally choose what to keep, what to release, and what to write anew. You are the programmer now. And the miracle is still waiting to be lived.

Going Deeper: Your Digital Companion

The questions above are meant to stir something in you—to begin the inner conversation. But real integration happens when you take time to explore your responses more fully.

In your digital companion, you'll find the following exercises for Chapter 2:

The World's Rewrites — A structured reflection on the messages you received from each programming source (family, education, culture, religion, relationships)

Your Life Code Audit — An examination of your Installed Programs, Default Settings, Background Processes, and Bugs & Glitches

The Cost Accounting — A clear-eyed look at what living someone else's program has cost you—and what purpose it served

Your Mindset Mind Map Update — Adding "The Wandering" layer: where and how you fragmented, and what programming you absorbed

---

The trail is becoming clearer. In Chapter 3, we'll descend below the waterline—into the iceberg that lies beneath your visible life, where the real drivers of your choices have been operating all along.

Chapter Three

The Iceberg Beneath Your Life

WHO do you think you are...below the waterline?

"Until you make the unconscious conscious, it will direct your life and you will call it fate." — Carl Jung

Now we go deeper.

In Chapter 1, you heard the call—the longing that brought you to this work. In Chapter 2, you saw how the world shaped you—how your Life Code was installed by forces you didn't choose. Now it's time to look beneath the surface, into the vast underwater territory where the real action happens.

Picture an iceberg.

Above the waterline, you see the gleaming white mass—just 10% of the iceberg. Invisible but immense, the other 90% lies beneath. Everything depends on this hidden bulk: how the iceberg moves, what it endures, and if it survives.

You are that iceberg. The life you show the world—your behaviors, achievements, and public persona—makes up just the visible 10%. Meanwhile, the remaining 90% consists of unconscious beliefs, unexamined values, hidden fears, and your shadow. These unseen forces shape nearly everything about how you navigate life.

This is why surface-level change rarely sticks. You can try to reshape the 10% all you want—new habits, new goals, new resolutions—but if the

90% beneath isn't aligned, the iceberg just drifts back to where it was. The underwater mass always wins.

To find your way home, you have to be willing to go below the waterline.

Above the Waterline: The 10% You Show the World

Let's start with what's visible—the part of you that you present to the world, the part you probably know pretty well.

Behaviors and Habits

How you act. What you do. The patterns that others can observe. Morning routines, work habits, social patterns—the ways you respond to stress, joy, or conflict. This is the most visible layer of you.

Achievements and Accomplishments

What you've done. Your resume, your credentials, the external markers of success. The degrees earned, the positions held, the goals accomplished. This is what the world often uses to measure your worth—and what you may have used to measure yourself.

Roles You Play

Parent, professional, partner, friend, sibling, community member. The various identities you inhabit depending on the context. Each role comes with expectations, and you've learned to perform them with varying degrees of authenticity.

Public Persona

The image you project. The desire to be seen in a particular way. The carefully curated version of yourself is presented in professional settings, on social media, and at social gatherings. The mask that may or may not resemble the face beneath.

None of this is false. Your behaviors, achievements, roles, and persona are part of who you are. But they're not your full story. They're just the tip of the iceberg. To understand why you act and feel as you do, or why patterns repeat, you must be willing to go below the surface.

Below the Waterline: The 90% That Drives Everything

Here's where the real territory lies. Here's where the Life Code from Chapter 2 actually operates. The underwater mass of the iceberg includes:

Values (Conscious and Unconscious)

Values matter to you—what you see as important, worthy, and meaningful. But there's complexity: you have espoused values (what you say matters) and enacted values (what your behavior reveals). These aren't always the same.

You might say you value health, but your enacted value—revealed by how you actually spend your time and energy—might be work. You might say you value family, but your calendar might reveal that career advancement gets more of your attention. This isn't about judgment; it's about awareness.

Below your conscious values are unconscious ones—drivers you don't see. You may value approval so much that it overrides your stated values. You may value safety so greatly that it keeps you from your desires. Many unconscious values were absorbed in childhood through family and culture without your noticing.

Beliefs About Yourself and the World

Beliefs are the assumptions you hold about how reality works. They operate like the operating system we discussed in Chapter 2—running in the background, filtering your perception, shaping what seems possible.

Some beliefs are explicit: *"Hard work leads to success"* or *"People can't be trusted."* But the most powerful beliefs are implicit—so deeply embedded that they feel like facts rather than beliefs. *"I'm not creative." "I'm not the kind of person who..." "There's something wrong with me."* These aren't thoughts you consciously think—they're the water you swim in, invisible and all-encompassing.

Psychologists call these core beliefs or schemas—deep structures that organize how you interpret everything. They were formed early, often before you had language, and they've been filtering your reality ever since.

Fears (Acknowledged and Hidden)

Some fears you know about. You know you're afraid of public speaking, or heights, or rejection. These acknowledged fears, while uncomfortable, are at least visible.

Beneath these lie deeper, more elusive fears: fear of being seen as you truly are; fear of possessing too much power; worry that if people knew the real you, they might leave; anxiety over success; fear of outshining others; the suspicion that your best isn't enough; or even the secret belief that you are fundamentally inadequate.

These hidden fears have a huge influence. They build invisible walls and apply brakes you don't see. Procrastination or self-sabotage often masks fears that protect you from imagined danger.

Unmet Needs

Every human has fundamental needs—for belonging, for significance, for autonomy, for safety, for love. When these needs go unmet, especially in childhood, they don't disappear. They go underground, driving behavior in ways that may seem irrational on the surface.

The adult who can't stop seeking approval may be running on an unmet childhood need to be seen as valuable. The person who can't commit to relationships may protect an unmet need for safety. The workaholic may be unconsciously trying to fill an unmet need for significance.

Understanding your unmet needs isn't about blame or victimhood. It's about compassion—and about finally being able to meet those needs in healthy ways rather than through unconscious compensations.

Shadow (The Disowned Parts)

Jung gave us the concept of the shadow—the parts of ourselves we've rejected, denied, or hidden because they weren't acceptable to ourselves or others.

The child who was told their anger was unacceptable may have pushed it into the shadows, becoming a person who "never gets angry"—but the anger didn't disappear. It went underground, perhaps emerging as passive aggression, depression, or physical symptoms. The person who learned that being too confident was arrogant may have disowned their natural self-assurance, becoming someone who chronically undersells themselves.

Shadow isn't just about negatives. Sometimes, your gifts go dark—creativity, sensuality, power, joy. In environments where these qualities felt discouraged or dangerous, you may have hidden them so well that even you forgot you possessed them.

The shadow is like a basement where we've stored everything we couldn't bring into the living room of our personality. It takes energy to keep that door closed. And everything stored there still influences us—often by projecting onto others what we can't acknowledge in ourselves.

Wounds and Programming

The experiences that shaped you—especially the painful ones—didn't just create memories. They created programming. A single experience of humiliation can install a lifelong pattern of avoiding vulnerability. A childhood of unpredictability can wire your nervous system to expect danger even in safe situations.

This isn't weakness—it's how the human system works. We are designed to learn from experience, especially painful experience, so that we can protect ourselves. The problem is that the lessons we learn in childhood aren't always accurate for adulthood. The protection strategies that helped us survive may now limit our ability to thrive.

Values Inherited vs. Values Chosen

One of the most powerful exercises in self-coaching is distinguishing between values you inherited and values you've consciously chosen.

You absorbed values from your family: what they praised, what they punished, what they modeled. You absorbed values from your culture: what society rewards, what it shames, what it holds up as worthy. You absorbed values from your religion, your education, your peer group, and the media you consumed.

Some of these inherited values genuinely resonate with who you are. They feel true when you examine them. Others—and this is the crucial part—don't actually fit. You've been carrying them without ever checking whether they're yours.

In your digital companion, you'll have the opportunity to do a thorough values inventory—to separate what you've absorbed from what you genuinely believe, to notice where your espoused and enacted values don't match, and to begin consciously choosing what you want to guide your life.

This isn't about rejecting everything you were taught. It's about making conscious choices rather than inheriting unconsciously. It's about moving from absorbed values to authored values.

Beliefs Running in the Background

Let's explore beliefs more deeply, as they're the most powerful part of what's below the waterline.

A belief is anything you hold to be true. But the most influential beliefs are the ones you don't even recognize as beliefs—they feel so obviously true that you've never questioned them. They're the water you swim in, the air you breathe, the ground you walk on.

Consider: *"I'm not good enough."* For many people, this doesn't feel like a belief—it feels like a fact. It feels so self-evidently true that it doesn't even occur to them to question it. But it *is* a belief—one that was installed, one that can be examined, one that can potentially be changed.

Core beliefs typically fall into a few categories:

Beliefs about yourself: "I'm capable/incapable." "I'm worthy/unworthy." "I'm lovable/unlovable." "I'm fundamentally flawed."

Beliefs about others: "People can be trusted/can't be trusted." "People will hurt you if you let them." "People only care about themselves."

Beliefs about the world: "The world is safe/dangerous." "Life is fair/unfair." "There's never enough." "Good things don't last."

Beliefs about what's possible: "People like me don't..." "That's not realistic." "I'm too old/young/different for that."

These beliefs function as self-fulfilling prophecies. If you believe you're unlovable, you'll likely behave in ways that push love away—not because the belief is true, but because you act as if it were. If you believe the world is dangerous, you'll find evidence for danger everywhere—not because it's objectively more dangerous, but because that's what you're looking for.

The good news is that beliefs can be examined. They can be questioned. And when you shine awareness on them, they often loosen their grip. You begin to see them as beliefs rather than facts—and that creates space for something new.

Making the Unconscious Conscious

Jung's quote at the beginning of this chapter is worth repeating: "Until you make the unconscious conscious, it will direct your life, and you will call it fate."

This is the whole point of exploring below the waterline. Not to wallow in psychological archaeology, but to reclaim authorship of your life. As long as your values, beliefs, fears, needs, and shadow remain unconscious, they run the show. You think you're making free choices, but you're actually executing old programming, reacting from unexamined patterns, living out scripts you never agreed to.

When you make the unconscious conscious, something shifts. You don't automatically change—awareness isn't a magic wand—but you gain something precious: choice. You can see the pattern and decide whether to follow it. You can recognize the belief and question whether it's true. You can notice the fear and choose to move forward anyway.

This is what it means to become the programmer of your own Life Code rather than running on code someone else installed.

How do you make the unconscious conscious? There are many doorways:

Patterns: What keeps happening in your life? What themes recur? The pattern is often a clue to the unconscious material driving it.

Triggers: What sets you off? What makes you react with intensity disproportionate to the situation? Strong reactions often point to something beneath the surface.

Projections: What do you criticize in others? What bothers you in ways you can't explain? Often, what we react to in others is something we've disowned in ourselves.

Body sensations: Where do you feel tension, constriction, or unease? The body often knows what the mind hasn't yet admitted.

Dreams: What visits you in sleep? Dreams are messages from the unconscious—not predictions or literal truths, but symbolic communications worth attending to.

Resistance: What do you avoid? What topics make you change the subject? What questions make you uncomfortable? Resistance often guards something important.

Throughout this book, and especially in your digital companion, we'll use all these doorways. But for now, simply begin to notice. Where might your unconscious be running the show? What patterns might point to something beneath the surface?

The Courage to Descend

I won't pretend this work is easy.

Looking beneath the waterline takes courage. There's a reason we keep things unconscious—usually because they were too painful, too threatening, or too unwelcome to remain in awareness. The defenses that keep the 90% hidden were built for a reason.

This is why we approach this work with compassion, not criticism. We're not diving beneath the surface to find what's wrong with us. We're diving to find what's been waiting in the dark—the exiled parts, the disowned gifts, the truths we couldn't handle until we were ready.

Sometimes what we find is painful--old wounds, buried grief, parts of ourselves we're ashamed of. But here's what I've learned after forty years of accompanying people into these depths: what we find beneath the surface is always survivable. It's not the looking that keeps us trapped.

And often, what we find is surprising. Alongside the pain, there's treasure. The anger you disowned might hold your boundaries and your passion. The grief you suppressed might hold the key to your capacity to love deeply. The parts you rejected might hold gifts you desperately need.

The iceberg's underwater mass isn't a problem to be fixed. It's territory to be known, integrated, reclaimed. It's where your wholeness has been waiting.

The Gift of the Iceberg

Here's the reframe I want to leave you with: your unconscious isn't your enemy.

The 90% below the waterline has been working for you, not against you. It installed protective beliefs when you needed protection. It suppressed what was too big to handle when you were too small to handle it. It kept running old programming because that programming once kept you safe.

The problem isn't that you have an unconscious. The problem is that you've been treating it like a haunted basement you dare not enter. When you can turn toward it with curiosity and compassion—when you can explore below the waterline not with a flashlight searching for monsters but with a lantern illuminating treasure—everything shifts.

Your iceberg isn't a liability. It's your depth. It's what makes you complex, fascinating, and capable of growth and transformation. It's where your authentic self has been waiting all along, beneath the performances and adaptations, beneath the roles and masks.

The journey home requires going below the waterline. But you don't have to go alone, and you don't have to go all at once. We're building awareness gradually, one layer at a time, one breadcrumb at a time.

Completing Part One: Realizing You're in the Woods

With this chapter, you've completed Part One of your journey.

You've heard the call and recognized why you're here. You've seen how the world programmed you—how your Life Code was installed by forces beyond your control. And now you've begun to explore what lies beneath the surface—the underwater mass of your iceberg where the real work happens.

In Part Two, we'll shift focus. Having realized you're in the woods, we'll start learning how to see the breadcrumbs—the signals from your authentic self that have been there all along, waiting to be recognized. We'll develop the capacity to witness your own life with compassion rather than judgment. And we'll begin learning to trust the trail you've been leaving yourself.

But first, take time with this chapter's work. The iceberg exploration isn't something to rush through. It's the foundation for everything that follows.

Pause and Reflect

Before moving to Part Two, take a moment to sit with these questions. You don't need perfect answers. Just let the questions work on you.

What's the gap between your espoused values (what you say matters) and your enacted values (what your behavior reveals matters actually)? Where does this gap show up most clearly in your life?

What beliefs have you been treating as facts—so obviously true that you've never questioned them? What if they're not facts at all, but outdated programming?

What fears might be operating beneath your awareness, influencing your choices in ways you haven't fully acknowledged?

What parts of yourself did you disown to become acceptable? What gifts might be waiting in your shadow?

If you could explore one thing from beneath your waterline—one value, belief, fear, or disowned part—with complete compassion and curiosity, what would it be?

The Breadcrumb

Each chapter closes with a single breadcrumb—a key insight to carry forward on your journey.

What lies beneath the surface isn't a problem to be fixed—it's a territory to be known. Your unconscious isn't working against you; it's been working for you with the information it had. When you bring compassionate awareness to what's below the waterline, you don't find evidence of your brokenness. You find evidence of your wholeness—parts that got set aside, waiting to be reclaimed. The monsters you've been avoiding are smaller than you think. And the freedom you're seeking lives on the other side of being willing to look.

Going Deeper: Your Digital Companion

The questions above are meant to stir something in you—to begin the inner conversation. But real integration happens when you take time to explore your responses more fully.

In your digital companion, you'll find the following exercises for Chapter 3:

Above and Below the Waterline — A visual exercise to map your personal iceberg: what you show the world above the waterline, and what operates beneath

Values Inventory: Inherited vs. Chosen — An assessment to distinguish values you absorbed from family, culture, and society versus values you genuinely hold when you're honest with yourself

Beliefs Running in the Background — A journaling exercise using sentence completions to surface the implicit beliefs that have been operating without your awareness

Mindset Mind Map Update: Below the Surface — Adding your iceberg elements, values, and beliefs to the evolving map of your inner landscape

Part One Integration: The Code I Inherited — Synthesizing your work from Chapters 1-3 into the first section of your Life Code Document

---

Part One complete. You've realized you're in the woods. In Part Two, we'll begin learning to see the breadcrumbs—starting with the most important skill of all: developing the witness within.

Part TWO: Learning to See the Breadcrumbs

Developing Your Inner Witness

Chapter Four

The Witness Within

WHAT do you think you are doing...when you watch yourself without judgment?

"Between stimulus and response there is a space. In that space is our power to choose our response." — Viktor Frankl

"What we observe is not nature itself, but nature exposed to our method of questioning." — Werner Heisenberg

Welcome to Part Two.

In Part One, you realized you were in the woods. You heard the call that brought you here; you saw how the world programmed you with a Life Code you didn't write, and you explored the vast underwater territory of your iceberg—the 90% beneath the surface that drives everything. You answered the question *WHO do you think you are?* From three different angles, and in doing so, you began to see yourself more clearly.

Now we shift from *realizing* to *seeing*. Part Two is about developing your capacity to recognize the breadcrumbs—the signals from your authentic self that have been there all along, waiting to be noticed. But before you can see the breadcrumbs, you need to develop the part of you that sees.

You need to meet your witness.

The Part of You That Watches

There's a part of you that watches.

It watches you lose your temper and then feel ashamed. It watches you say "yes" when you mean "no". It watches you perform, people-please, and push down what you really feel. It notices when you abandon yourself, and it notices when you come back.

This is your inner witness—the aspect of your awareness that simply observes your thoughts, feelings, and actions. The witness does not judge or criticize; it observes with patient neutrality, waiting for you to notice what it already sees.

Right now, as you read these words, the witness within you is present. It is the awareness that notices you are reading, that senses your posture, your breath, a slight tension in your shoulders, or a stirring of curiosity in your chest. This witness is the observing presence in your mind.

The witness is not your thoughts—it is the aspect of you that is aware of your thoughts. It is not your emotions—it is the part that notices emotions as they arise and pass. It is not the voice in your head—it is the silent presence that observes that voice.

Most of us have lost touch with this witness. We're so identified with our thoughts, our reactions, our roles, that we forget there's a part of us that exists beneath all of it—watching, waiting, holding the thread of who we really are even when we've wandered far from home.

The journey back to wholeness is, in many ways, a journey back to the witness within.

Identification vs. Observation

Here's the problem: most of the time, we don't *have* thoughts and emotions—we *are* them.

When anger arises, we don't notice, "There's anger moving through me." We become the anger. We *are* angry. When fear shows up, we don't observe "fear is present." We collapse into the fear. We *are* afraid.

This is what psychologists call *identification*—the complete merging of awareness with its contents. When you're identified with a thought, you can't see it. You can only see *from* it. When you're identified with an emotion, you can't witness it. You can only *be* it.

And here's why this matters: when you're completely identified with your thoughts, beliefs, and emotional reactions, you have no leverage. You're inside the system, with no way to see it. You're running on the Life Code from Chapter 2 with no ability to question whether that code still serves you.

Viktor Frankl discovered something profound in the concentration camps of Nazi Germany—something that kept him alive when so many others perished. He discovered that between what happens to us and how we respond, there is a space. A gap. A moment of freedom where choice lives.

That space *is* the witness.

When you can observe your anger rather than *be* your anger, you gain choice. You can still feel the anger fully—this isn't about suppression—but you're no longer possessed by it. You can notice "anger is here" and then decide how to respond rather than simply reacting from the anger.

When you can witness your fear rather than collapse into it, you gain freedom. The fear doesn't disappear, but it's no longer running the show. You can feel the fear and choose to move forward anyway.

This is the core shift: from identifying with your thoughts and emotions to observing them. From being unconsciously driven by old patterns, to consciously choosing your response.

The Practice of Noticing

Developing your inner witness isn't complicated, but it does take practice. The mind has spent decades identifying with its contents. Learning to step back and observe requires patience and repetition.

The simplest practice is this: **"I notice that I am..."**

When you catch yourself in a reactive pattern, pause and complete that sentence:

I notice that I am feeling anxious about this conversation.

I notice that I am telling myself I'm not good enough.

I notice that I want to check my phone to avoid this feeling.

I notice that I am judging myself for judging myself.

The phrase "I notice that I am" creates just enough distance between awareness and experience for the witness to emerge. You're no longer lost in the anxiety—you're the one noticing the anxiety. You're no longer fused with the self-critical thought—you're the awareness observing the thought.

This might seem like a small shift, but it changes everything.

Try it right now. Notice what's happening in your body. Notice any thoughts passing through. Notice any emotions present. And notice the *noticing* itself—the awareness that's aware of all of it.

That awareness is your witness. It's been there your whole life. You just haven't been formally introduced.

Self-Compassion vs. Self-Criticism

Here's where most people get stuck: they develop a witness, but it's a harsh one.

Their observation becomes: *Look at you, doing it again. What's wrong with you? Why can't you just get it together? You should know better by now.*

This isn't witnessing. This is the inner critic wearing a witness costume.

A true witness offers compassionate neutrality. It observes clearly, without judgment or criticism. It recognizes your patterns without defining your worth by them. It sees your entirety—light and shadow—and remains by your side.

Think about what it feels like to be truly witnessed by another person. Not advised. Not fixed. Not the rushed, half-listening we've all grown accustomed to. But the experience of being fully seen—without judgment, without agenda, without the other person waiting for their turn to speak.

When we are truly witnessed by another, something in us settles. We stop performing. We stop defending. We begin to tell the truth—sometimes for the first time.

Your inner witness needs to offer you that same quality of presence.

This is where self-compassion enters. Self-compassion isn't self-indulgence or self-pity. It's simply offering yourself the same kindness you would offer a good friend. When you notice yourself struggling, instead of attacking, you acknowledge: "*This is hard. You're doing your best. It's okay to be human.*"

Research by Kristin Neff and others has shown that self-compassion—far from making us weak or complacent—actually increases resilience, motivation, and the capacity for change. It turns out that beating yourself up doesn't help you grow. But witnessing yourself with kindness does.

So as you develop your inner witness, pay attention to its tone. Is it harsh or gentle? Critical or curious? Does it observe with contempt or with compassion?

The goal is a witness who sees everything clearly and holds it all with kindness. This is the witness that can accompany you anywhere—into your shadow, into your wounds, into the parts of yourself you've been afraid to face. Because it won't abandon you there. It won't turn on you. It will simply stay, observing with love, until you're ready to integrate what you find.

What the Witness Makes Possible

When you have access to your inner witness, several things become possible that weren't possible before.

You can see your patterns. Remember the iceberg from Chapter 3? The 90% that operates below the level of awareness? With a developed witness, you start catching glimpses of what's beneath the waterline. You notice the same reaction arising in different situations and think, *Interesting—there's that pattern again.* You observe beliefs operating and recognize them as beliefs rather than facts.

You can work with triggers. A trigger is any stimulus that bypasses your conscious mind and activates an automatic response. Without a witness, triggers run you. With a witness, you can notice yourself being triggered and create that Frankl space—the gap between stimulus and response where choice lives.

You can hold paradox. Life is full of contradictions. You can love someone and be angry with them. You can be grateful for your life and want something to change. You can feel confident in some areas and insecure in others. Without a witness, these contradictions create confusion and internal warfare. With a witness, you can hold multiple truths simultaneously: *I notice that part of me wants to stay and part of me wants to leave. Both are true.*

You can companion yourself. This might be the most important gift of all. With a developed inner witness, you're never truly alone. There's always a presence with you, observing your experience and offering silent companionship. You become your own faithful friend—the one who stays no matter what arises.

The Grand Witness

And yet, there's something larger still.

Quantum physics has revealed something the mystics have always known: observation matters. At the subatomic level, the act of witnessing changes what is witnessed. Particles behave differently when observed. Reality, it seems, is not indifferent to attention. It responds to being seen.

Heisenberg's insight—that what we observe is nature exposed to our method of questioning—suggests that the observer and the observed are not separate. We don't stand outside reality watching it. We participate in its unfolding through the very act of attention.

This points to something profound—what I call the Grand Witness. A universal awareness that holds all of existence in its gaze. Call it consciousness, call it source, call it the field, call it God. The name matters less than the recognition: we are not witnessing in isolation. We are participating in something vast.

As above, so below.

The same awareness that observes the unfolding of galaxies is present in the quiet moment when you finally see yourself clearly. The witness within you is not separate from the witness that holds the cosmos. When you turn your attention inward with compassion, you are not just healing yourself—you are participating in the universe's way of knowing itself.

This is the great mystery: consciousness witnessing consciousness. You, observing your own life. And something infinite, observing it not with judgment, but with the same patient presence we're learning to offer ourselves.

You have never been unwatched. You have never been unseen. Even in your darkest moments, even when you felt most alone, there was a witness that never looked away.

The Collective Witness

There's another dimension to this that deserves mention: the power of collective witnessing.

When we witness each other—truly see one another without trying to fix or change—something happens that is greater than the sum of its parts. A field opens. Healing accelerates. Truth becomes easier to tell. It's as if our individual witnessing plugs into something larger, a collective awareness that amplifies what any one of us could do alone.

I've seen this in forty years of coaching and group work. I've seen it in workshops where strangers become sacred mirrors for each other. I've seen it in the simple act of one person saying to another, *"I see you. I see what you're carrying. You're not alone."*

This is why your journey home matters beyond just you.

When you learn to witness yourself with compassion, you become capable of witnessing others without judgment. And when enough of us do this—when enough of us reclaim the inner witness and offer that presence to the world—we participate in a collective healing. We become part of how the Grand Witness sees itself more clearly through human eyes.

As within, so without.

Your wholeness ripples outward.

Becoming Your Own Witness

The work of this chapter—and the practice you'll continue throughout this book—is learning to witness yourself the way I would witness you if we were sitting together.

Not fixing. Not rushing. Trusting that you already have what you need—you've just lost sight of it. Holding space for you to remember.

This is the capacity that makes everything else in this book possible. You can explore your shadow with a compassionate witness accompanying you into the dark. You can examine painful patterns with a loving presence that won't abandon you in difficulty. You can face hard truths about yourself when you know that the witnessing won't turn to condemnation.

The witness is what makes the journey safe enough to take.

And here's the beautiful paradox: the witness has been there all along. You're not creating something new. You're simply remembering—reconnecting with a capacity that got buried under all the identification, all the reactivity, all the years of being swept away by thoughts and emotions rather than observing them.

Your witness has been waiting for you to come home to it, just as patiently as it waits for everything else.

Part Two Begins

With your inner witness awakening, you're ready for what comes next.

In Chapter 5, we'll explore what breadcrumbs actually are—those signals from your authentic self that have been there all along, waiting to be noticed. You'll learn to recognize the unexpected tears, the recurring dreams, the quiet longings that point the way home.

In Chapter 6, we'll examine what gets your attention—and what doesn't. You'll discover the filters and biases that have been hiding the breadcrumbs from view, and you'll learn to clear the lens so you can see what's really there.

But first, spend time with this chapter. The witness is foundational. Everything else rests on it.

Pause and Reflect

Before moving to the next chapter, take a moment to sit with these questions. Let them work on you.

When you make a mistake or fall short, what does your inner voice sound like? Is it harsh and critical, or kind and understanding? What would shift if you could witness yourself with more compassion?

Can you recall a moment when someone truly witnessed you—saw you without judgment, without trying to fix you? What did that feel like? What became possible in that presence?

What patterns or reactions might you be able to see more clearly if you could step back and observe rather than being lost inside them?

What would it mean to know—really know—that you have never been unwatched, that something larger than you has been witnessing your entire journey with patience and love?

Right now, in this moment, what do you notice? What is your witness aware of?

The Breadcrumb

Each chapter closes with a single breadcrumb—a key insight to carry forward on your journey.

You are not your thoughts. You are not your emotions. You are not your reactions, *or your patterns, or your pain. You are the awareness that witnesses all of it—the vast, compassionate presence that observes your life unfolding and remains unchanged by what it sees. When you remember this, you gain something precious: the space between stimulus and response, where freedom lives. Your witness has been waiting your whole life for you to notice it. It's still here. It's always been here. And it's not going anywhere.*

Going Deeper: Your Digital Companion

The questions above are meant to stir something in you—to begin the inner conversation. But real integration happens when you take time to explore your responses more fully.

In your digital companion, you'll find the following exercises for Chapter 4:

Developing Your Inner Witness — A guided practice in observing without judging, using the "I notice that I am..." technique to create space between awareness and experience.

Self-Compassion vs. Self-Criticism Inventory — An assessment of how you typically respond to yourself when you make mistakes or fall short, with practices for developing a kinder inner voice

The Witness Meditation — A simple meditation practice for strengthening your capacity to observe thoughts and emotions without identification

Mindset Mind Map Update: The Observer — Adding your relationship with your inner witness, your self-talk patterns, and your growing awareness to your evolving map

Letter from Your Witness — An imaginative exercise where you write to yourself from the perspective of your compassionate inner witness

---

The witness is awake. In Chapter 5, we'll put it to use—learning to recognize the breadcrumbs that your authentic self has been leaving all along, waiting for you to finally see them.

CHAPTER FIVE

RECOGNIZING YOUR BREADCRUMBS

WHAT do you think you are doing...when you follow the longing?

"Before I can tell my life what I want to do with it, I must listen to my life telling me who I am." — Parker Palmer

"Tell me, what is it you plan to do with your one wild and precious life?" — Mary Oliver

NOW THAT YOU'VE AWAKENED your inner witness, you have the capacity to see what's been there all along. Let's explore what those discoveries might reveal.

In Chapter 1, I introduced the concept of breadcrumbs—trail markers you've been leaving yourself throughout your life, signals from your authentic self pointing the way home. You understood the idea. But recognizing them differs from understanding them.

With this in mind, this chapter is about learning to *see* the breadcrumbs: to notice them when they appear, to trust them when they call, and to follow them, even when you can't yet see where they lead.

Your authentic self has communicated with you your entire life through your body, emotions, dreams, longings, and your responses to music, places, or people—through what makes you feel alive or moved for reasons that are hard to explain.

The question isn't whether the breadcrumbs are there. They are. The question is whether you've learned to recognize them—and whether you're willing to trust what they're telling you.

What Breadcrumbs Actually Are

Let's get clear about what we're looking for.

Breadcrumbs are signals from your authentic self—the self that existed before conditioning. They're reminders of who you really are, appearing amid a life that may have drifted from that truth.

Breadcrumbs are *not*: random impulses or fleeting whims; escapist fantasies designed to avoid reality; someone else's idea of what you should want; the ego's desire for approval, status, or validation.

Breadcrumbs *are* persistent signals that return no matter how often you dismiss them. They arise from somewhere deeper than your conditioned mind and connect to a larger pattern, offering invitations toward wholeness.

Here's the key distinction: breadcrumbs feel like *recognition*, not ambition. When you encounter a true breadcrumb, there's often a sense of "yes, this"—not because it's new, but because it's familiar. It's the feeling of remembering something you forgot you knew.

The breadcrumb doesn't say "become this new person." It says, "Remember who you've always been."

The Language of Breadcrumbs

Your authentic self doesn't speak in words. It can't send you a memo or leave a voicemail. So, it communicates through other channels—channels that bypass the rational mind and its elaborate defenses.

Learning to recognize breadcrumbs means learning to read a different language. Here's what that language sounds like:

The Unexpected Tears

You're watching a movie, and suddenly you're crying—not at the sad part, but at the moment when a character finally does the thing they were always meant to do. You hear a song and something in your chest cracks open. You witness a stranger's act of courage and find yourself unexpectedly moved.

These tears aren't random. They're breadcrumbs.

When tears arrive without an obvious cause, your authentic self is responding to something. Often it's recognition—seeing on the outside what's been longing to live on the inside. The character who finally speaks their truth moves you because *your* own truth longs to be spoken. The song breaks you open because it's touching something in you that wants to be touched.

Pay attention to what makes you cry when you "shouldn't" be crying. There might be a breadcrumb there.

The Recurring Dreams

Not all dreams are breadcrumbs, but the ones that repeat usually are.

The dream of flying has visited you since childhood. The recurring search for a room in a house you've never seen. The dream where you're back in school, unprepared for an exam. The one where you're trying to get somewhere but can't move fast enough.

Dreams process what the conscious mind avoids. A recurring dream means the message remains unreceived. Your authentic self repeats the signal, waiting for you to notice.

What dreams keep visiting you? What might they be trying to say?

The Quiet Longings

There's a difference between wanting and longing.

Wanting is surface level: I want a new car, a vacation, recognition. Wanting can be satisfied. Once you get what you want, the wanting stops.

Longing is deeper; it persists beyond achievement. It's about being, not having. The longing for meaningful work. The longing to create. The longing for depth, contribution, or a sense of home in yourself.

These longings are breadcrumbs—perhaps the most important ones. They're your authentic self telling you what it needs to thrive. And no amount of achievement, accumulation, or external success will satisfy them. Only alignment will.

What have you been longing for beneath all the wanting?

The Inexplicable Joy

What makes you come alive?

It's not about proficiency or praise, though those may overlap. What truly lights you up inside, no matter who notices?

For some people, it's making things with their hands. For others, it's solving complex problems. Some come alive in nature, others in cities. Some in solitude, others in community. Some through movement, others through stillness. Some through creating, others through organizing, and others through connecting.

There's no right answer. The only right answer is *your* answer.

You already know. Maybe you hid it under the guise of practicality or dismissed it as childish, unrealistic, or unimportant. But somewhere in you, you know what makes you come alive.

That knowing is a breadcrumb.

The Envy That Points

Envy gets a bad reputation, but it's actually one of the most useful breadcrumbs you have.

When you feel a pang of envy—not the bitter, resentful kind, but the wistful, longing kind—pay attention. You're not actually envying the person. You're recognizing something in them that wants to live in you.

The friend who left their corporate job to start something of their own—and something in you aches. That ache isn't about their choice; it's about yours. The acquaintance who speaks their mind freely—and something in you stirs. That stirring isn't about them; it's about the voice in you that's been silenced.

Envy, read correctly, maps your unlived life. It shows what you've wanted but haven't let yourself pursue.

Who do you envy? What does that tell you about what your authentic self is longing for?

Behavioral Breadcrumbs: What Your Actions Reveal

Beyond emotions and dreams, your authentic self leaves breadcrumbs in your *behavior*—often without your conscious awareness. Your actions reveal who you are, even when your mind is telling a different story.

What You Do When No One Is Watching

How you spend your discretionary time—the hours that belong only to you—reveals what actually matters to you, not what you say matters. The person who claims to value creativity but never creates. The person who insists relationships are their priority but spends every free moment alone. The person who says health is important but consistently chooses otherwise.

This isn't about judgment. It's about information. Your behavior is data about your actual values and authentic inclinations. What do you find yourself doing when no one is keeping score?

What You Procrastinate On

Procrastination is usually framed as a character flaw—laziness, lack of discipline, poor time management. But procrastination is often a breadcrumb.

We don't chronically procrastinate on things that feel aligned with who we really are. We procrastinate on tasks that violate our values, undermine our sense of meaning, or conflict with our authentic interests. The report you keep putting off might not be about poor work habits; it might be about work that doesn't fit who you are. The project that never gets started might be someone else's dream that you've been carrying.

What do you consistently avoid? The avoidance itself might point toward misalignment.

What You Volunteer For

Notice the difference between what you're assigned and what you naturally gravitate toward. In meetings, which problems do you want to solve? In your community, which causes call to you? In your relationships, what kind of help do you instinctively offer?

You volunteer for what matters to you. You gravitate toward what fits. The tasks you have to force yourself to complete versus the ones you'd do even if no one asked—this gap is a breadcrumb about where your authentic gifts and interests actually lie.

How You Help Others

There's a fascinating pattern in human behavior: we often give others the very thing we most need ourselves. The person who offers encouragement to everyone may be starving for it themselves. The person who helps everyone get organized may be longing for order in their own life. The person who always listens may be desperate to be heard.

How do you instinctively help others? What you offer reveals what you value—and often what you need. There's a breadcrumb in your generosity.

What You Notice That Others Miss

Your attention has a signature. In any environment, you notice certain things that others overlook. The designer notices aesthetic details. The systems thinker notices patterns and connections. The empath notices emotional undercurrents. The naturalist notices what's alive and growing.

What do you consistently notice that others seem to miss? Your perceptual filters are tuned to what matters to your authentic self. What you see says something about who you are.

Breadcrumbs Across the Six Dimensions

In Chapter 2, we explored the six layers of your Life Code—biological, neurological, psychological, cultural, relational, and spiritual. Your authentic self leaves breadcrumbs in these dimensions. Learning to recognize them means listening with your whole being, not just your mind.

Biological Breadcrumbs: The Body Knows

Your body is constantly communicating. It knows things your conscious mind hasn't admitted yet.

Energy and vitality are breadcrumbs. Notice when you feel energized versus drained. Certain activities, certain people, and certain environments give you energy. Others deplete you. This isn't random information about what aligns with your authentic self and what doesn't.

Physical sensations are breadcrumbs. The chest that tightens when you're about to say yes to something you should decline. The shoulders that relax when you're finally doing what you love. The gut that churns when something's wrong, even if you can't explain why.

Illness and symptoms can be breadcrumbs. Not always; sometimes illness is just illness. But chronic conditions that resist treatment sometimes carry messages. The back pain that appears when you're carrying too much that isn't yours. The fatigue deepens the further you drift from your truth. The body has wisdom that the mind ignores.

Neurological Breadcrumbs: The Brain's Signals

Your brain leaves breadcrumbs through its patterns of activation and attention.

What captivates your attention is a breadcrumb. In a world of infinite information, what do you find yourself drawn to? What topics make you lose track of time? What problems do you find yourself wanting to solve? Where your attention naturally flows—not where you force it, but where it wants to go—is data about your authentic interests and gifts.

Flow states are breadcrumbs. Those experiences where time disappears, where you're so absorbed in an activity that the sense of separate self dissolves—these are your brain telling you that you're doing what you're designed to do. When does time disappear for you?

Memory and nostalgia are breadcrumbs. The memories that persist, the periods of your life you return to in your mind, the moments that still feel vivid decades later—your brain has preserved these for a reason. What are they trying to remind you of?

Psychological Breadcrumbs: The Psyche's Wisdom

Your psychological patterns, including the ones you might consider problems, often contain breadcrumbs.

What you resist is a breadcrumb. Resistance is a signpost pointing toward something important. If you feel strong resistance to a particular path, question, or possibility, don't just push through it or avoid it—get curious. What is the resistance protecting? What might be on the other side?

Your wounds are breadcrumbs. This isn't to minimize pain, but our deepest wounds often point toward our deepest gifts. The person who was made to feel invisible often has a profound capacity to truly see others. The person whose voice was silenced often becomes a powerful advocate. The wound and the gift are often two sides of the same coin.

Your "unrealistic" dreams are breadcrumbs. The dreams you've labeled impractical, impossible, or "not for someone like me"—these labels were often applied by your conditioning, not your wisdom. The dream itself may be a breadcrumb worth following, even if the path looks different from what you imagined.

Cultural Breadcrumbs: What Transcends Your Programming

Some of your breadcrumbs show up as friction with the cultural water you swim in.

Values that don't fit are breadcrumbs. If you've always felt slightly at odds with the values of your family, your community, or your culture—if something in you has never fully accepted the "way things are done"—that dissonance isn't a problem. It's your authentic self signaling that it has different values than the ones you inherited.

The "different" feeling itself is a breadcrumb. If you've always felt like you didn't quite belong, like you were observing life from slightly outside it—that perspective isn't a flaw. It may be your authentic self refusing to fully merge with programming that wasn't yours.

Relational Breadcrumbs: What Your Connections Reveal

Your relationships are rich with breadcrumbs about who you really are.

Who you're drawn to is a breadcrumb. The people you feel inexplicably connected to, the qualities in others that magnetize you—these reveal something about what you value and who you're becoming.

The feedback you keep receiving is a breadcrumb. What do people consistently see in you that you dismiss? The compliment you deflect, the quality others appreciate that you take for granted—there's often a breadcrumb in the gap between how others see you and how you see yourself.

Spiritual Breadcrumbs: The Soul's Communications

Whether or not you frame it religiously, there's a dimension of experience that transcends the material—and it leaves breadcrumbs too.

Moments of awe are breadcrumbs. The times you've been stopped in your tracks by beauty, vastness, or mystery—these aren't just pleasant experiences. They're your consciousness recognizing something larger than your everyday identity.

Synchronicities are breadcrumbs. Those meaningful coincidences that seem too precise to be random—the book that falls off the shelf with exactly the message you needed, the person who appears at exactly the right moment. You can explain these away, or you can receive them as communications from a universe that's paying attention.

The call toward meaning is a breadcrumb. The persistent sense that your life is meant to mean something, that you're here for a purpose. This call doesn't go away just because you can't articulate it. It's your authentic self—perhaps your soul—trying to get your attention.

Why We Miss the Breadcrumbs

If breadcrumbs are everywhere, why don't we see them?

The answer lies in the psychology of perception. Your brain isn't a neutral recording device—it's a filtering system, constantly deciding what to let in and what to screen out. And much of that filtering happens outside your awareness.

We have biases that dismiss information conflicting with our constructed identity. We have filters installed by our conditioning that evaluate everything against "what we should want" rather than what we actually want. We have blind spots we don't even know we have.

This is such an important territory that we'll explore it fully in the next chapter. For now, simply know this: if you've been missing the breadcrumbs, it's not because they aren't there. It's because you haven't yet learned to see past the filters. That's learnable. That's exactly where we're headed.

When Breadcrumbs Get Louder

Sometimes life turns up the volume.

There are seasons when the usual filters thin, and the breadcrumbs become impossible to ignore. If you're in such a season now, it may be why you picked up this book.

Midlife Awakening

There's a reason the term "midlife crisis" exists—though I prefer "midlife awakening." Somewhere in the forties or fifties, many people find that the breadcrumbs they've been dismissing for decades suddenly demand attention.

The achievements that were supposed to fulfill you clearly haven't. The life you built doesn't fit the person you've become. The questions you postponed—*Is this all there is? What am I really here for?*—refuse to stay postponed any longer.

This isn't a crisis; it's consciousness. The filters that kept you focused on building are dissolving, and what's been waiting beneath is finally becoming visible.

Loss and Grief

Loss has a way of stripping away the noise. When someone you love dies, when a relationship ends, when a chapter of life closes—suddenly the trivial falls away, and the essential becomes audible.

Grief creates an opening. In the rawness of loss, breadcrumbs that were previously invisible become unmistakable. What matters becomes clear. What you've been postponing becomes urgent. The breadcrumbs you've been dismissing for years suddenly look like the only trail worth following.

Illness as Messenger

Sometimes the body forces a pause that finally allows the breadcrumbs to be heard.

Illness can be a threshold—an involuntary stopping that creates space for reflection. When you can't maintain the pace that kept you distracted, when you're forced to rest, when the roles you've been playing are stripped away—the quieter signals finally have room to speak.

This isn't to romanticize illness or suggest that all illness carries meaning. But for many people, health crises become turning points not despite the difficulty but because of it.

Liminal Spaces

Any major transition—job loss, divorce, children leaving home, retirement, relocation—creates what anthropologists call a liminal space: a threshold between what was and what will be.

In liminal spaces, the usual structures dissolve. The identity that was tied to the old context doesn't work in the new one. This is disorienting, but it's also clarifying. The filters that kept the breadcrumbs hidden were part of the old structure. When the structure dissolves, the breadcrumbs become visible.

If you're in a liminal space right now, pay attention. The transition isn't just an ending—it's a window. The breadcrumbs are easier to see from here.

Learning to Trust the Trail

Recognizing breadcrumbs is one thing. Trusting them is another.

Your conditioning has taught you to trust external authority—experts, credentials, data, and others' approval. It hasn't taught you to trust your own deep knowing. In fact, it may have actively taught you to distrust it.

So when a breadcrumb appears—when your body says no even though your mind says you should say yes, when a quiet longing persists despite all the reasons it's impractical, when a dream keeps visiting with its mysterious images—your first instinct may be to dismiss it.

That's just a feeling. That's not realistic. I can't trust myself. What do I know?

This is where your witness becomes essential. The witness can observe these dismissing thoughts without being ruled by them. The witness can notice the breadcrumb and hold it gently, allowing it to speak without immediately shutting it down.

Trusting the trail doesn't mean blindly following every impulse. It means giving your breadcrumbs the same respect you give external evidence. It means treating signals from your authentic self as *data*—not the only data, but data worth considering.

Here's a practice: when you notice a potential breadcrumb, instead of immediately dismissing or following it, simply witness it. Say to yourself:

"I notice this. I'm curious about it. I will decide nothing right now. I'm just going to let it be here and see what else emerges."

Over time, patterns will reveal themselves. Individual breadcrumbs will connect into a trail. And the trail will become trustworthy because you've watched it long enough to see that it's real.

The Trail Is Already There

Here's what I want you to understand: you don't have to create the trail. You just have to see it.

Your authentic self has been leaving breadcrumbs your entire life. Every joy without purpose, every recurring dream, every inexplicable longing, every moment of envy or awe or unexpected tears—these weren't random. They were signals. They were your deepest self trying to communicate through the only channels available to it.

The breadcrumbs didn't disappear because you ignored them. They're still there, scattered across the landscape of your life, waiting for you to notice them.

Parker Palmer says we must listen to our lives as they tell us who we are. Mary Oliver asks what we plan to do with our one wild and precious life. These aren't separate questions. They're two movements of the same dance: listening and responding, receiving and acting, recognizing the breadcrumbs and following them home.

You've already been leaving yourself the trail. Now you're learning to see it.

Pause and Reflect

Before moving to the next chapter, take a moment to sit with these questions. Let them work on you.

What makes you cry when you "shouldn't" be crying? What might those unexpected tears be responding to?

What do you do when no one is watching? What does your discretionary time reveal about what actually matters to you?

What do you chronically procrastinate on—and what might that avoidance be telling you about alignment or misalignment?

What dreams—sleeping or waking—keep visiting you? What might they be trying to say?

Are you in a liminal space right now—a transition, a loss, a threshold? What breadcrumbs are becoming visible that weren't visible before?

Which dimension of breadcrumbs—biological, neurological, psychological, cultural, relational, or spiritual—have you been most ignoring? What might you notice if you started paying attention?

The Breadcrumb

Each chapter closes with a single breadcrumb—a key insight to carry forward on your journey.

Your authentic self has never stopped communicating with you. It speaks through your body, your emotions, your dreams, your longings, your behaviors, your inexplicable responses to beauty and truth. These aren't random experiences—they're breadcrumbs, trail markers left by the part of you that remembers wholeness. The trail home isn't something you have to create. It's already there, scattered across your life, waiting for you to recognize it. Every persistent longing, every recurring dream, every moment that makes you come alive, is your authentic self saying, "This way, this way, this way." The breadcrumbs are speaking. The only question is whether you're ready to listen.

Going Deeper: Your Digital Companion

The questions above are meant to stir something in you—to begin the inner conversation. But real integration happens when you take time to explore your responses more fully.

In your digital companion, you'll find the following exercises for Chapter 5:

Expanding Your Breadcrumb Inventory — Building on Chapter 1, going deeper into the types of breadcrumbs: physical sensations, emotional signals, synchronicities, recurring themes, the body's wisdom, and the soul's longings

Behavioral Breadcrumbs Audit — An examination of what your actions reveal about your authentic self: how you spend discretionary time, what you avoid, what you volunteer for, how you help others

Breadcrumbs Across Dimensions — A guided exploration of how your authentic self communicates through each of the six Life Code layers

The Dreams That Won't Leave — A journaling practice for working with recurring dreams and persistent imaginings

Mindset Mind Map Update: The Trail Markers — Adding the breadcrumbs you're learning to recognize to the evolving map of your inner landscape

---

You're learning to see the trail. In Chapter 6, we'll examine what gets your attention—the power of focus, the phenomenon of unintentional blindness, and how to clear the lens so you can see what's really there.

CHAPTER SIX

WHAT GETS YOUR ATTENTION

WHAT do you think you are doing...with your precious attention?

"We don't see things as they are, we see them as we are." — Anaïs Nin

"The eye sees only what the mind is prepared to comprehend." — Robertson Davies

IN CHAPTER 5, YOU learned to recognize the breadcrumbs—those signals from your authentic self that have been there all along. But here's the core challenge: true recognition isn't just about seeing breadcrumbs. It's about understanding the filters through which you notice them and realizing that your own perceptual system shapes what you recognize.

You don't see the world as it is. You see it through a complex system of filters, biases, and distortions that has been shaping your perception your entire life—largely without your awareness. This system determines what reaches your conscious mind and what gets screened out before you even know it existed.

This chapter is about understanding that system. About seeing how information moves from raw reality to your conscious experience—and all the ways it gets altered along the way. About why you've been missing breadcrumbs that were right in front of you. And about how to work with your perceptual system rather than being unconsciously controlled by it.

Because here's what I've learned in forty years of coaching: people don't struggle to change because they're lazy or weak or broken. They struggle because they literally cannot see what needs changing. Their perceptual system has been filtering it out, biasing their interpretation, and distorting the meaning before conscious awareness even enters the picture.

The good news? Once you understand how this system works, you can begin to see more clearly.

The Flood You Cannot See

Let's start with a number that might stagger you: approximately *eleven million*.

That's how many bits of sensory information are hitting your nervous system every single second. Eleven million bits—from your eyes, ears, skin, nose, tongue, and proprioceptive system—are flooding into you right now as you read these words.

Now here's the number that should really get your attention: *forty to fifty*.

That's how many bits of information your conscious mind can actually process per second. Not eleven million. Forty to fifty.

Think about what that means. Of the vast ocean of information available to you in any moment, you are consciously aware of approximately 0.00 05% of it. Less than one-thousandth of one percent.

This isn't a design flaw. It's a survival necessity. If you had to consciously process eleven million bits of information every second, you would be completely overwhelmed. You couldn't function. You couldn't walk across a room, hold a conversation, or make the simplest decision. Your brain would crash like a computer running a million programs simultaneously.

So, your brain does something remarkably intelligent: it filters, it screens, it selects. Out of the eleven million bits available, it chooses the forty to fifty that seem most relevant to your survival, your goals, and your current focus—and it discards the rest before you ever know it existed.

This is happening right now. As you read these words, your brain is ignoring the feeling of your clothes against your skin (until I mentioned it), the ambient sounds in your environment, the temperature of the air, and the subtle movements of your body as you breathe. All of that information is hitting your nervous system. Almost none of it is reaching your conscious awareness.

Your experience of reality is not reality. It's a tiny, curated slice of reality—selected by systems operating far below your conscious awareness.

The Three Levels of Knowing

This brings us to a framework that's essential for understanding how we navigate the world.

There's what we know. This is our conscious awareness—the explicit knowledge we can access and articulate. It includes facts we've learned, skills we've developed, beliefs we can state, and experiences we remember. This is the territory we are aware of being aware of. Most researchers estimate this represents only 10-20% of what's actually driving our lives.

There's what we know we don't know—our acknowledged ignorance. These are the questions we know we can't answer, the skills we know we haven't developed, and the information we know we're missing. This area, while uncomfortable, is manageable because we are aware of the gaps and can choose to learn or explore.

And then there's what we don't know we don't know. This is the vast unconscious territory—the beliefs we don't know we hold, the patterns we don't know we're running, the assumptions so embedded we don't recognize them as assumptions at all. We can't question these beliefs because we don't know they're beliefs. We can't change these patterns because we don't know they exist. We can't examine these assumptions because they feel like reality itself.

Here's the crucial insight: what we don't know we don't know is the powerful hidden force driving our perceptions, decisions, and actions. This unconscious filtering is the main reason change is so hard—because we can't confront or question filters we don't even know exist.

The beliefs running in the background that we've never examined. The patterns installed in childhood that we've never questioned. The cultural conditioning is so pervasive that we mistake it for truth. The family dynamics are so normalized that we think they're just "how things are."

This is also where most of the filtering takes place. The eleven million bits get reduced to forty or fifty, not by your conscious choice, but by systems operating in the realm of what you don't know you don't know. You never chose these filters, yet they're determining your entire experience of reality.

The journey home requires making the unconscious conscious—bringing what you don't know you don't know into the territory of what you know you don't know, and eventually into what you know. This chapter is a step in that direction.

How Perception Actually Works: A Three-Stage Process

Comprehending perception requires recognizing that it's not a single event but a process—a series of stages through which information passes, being filtered, shaped, and interpreted along the way.

Think of it like water flowing through a treatment plant. Raw water enters, containing everything—minerals, organisms, debris, chemicals. At each stage of treatment, something is removed or altered. What comes out the other end is clean and drinkable, but it's not the same water that went in. It's been transformed by the process.

Your perception works similarly. Raw reality enters through your senses. What emerges as your conscious experience has been transformed at every stage. Let's look at those stages.

Stage One: Sensory and Environmental Filtering

Before any psychological processing can occur, information must first pass through your biological gatekeeping system.

Your **Reticular Activating System (RAS)** is a network of neurons in your brainstem that acts as a filter between your body and your brain. Its primary job is to determine what's worthy of conscious attention and what should be screened out.

The RAS prioritizes based on several criteria:

Survival relevance. Anything that might threaten your physical safety gets priority processing. This is why you can hear your name whispered across a crowded room—your RAS is always scanning for identity-relevant information—and why a sudden movement in your peripheral vision immediately captures your attention.

Current goals. Once you decide to buy a red car, you suddenly see red cars everywhere. They were always there; your RAS just wasn't flagging them as relevant. Whatever you're focused on, your RAS helps you find more of it.

Novelty. Your brain is wired to notice what's different. Familiar, predictable information gets filtered out because it doesn't require conscious attention. Novel information gets flagged because it might require a response.

Emotional charge. Information associated with powerful emotion—positive or negative—is prioritized. This is why you remember where you were on September 11, 2001, but not what you had for lunch three Tuesdays ago.

Beyond the RAS, your **physical environment** also filters what you perceive. You can't see what isn't in your environment. You can't hear conversations you're not near. The people you spend time with, the media you consume, the places you frequent—all of this shapes what information is even available to be filtered.

This first stage is primarily **biological**—it's your nervous system doing its job. But notice how it's already shaping your reality before any conscious processing begins.

Stage Two: Dimensional Filtering

Whatever makes it past the sensory gates now passes through a second level of filtering—the filters installed by each dimension of your Life Code.

Biological filters continue operating here. Your nervous system state—whether you're in fight-or-flight or rest-and-digest—dramatically affects what you perceive. In a threat state, your perception narrows; you literally see less. In a calm state, your perception widens. Your physical health, energy level, hormonal state, and even hunger affect how you filter information.

Neurological filters shape perception through your brain's existing patterns. Your attention habits determine what you notice. Your memory systems compare incoming information to stored experiences. Your default mode network—the part of your brain active when you're not focused externally—generates a constant stream of self-referential thinking that filters everything through the question, "What does this mean for me?"

Psychological filters screen information through your beliefs about yourself and the world. Your self-concept acts as a filter—information that conflicts with how you see yourself gets screened out or minimized. Your mental models of how the world works determine what seems possible and what seems impossible.

Cultural filters evaluate information against the norms, values, and assumptions of your cultural context. What your culture considers important gets attention; what it considers irrelevant gets ignored. What your culture considers possible gets through; what it considers impossible gets filtered out as "not realistic."

Relational filters process information through the lens of your attachment patterns and social learning. How you learned to relate shapes what you notice in relationships. The dynamics you grew up with feel "normal," so information that challenges them gets filtered out as aberrant.

Spiritual filters screen information through your meaning-making frameworks. Your beliefs about purpose, the nature of existence, and what matters ultimately shape what registers as significant and what seems trivial.

Each dimension adds another layer of filtration. By the time information passes through all of them, it has been dramatically reduced and shaped. And all of this happens automatically, without conscious awareness.

Stage Three: Interpretation Through Biases and Distortions

Whatever information survives the first two stages now reaches the level where it begins to be interpreted, where you start to make meaning of it. But this interpretation doesn't happen neutrally. It happens through systematic patterns called biases and distortions.

This is where many people get confused, because filters, biases, and distortions are related but distinct. Let me clarify:

Filters are gatekeepers. They determine what information reaches your awareness and what is screened OUT. Filters operate largely before conscious awareness—you don't know what you're not seeing because it never reaches you. Filters answer the question: "What do I perceive?"

Biases are slants. They are systematic patterns in HOW you interpret the information that makes it through the filters. Biases don't block information; they tilt your interpretation in consistent, predictable directions. Biases answer the question: "What does this mean?"

Distortions are warps. They are ways that you twist, exaggerate, minimize, or alter information based on conditioning and psychological patterns. Distortions change the shape of information, making it conform to pre-existing templates. Distortions answer the question: "What story do I tell about this?"

All three work together to create your experience of reality. Filters select what you perceive. Biases interpret what you perceive. Distortions shape the narrative you construct about what you perceive.

Let's look at each more closely.

The Filters That Block Your View

Filters operate as gatekeepers, determining what reaches your conscious awareness. Here are some of the most significant:

Inattentional Blindness

This is the psychological phenomenon of failing to perceive what is right in front of you in plain sight—because your attention is elsewhere.

The famous "gorilla experiment" demonstrates this perfectly. Participants who were asked to count basketball passes failed to notice a person in a gorilla suit walking through the middle of the scene. The gorilla was clearly visible. Their eyes received the visual information. But their attention filter screened it out.

This isn't stupidity or carelessness. It's how attention works. What you focus on determines what you're capable of seeing—and, equally important, what you're incapable of seeing.

Dimension: This is primarily a **neurological** filter, but what you focus on is shaped by **psychological** and **cultural** factors.

The Familiarity Filter

Your nervous system prefers the known over the unknown. Familiar information passes through easily because it matches existing patterns. Unfamiliar information—especially information that suggests change—gets flagged as a potential threat and filtered more heavily.

This is why you can miss opportunities that don't look like opportunities you've seen before. Why do solutions that require becoming someone different get screened out? Why the breadcrumbs pointing toward unfamiliar territory often don't register.

Dimension: This operates at the **biological** level (the nervous system's preference for predictability) and is reinforced by **psychological** patterns.

The "Should" Filter

From childhood, you accumulated a vast collection of "shoulds"—what you should want, should value, should be. These shoulds become a filter that screens out information that doesn't fit the approved template.

A longing arises that conflicts with what you "should" want, and the filter minimizes it before it fully registers. An opportunity arises that doesn't align with what someone "like you" should pursue, and it gets screened out as "not for me."

Dimension: This is primarily a **cultural** and **relational** filter that has become internalized as **a psychological one**.

The Biases That Slant Your Interpretation

Once information passes through your filters, biases shape how you interpret it. These are systematic patterns—predictable tendencies that tilt your meaning-making in consistent directions.

Confirmation Bias

This is the tendency to seek, interpret, and remember information in ways that confirm your existing beliefs—while dismissing or minimizing information that contradicts them.

If you believe you're not creative, you'll interpret every creative attempt through that lens. The successful project was "not really creative." The compliment was "just being nice." Meanwhile, any failure becomes proof: "See, I knew I wasn't creative."

Your beliefs don't just influence what you look for—they influence how you interpret everything you find.

Dimension: This operates at the **psychological** level but is heavily shaped by **cultural** and **relational** programming about what's true.

Anchoring Bias

Your brain over-relies on the first piece of information it receives about something. This "anchor" then influences all subsequent interpretations.

If your first experience of speaking up was being shamed, that anchor shapes every subsequent speaking-up situation. Even years later, even in supportive environments, the interpretation tilts toward "this could go badly."

Early conclusions about who you are and what you're capable of become anchors that bias every subsequent self-interpretation.

Dimension: This is **neurological** in mechanism—it's how the brain builds mental models—but the content of anchors often comes from **relational** and **cultural** experiences.

The False Consensus Effect

People systematically overestimate how many others share their beliefs, values, and perspectives. You assume that reasonable people see things the way you do.

This bias prevents questioning. Why examine your beliefs when everyone agrees with them? Why consider your view might be limited when it's obviously correct?

Dimension: This is **psychological, but it is** strongly reinforced by **relational** patterns—we surround ourselves with people who confirm our views.

Self-Serving Bias

People tend to attribute successes to their own efforts and abilities, while attributing failures to external circumstances.

You got the promotion because you're talented. You didn't get the promotion because the system is unfair. This bias protects self-esteem but prevents accurate self-assessment.

Dimension: Primarily **psychological**, serving ego protection.

Projection Bias

You attribute your own unacknowledged feelings, motives, or characteristics to others. What you can't accept in yourself, you see in them.

The person whose ambition triggers your judgment may be reflecting your own disowned ambition. The person whose neediness irritates you may mirror needs you've refused to acknowledge.

Dimension: Psychological in origin, manifesting in the **relational** dimension.

The Distortions That Warp Your Perception

Distortions go beyond biased interpretation; they actively alter information, twisting it to fit pre-existing templates. These are habitual ways of warping reality based on conditioning.

All-or-Nothing Thinking

You see things in black-and-white categories. If a situation isn't perfect, it's a failure. If someone isn't completely trustworthy, they're completely untrustworthy. This distortion eliminates nuance and creates false dichotomies.

Dimension: Psychological, often rooted in **relational** experiences where nuance wasn't modeled or permitted.

Catastrophizing

You expect the worst possible outcome and treat it as inevitable. A small setback becomes evidence of total failure. A minor conflict ends the relationship. The distortion magnifies negative possibilities while minimizing positive ones.

Dimension: Psychological and **neurological** (an overactive threat-detection system), often rooted in **relational** experiences of unpredictability.

Mind Reading

You assume you know what others are thinking—usually something negative about you. Without evidence, you're certain they're judging, rejecting, or disapproving.

Dimension: Psychological, manifesting in the **relational** dimension.

Discounting the Positive

Positive experiences "don't count" for various reasons. The compliment was just politeness. The success was just luck. The good day was just temporary. This distortion maintains a negative self-concept by invalidating contradicting evidence.

Dimension: Psychological, often installed through **relational** experiences where positives were minimized or criticized.

How They Compound: A Breadcrumb Example

Let's see how filters, biases, and distortions work together to hide a breadcrumb.

Imagine you feel a pull toward writing. This is a breadcrumb from your authentic self—a signal pointing toward something real about who you are.

First, the filters:

Your familiarity filter screens it: "Writing isn't what I do. That's unfamiliar territory." Your should filter evaluates it: "I should be practical. Writing isn't a real career." Inattentional blindness means you've been so focused on your current path that you barely register the pull.

Then, the biases:

Confirmation bias interprets the few times you did write through your "I'm not a writer" belief: "That thing I wrote wasn't that good." Anchoring bias references your seventh-grade teacher who said your essay was "adequate": "I was never particularly talented." False consensus tells you: "Nobody actually makes a living writing. Everyone knows that."

Finally, the distortions:

All-or-nothing thinking declares: "Either I'm a successful published author or writing is pointless." Catastrophizing imagines: "If I tried, I'd fail, and everyone would see I'm not good enough." Discounting the positive dismisses: "That one piece people liked was just a fluke."

The breadcrumb was real. The pull toward writing was a genuine signal from your authentic self. But by the time it passed through your filters, got interpreted through your biases, and was warped by your distortions, it barely registered. Or if it did register, it was immediately dismissed as unrealistic, impractical, and not for "someone like you."

This is happening with breadcrumbs in your life right now.

Clearing the Lens

Understanding this system is the first step toward working with it. You can't eliminate your filters, biases, and distortions—they're part of how your brain functions. But you can become more aware of them, which loosens their grip.

Expand what you know you don't know. The more you can move from the third category (don't know you don't know) to the second (know you don't know), the more conscious choice you have. Ask yourself regularly: "What might I be missing? What assumptions am I making that I don't recognize as assumptions?"

Engage your witness. Your inner witness—the part of you that observes without being caught in what it observes—is your primary tool for seeing your perceptual system at work. When you can notice "I'm filtering this" or "I'm interpreting this in a biased way," you create space for different possibilities.

Seek disconfirming evidence. Deliberately look for information that challenges your existing beliefs. If confirmation bias leads you to seek supporting evidence, consciously seek the opposite.

Question strong reactions. Your emotional intensity is data. When you have a disproportionate reaction—strong judgment, fierce resistance, unusual attraction—that's often your perceptual system at work. Get curious rather than acting on it.

Listen to feedback. Others can often see what you can't. The feedback you've been dismissing might contain information about your blind spots.

Name the pattern. When you can identify "That's my familiarity filter," or "That's confirmation bias," or "That's catastrophizing," you create distance from it. Naming a pattern breaks its automatic hold.

Attention as a Superpower

Here's the empowering truth embedded in all of this: if attention determines what you perceive, then attention is also your point of leverage.

You can't control the eleven million bits of information hitting your nervous system. But you can increasingly influence where you direct your conscious attention. And where you direct attention shapes what you perceive, which shapes what you believe, which shapes what you do, which shapes the results you get.

Thoughts → Feelings → Actions → Results

This chain starts with perception. And perception starts with attention.

Your breadcrumbs are real. They exist in the eleven million bits. They've been there all along, waiting to be noticed. The question is whether your perceptual system will let them through—or whether your filters will screen them, your biases will minimize them, and your distortions will explain them away.

Now you understand the system. Now you can begin to work with it.

Pause and Reflect

Before moving to the next chapter, take a moment to sit with these questions. Let them work on you.

What might exist in the territory of what you don't know you don't know? What beliefs might be running your life without your awareness?

At which stage do you think most of your breadcrumbs get lost—sensory filtering, dimensional filtering, or interpretation through biases and distortions?

Which filters do you most recognize in yourself—inattentional blindness, the familiarity filter, the should filter?

Which biases most shape your interpretation—confirmation bias, anchoring, false consensus, self-serving bias, or projection?

Which distortions most warp your perception—all-or-nothing thinking, catastrophizing, mind reading, or discounting *the positive?*

What feedback have you been receiving that your perceptual system might be filtering out or distorting?

The Breadcrumb

Each chapter closes with a single breadcrumb—a key insight to carry forward on your journey.

Eleven million bits of information hit your senses every second, and you consciously perceive perhaps fifty. The rest is filtered, biased, and distorted before it ever reaches your awareness—shaped by systems operating in the vast territory of what you don't know you don't know. This isn't a flaw; it's how perception works. But it means your experience of reality is not reality itself. It's a tiny, curated slice, selected and shaped by patterns you didn't choose. The breadcrumbs from your authentic self exist in the eleven million bits. They've been there all along. Your filters have been screening them out. Your biases have been minimizing their significance. Your distortions have been explaining them away. But now you see the system. Now you can begin to question it. Now you can start to let more through. The breadcrumbs are waiting. Clean the lens. Trust what appears.

Going Deeper: Your Digital Companion

The questions above are meant to stir something in you—to begin the inner conversation. But real integration happens when you take time to explore your responses more fully.

In your digital companion, you'll find the following exercises for Chapter 6:

The Attention Audit — A week-long tracking exercise: Where does your attention naturally go? What do you avoid looking at? What captures you without your permission?

Mapping Your Filters — Identifying which Stage One and Stage Two filters most affect your perception, with specific examples from your own life

Bias Inventory — Examining which interpretive biases most shape your meaning-making and how they've affected significant life decisions

Distortion Patterns — Recognizing your habitual ways of warping information and tracing their origins

The Feedback Review — Examining feedback you've received from others and considering what your perceptual system might have caused you to dismiss

Mindset Mind Map Update: Filters, Biases & Distortions — Adding your perceptual patterns to the evolving map of your inner landscape

---

You've now completed Part Two: Learning to See the Breadcrumbs. You've awakened your inner witness, learned to recognize the signals from your authentic self, and understood what's been hiding them from view. In Part Three, we'll turn to Understanding the Territory—exploring the cast of characters within you, the stories and patterns that have shaped your life, and the boundaries that define where you end, and others begin. The trail is becoming clearer. Let's keep walking.

Part Three: Understanding the Territory

Mapping Your Inner Landscape

Chapter Seven

The Cast of Characters

WHEN will you ever learn...that your defenses were trying to help?

"The curious paradox is that when I accept myself just as I am, then I can change." — Carl Rogers

"Nothing ever goes away until it has taught us what we need to know." — Pema Chödrön

Welcome to Part Three.

In Part One, you realized you were in the woods. You heard the call, discovered the Life Code you didn't write, and explored the vast territory beneath the waterline of your iceberg. In Part Two, you developed your inner witness, learned to recognize the breadcrumbs from your authentic self, and understood the filters, biases, and distortions that have been shaping your perception without your knowledge.

Now it's time to map the territory you're navigating. Part Three—Understanding the Territory—is where you meet the inner landscape more directly. The cast of characters who live inside you. The stories and patterns that connect the dots of your life. The boundaries that define where you end, and others begin. And the things you've hidden from yourself in what we'll call the Denial Box.

Part Three asks the question every parent, teacher, and authority figure has asked at some point: *WHEN will you ever learn?*

Except here, the question isn't a reprimand. It's an invitation. Because what you're about to learn—about your own protective strategies, your recurring patterns, your relationship to boundaries, and your hidden places—is some of the most liberating knowledge you'll ever encounter.

Let's start by meeting the characters who've been running the show.

A Play You Never Auditioned For

Imagine you're sitting in a theater. The houselights dim. The curtain rises. And there on stage, acting out the drama of your daily life, is a full ensemble cast—characters you recognize, characters you didn't know existed, and a few who've been running entire scenes without ever asking your permission.

There's The Perfectionist, rehearsing every line until it's flawless. The People Pleaser, rewriting the script to keep the audience happy. The Controller manages every blocking note and stage direction. The Achiever, making sure the reviews are always stellar. The Invisible One, staying backstage entirely, hoping no one notices them in the wings.

These aren't flaws. They're not diagnoses. They're characters—roles that developed for very good reasons at specific points in your life. And here's what makes this chapter different from what you might expect: we're not here to get rid of them. We're here to get to know them. To understand why they showed up, what they're protecting, and how to direct the play with more awareness and choice.

Because right now, these characters are directing themselves. And a play with no director is a chaotic production, no matter how talented the cast.

How the Cast Was Assembled

In Chapter 6, you learned that your perception operates through a three-stage system of filters, biases, and distortions—shaping what you see and how you interpret it before conscious awareness even enters the picture. Your defense mechanisms happen *downstream* of that system. They are the behavioral strategies your brain created in response to what your filters let through, what your biases interpreted, and what your distortions made it mean.

Think of it this way: if your filters, biases, and distortions are the intelligence-gathering operation—deciding what information gets through and how it's interpreted—then your defense mechanisms are the response team. They're the strategies your system deploys based on the intelligence it receives.

And they were assembled remarkably early.

As a child, you didn't have the resources to handle overwhelming experiences directly. You couldn't leave an unsafe home. You couldn't change a critical parent. You couldn't opt out of a school system that shamed you for being different. So your brain did something brilliant: it developed strategies to manage what it couldn't control.

If being visible meant being criticized, a part of you learned to become invisible. If showing emotions meant being ridiculed, a part of you learned to lock them down. If achieving earned the only approval available, a part of you became a relentless achiever. If controlling every variable reduced unpredictability, a part of you became a world-class controller.

These weren't conscious decisions. They were adaptive responses—your brain's way of saying, *"I can't change this situation, but I can develop a strategy to survive it."*

And here's the crucial coaching insight: **they worked.** Whatever strategies you developed got you through. You're here, reading this book, which means your protective system did its job. The question isn't whether these strategies served you. They did. The question is whether they're still serving you—or whether strategies designed for a five-year-old's challenges are now running a forty-five-year-old's life.

Defense Mechanisms: A Quick Education

The concept of defense mechanisms has been around since Freud, but our understanding has evolved significantly. Modern research in neuroscience, developmental psychology, and coaching psychology gives us a much more nuanced and empowering picture.

Here's what we now know:

Defense mechanisms are neurologically real. They aren't just psychological concepts—they're actual neural pathways that your brain built through repeated use. Every time a strategy "worked" (meaning it reduced distress), the neural pathway strengthened. Over time, these pathways became automatic—the default route your brain takes when certain triggers appear. This is why you can't simply decide to stop using a defense mechanism. It's wired in. But neural pathways can also be redirected, which is why awareness and practice can create new defaults over time.

Defense mechanisms exist on a spectrum. Researchers like George Vaillant organized defenses into levels—from what he called "immature" defenses (such as denial and projection) to "mature" defenses (such as humor and sublimation). But I want to reframe that hierarchy. Rather than immature versus mature, think of defenses as existing on a spectrum from *automatic and rigid* to *flexible and chosen.* A defense isn't good or bad—it's either serving you in this moment, or it isn't. And the goal isn't to eliminate defenses—it's having more choice about which ones you deploy and when.

Defense mechanisms are relational. Most of your protective strategies were built in the context of relationships—with parents, siblings, teachers, peers, and culture. They were your best attempts to maintain a connection while protecting yourself. This means they show up most powerfully in relational contexts—in your partnerships, friendships, work dynamics, and parenting.

Defense mechanisms operate across all six dimensions of your Life Code. They aren't just psychological. They show up biologically (in your body's stress responses), neurologically (in your brain's automatic pathways), psychologically (in your thought patterns and emotional management), culturally (in the roles your culture reinforced), relationally (in how you connect and disconnect), and spiritually (in how you relate to meaning and purpose). We'll explore this shortly.

A Defense in Action: How It Forms

Let me show you how this works with a concrete example, because it connects directly to what you learned in Chapter 6.

Imagine a seven-year-old who comes home excited about a painting she made at school. She's proud of it—it's bright and messy and full of joy. Her parent glances at it and says, "That's nice, honey, but don't get paint on the carpet."

That's one experience. But it doesn't stay one experience.

Her filters begin to form: enthusiasm becomes something to be cautious about. Her biases begin to tilt: creative expression gets filed under "messy" and "inconvenient." Her distortions begin to warp: "My creativity causes problems."

Now add a few more experiences like this—a teacher who favors the neatest work, a peer who laughs at an imperfect drawing, a culture that measures value in grades rather than self-expression—and something begins to solidify. A character steps onto the stage.

Maybe it's The Perfectionist, deciding that nothing leaves her hands until it's beyond criticism. Maybe it's The Invisible One, deciding it's safer not to show anything at all. Maybe it's The Achiever, redirecting all that creative energy into academics, where effort is reliably rewarded.

By the time this seven-year-old is forty-two, she may have no idea why she "just isn't creative." She may feel a pull toward artistic expression—a breadcrumb from Chapter 5—but her perceptual system from Chapter 6 filters it out, her biases dismiss it, and her defense mechanism from this chapter has a well-practiced strategy for keeping her away from anything that might repeat that original vulnerability.

Filters, biases, distortions, and defenses. They're a system. And now you're learning to see the whole thing.

Meeting the Usual Suspects

Now comes the fun part.

Rather than approaching defense mechanisms as clinical categories to be analyzed, I want you to approach them as characters to be met. Think of this as a casting call. You're the director now, sitting in the theater, watching each character walk onto the stage and introduce themselves. Your job is simply to notice—with curiosity, not judgment—which ones are in *your* production.

As you read through these characters, you may recognize some immediately. Others may surprise you. A few may make you uncomfortable—which, by the way, is information. Remember your witness from Chapter 4. Let it do its job: watching, noticing, staying curious.

Here are some of the most common characters that show up in the human production. See who you recognize.

The Perfectionist

What they do: Hold everything—and everyone, including you—to impossibly high standards. Rehearse, revise, and polish until there's no risk of criticism. Delay or avoid entirely if perfection isn't guaranteed.

What they protect you from: The vulnerability of being seen as flawed, inadequate, or "not enough." Often born in environments where love or approval was conditional on performance.

Their favorite line: *"If I do it perfectly, no one can criticize me."*

The People Pleaser

What they do: Scan the room for what others need and deliver it—often before being asked. Say yes when they mean no. Prioritize everyone else's comfort over their own truth.

What they protect you from: Rejection, abandonment, conflict. Often born from environments where being "good" and accommodating was the surest path to belonging and safety.

Their favorite line: *"If I keep everyone happy, I'll be safe."*

The Controller

What they do: Manage, organize, plan, and direct—not just tasks, but people, outcomes, and environments. Struggle to delegate or let things unfold naturally. Feel anxious when things are unpredictable.

What they protect you from: Chaos, helplessness, vulnerability. Often born from environments that felt unpredictable or unsafe—where controlling the variables was the only way to feel secure.

Their favorite line: *"If I stay in control, nothing bad can happen."*

The Achiever

What they do: Pursue accomplishment relentlessly. Set goal after goal, often reaching one only to immediately set the next. Tie their sense of worth to what they produce, earn, or achieve.

What they protect you from: The fear that, without achievements, you're worthless. Often born from environments where doing was valued over being, where your output defined your value.

Their favorite line: *"If I achieve enough, I'll finally feel like I'm enough."*

The Intellectual

What they do: Move everything into the head. Analyze rather than feel. Explain rather than experience. Turn emotional situations into intellectual problems to be solved.

What they protect you from: The intensity and unpredictability of emotions. Often born from environments where feelings were overwhelming, unwelcome, or dangerous.

Their favorite line: *"If I can understand it, I don't have to feel it."*

The Invisible One

What they do: Stay small. Avoid attention. Shrink in groups. Minimize accomplishments and deflect praise. Make sure they're never the center of focus.

What they protect you from: The danger of being seen—because visibility once led to criticism, punishment, or harm. Often born in environments where standing out was met with negative consequences.

Their favorite line: *"If no one notices me, no one can hurt me."*

The Comedian

What they do: Use humor to deflect, redirect, or manage tension. Turn pain into punchlines. Keep things light when they're getting heavy. Make others laugh to avoid being seen too deeply.

What they protect you from: Depth that feels dangerous. Vulnerability that feels exposed. Emotions that feel too big to sit with directly.

Their favorite line: *"If I'm funny, no one will see that I'm hurting."*

The Rebel

What they do: Push back against authority, expectations, and norms—sometimes productively, sometimes reflexively. Resist being told what to do. Define themselves by what they're against rather than what they're for.

What they protect you from: The loss of autonomy. Being controlled, confined, or made to conform in ways that feel like a betrayal of self. Often born in environments that are overly rigid or controlling.

Their favorite line: *"If I refuse to play by their rules, they can't own me."*

The Caretaker

What they do: Focus energy on others' needs, problems, and feelings—often at the expense of their own. Become the one everyone leans on. Feel most comfortable when they're helping someone else.

What they protect you from: Having to face your own needs, your own pain, your own emptiness. Often born from environments where taking care of others earned belonging, or where no one was taking care of you, so you learned to earn love by providing what you never received.

Their favorite line: *"If I take care of everyone else, I don't have to face what's missing in me."*

This isn't an exhaustive list. Your cast may include characters I haven't named here—The Skeptic, The Worrier, The Martyr, The Fixer, The Judge. You might have characters that are unique to your specific history and conditioning. The point isn't to match a category. It's beginning to recognize the strategies that operate inside you—and to recognize them with the warmth of a director who appreciates every member of the cast, even the ones who've been going off-script.

How the Characters Show Up Across Dimensions

One of the most useful things about understanding your cast of characters recognizes that they don't just show up in your thoughts. They manifest across every dimension of your Life Code. Let's look at how a single character—say, The Controller—might show up in each dimension:

Biologically, The Controller lives in your nervous system as a chronic state of vigilance. Your body stays slightly activated—shoulders tense, jaw tight, scanning for what might go wrong. Over time, this shows up as headaches, digestive issues, sleep disruption, or that persistent feeling that you can't fully relax. Your body has become a control station, always monitoring.

Neurologically, The Controller has built well-worn neural pathways for planning, anticipating, and problem-solving. Your brain is exceptionally good at running scenarios and spotting potential problems—because that circuit has been strengthened through decades of practice. It may also mean your brain struggles with open-ended situations, uncertainty, or activities without a clear endpoint.

Psychologically, The Controller manifests as core beliefs like *"If I don't manage this, it will fall apart"* or *"The only person I can rely on is myself."* These beliefs feel like facts—remember Chapter 3—but they're the operating code that The Controller installed to keep you functioning in an unpredictable world.

Culturally, The Controller may have been reinforced by a culture that values competence, self-reliance, and having it all together. In many professional cultures, the controlling style is actually *rewarded*—it looks like leadership, initiative, and excellence. This cultural reinforcement makes it harder to see The Controller as a defense mechanism because the world keeps telling you it's a strength.

Relationally, The Controller shows up in dynamics with others—micromanaging a partner, overparenting children, struggling to let colleagues handle tasks their own way. People around you may experience The Controller as suffocating, even when The Controller's intention is to keep everyone safe. Intimacy requires vulnerability, and vulnerability requires relinquishing control—which is exactly what this character was designed to prevent.

Spiritually, The Controller may struggle with surrender, trust, or any framework that asks you to release the steering wheel. Practices like meditation or prayer that require letting go can feel deeply uncomfortable—not because you don't believe in them, but because The Controller experiences letting go as a threat.

Every character in your cast shows up across all six dimensions. The People Pleaser has a body signature (smiling when you're hurting), a neural pathway (scanning for others' emotional states), a psychological belief system ("My needs don't matter"), cultural reinforcement ("she's so selfless and giving"), relational patterns (attracting people who take more than they give), and a spiritual dimension (confusing self-abandonment with love or service).

When you can see how a character operates across *all* the dimensions, it stops being just a quirk or a habit. You begin to see the whole system—and that's where your power to make different choices begins.

When Characters Collide

Here's something that rarely gets talked about: your characters don't always agree with each other.

The Achiever wants to step up and volunteer for the big project. The Perfectionist says, "Not unless you can guarantee you'll nail it." The People Pleaser has already said yes to something else and is panicking about letting someone down. The Invisible One suggests you skip the meeting entirely.

This internal tug-of-war is one of the most exhausting aspects of living with an undirected cast. You feel pulled in multiple directions—not because you're indecisive or confused, but because several characters are fighting for the microphone at the same time, each with a different strategy and a different fear.

If you've ever found yourself stuck—wanting to move forward but unable to—it may be because two or more characters have opposing agendas. The Rebel wants to break free, while The People Pleaser needs everyone's approval for the breakout. The Caretaker wants to focus on others, while some buried part of you is desperate to be cared for. These internal conflicts can feel like being stuck in gridlock, and no amount of willpower resolves them because willpower addresses only one character at a time.

What resolves the gridlock is what we're building here: the capacity to see all the characters, hear all their concerns, and then make a conscious choice about how to proceed. Not silencing anyone. Not pretending a concern doesn't exist. Simply choosing, with full awareness, which response best serves you and the situation.

The Characters Aren't the Problem

Here's where this chapter might surprise you.

In many books, this is the part where you'd be told to identify your defense mechanisms so you can *overcome* them. Fight them. Dismantle them. Replace them with healthier behaviors.

I will not tell you that.

Your characters aren't the problem. They never were. They were the solution—the best solution available to a young person navigating a world where they didn't have the power to change. The Perfectionist didn't show up to ruin your life. It showed up to protect you from criticism that felt like a matter of survival. The People Pleaser didn't emerge to erase your identity. It emerged to maintain connections that you desperately needed.

The problem isn't the characters. The problem is that they're running on autopilot—still executing strategies designed for situations that no longer exist, without your conscious awareness or consent.

This is the crucial shift from automatic to chosen. And it's what makes coaching different from trying to "fix" yourself. You don't need to be fixed. You need to be *aware* and *at choice.*

Becoming the Director

So, what does it look like to move from being run by your characters to being the director of the production?

It looks like awareness followed by choice.

First, recognize who's on stage. In any moment—especially moments of stress, conflict, or powerful emotion—you can ask: *Which character just took over? Who grabbed the microphone?* This isn't about analyzing yourself to pieces. It's a quick, light recognition. "Oh, there's The Perfectionist. Hello." Your witness from Chapter 4 is your greatest asset here. It can see the character without becoming the character.

A client I'll call Patricia had been described her whole life as "intense." She'd heard it from colleagues, from partners, from friends who meant it as a compliment and didn't quite hide that they also meant it as a complaint. By the time she came to coaching, she'd accepted it as a fixed fact about herself — like eye color. Just who she was.

In one of our sessions, she described arriving at a team meeting to find that a decision had been made without her input. She'd spent the next forty minutes running what she called "damage control" — clarifying, correcting, redirecting. By the end, the decision had been reversed. The team was tense. And Patricia felt, she said, "like I'd won something I didn't actually want."

I asked her what she thought had driven those forty minutes.

She thought for a moment. "Someone made a move I didn't see coming. I couldn't let it stand."

"Which character was in the room?" I asked.

She was quiet. Then, slowly: "The Controller."

We sat with that for a moment.

"What was it protecting?" I asked.

"Being left out. Being irrelevant." Another pause. "Being the kid at the table who doesn't get a vote."

She was forty-seven years old. The meeting had been perfectly safe. But The Controller didn't know that — because The Controller was still running a program written for a child who genuinely had no vote.

That recognition didn't make The Controller disappear. But it created something that hadn't been there before: a moment of space between the trigger and the response. The next time someone moved without her,

Patricia noticed the character stepping forward—and, for the first time, she got to choose whether to hand the microphone over.

Second, acknowledge what the character is protecting. Instead of criticizing the character's appearance, get curious about its intention. "The People Pleaser just said yes to something I don't actually want to do. What was it protecting me from? Probably the discomfort of disappointing someone." This isn't a twenty-minute analysis. It's a moment of recognition—a nod of understanding toward a part of you that's been working very hard on your behalf.

Third, assess whether the strategy serves you right now. This is the choice point. Is this the scene where The Perfectionist is needed, or is "good enough" actually good enough? Is this the moment for The People Pleaser to step in, or can you handle the discomfort of a boundary? Is The Controller's vigilance appropriate here, or is this actually a safe situation where you can relax the scanning?

Fourth, choose your response. Sometimes you'll let the character do its thing—because sometimes the strategy is exactly right for the situation. Other times, you'll gently redirect: "Thank you, Perfectionist. I appreciate your commitment to quality. But this email doesn't need to be a masterpiece. I'm going to hit send."

Notice what this process is *not.* It's not a battle. It's not suppressing or silencing parts of yourself. It's not performing internal surgery. It's directing—the way a skilled director works with a talented but unruly cast. With respect. With appreciation. With clarity about what the scene actually calls for.

And it gets easier with practice. The more you notice, the more you recognize. The more you recognize, the more space opens between the character's automatic response and your chosen response. That space—the one Viktor Frankl described between stimulus and response—is where your freedom lives.

A Word About Inner Collaboration

The ultimate goal isn't to fire anyone from the cast. It's inner collaboration—a production where every character has a role, every voice is heard, and *you* are directing from the center.

The Perfectionist becomes an ally when channeled—it's the part of you that cares about quality, that takes pride in craft, that refuses to be careless with things that matter. Under your conscious direction, it knows when precision is called for and when "done" is better than "perfect."

The People Pleaser carries genuine empathy and relational awareness. Under your direction, it helps you read a room and care for others—without abandoning yourself in the process.

The Controller brings organizational skills and foresight. Under your direction, it handles what genuinely needs managing while releasing what doesn't.

Every character in your cast holds a gift. The defense mechanism is the gift in its rigid, automatic form. The *strength* is the gift in its flexible, chosen form. Your work isn't to eliminate the characters. It's transforming the defense into a resource by bringing it under the direction of your conscious, aware self.

That's what it means to move from inner conflict to inner collaboration. Not a war inside yourself, but a team—with you at the helm.

Pause and Reflect

Before moving to the next chapter, take a moment to sit with these questions. Let them work on you.

Which characters did you recognize immediately? Which ones surprised you?

Pick one character who has been especially active in your life recently. What is it protecting you from? Was that protection necessary in the current situation, or was it running an old program?

In which dimension do your characters show up most strongly—in your body? Your thoughts? Your relationships? Your cultural roles?

Can you recall a recent moment when a character took over, and you recognized it happening—even after the fact? What would you have done differently if you had more choice in that moment?

Which character's gift are you most ready to reclaim—to transform from a rigid defense into a flexible strength?

What would it be like to appreciate your characters rather than fight them?

The Breadcrumb

Each chapter closes with a single breadcrumb—a key insight to carry forward on your journey.

You have a cast of characters inside you—protectors who showed up when you needed them most, strategies that got you through what you couldn't otherwise survive. They are not your enemies. They are not evidence of something broken. They are proof of your extraordinary capacity to adapt, to cope, to find a way forward when no other way was available. But they've been running on autopilot—performing the same roles in every scene, regardless of whether the scene calls for them. You are no longer the child who needed these defenses to survive. You are the adult who can choose. See the character. Appreciate what it did for you. Assess whether it's needed now. And then choose—consciously, freely, from the director's chair—how you want to play this scene. Your defenses were never the problem. Your relationship to them is what's up for transformation. The cast stays. The direction changes. That's where your freedom lives.

Going Deeper: Your Digital Companion

The questions above are meant to stir something in you—to begin the inner conversation. But real integration happens when you take time to explore your responses more fully.

In your digital companion, you'll find the following exercises for Chapter 7:

Meeting Your Protectors — A guided exercise to identify and name the protective characters within you. What do they protect you from? When did they first appear? What's their gift when channeled with awareness?

The Roles You Play — An inventory of the roles you inhabit across different contexts—at work, at home, with friends, in your community. Which feels authentic? Which are performances? Where does the line blur?

The Director's Chair — A practice exercise for the four-step process: recognize, acknowledge, assess, choose. Apply it to three recent situations where a character took the lead.

Defense to Strength — For each character you've identified, map the rigid defense to its flexible strength. What does each character offer when it's directed rather than automatic?

Mindset Mind Map Update: The Protectors — Adding your cast of characters and their roles to the evolving map of your inner landscape

---

You've just met the cast of characters who've been running much of the show. In Chapter 8, we'll look at the scripts they've been performing—the stories, patterns, and recurring themes that connect the dots of your life in ways you may not have seen before. The cast is assembled. Now let's look at what they've been rehearsing.

Chapter Eight

Stories, Patterns, and the Dots Between

WHEN will you ever learn...to see the pattern instead of the event?

"The universe is made of stories, not of atoms." — Muriel Rukeyser

"What happens is of little significance compared with the stories we tell ourselves about what happens." — Rabih Alameddine

In Chapter 7, you met the cast of characters who've been running much of your internal show—the protectors, the performers, the strategies that developed to keep you safe. But characters don't just stand on a stage. They perform scripts. They follow storylines. They play out the same scenes over and over again.

This chapter is about those scripts—the stories you tell yourself about who you are, what's possible, and how life works. It's about the patterns that connect seemingly random events into recognizable themes. And it's about learning to see the dots between the dots—the invisible threads that weave your experiences into a coherent narrative, whether or not that narrative serves you.

Because here's what forty years of coaching has shown me: people don't live random lives. They live patterned lives. The same dynamics show up in relationship after relationship. The same struggles appear in job after job. The same fears surface again and again. These aren't coincidences. They're patterns—and patterns are breadcrumbs pointing to something beneath the surface that's asking to be seen.

Why Your Brain Loves Patterns

Before we explore your specific patterns, let's understand why patterns exist in the first place—because this isn't a flaw in your thinking. It's a feature of your brain's design.

Your brain is, above all else, a pattern-recognition machine. This isn't metaphor—it's neuroscience. The human brain evolved to detect patterns because pattern recognition kept our ancestors alive.

The rustle in the grass that preceded a predator attack. The cloud formations signaled an approaching storm. The facial expression that indicated a tribal member was about to become aggressive. Survival depended on noticing these patterns quickly—often before conscious thought could catch up.

Your brain is constantly and unconsciously scanning for patterns in everything you experience. It looks for what connects, predicts, or follows—asking: *Have I seen this before? What happened last time? What's likely to happen next?*

This pattern-seeking happens at a neurological level through a process researchers call "predictive processing." Your brain doesn't passively receive information from the world—it actively predicts what it's about to encounter based on past patterns, then checks incoming data against those predictions. When reality matches the prediction, everything feels normal.

When it doesn't, your brain flags the discrepancy as something requiring attention.

This is remarkably efficient. Instead of processing every piece of information as completely new, your brain uses patterns to take shortcuts—to fill in expected details without requiring conscious processing.

But here's where it gets interesting for our work together: your brain doesn't distinguish between patterns that are objectively true and patterns it has constructed from limited data. Once a pattern is established, your brain treats it as reality—and then looks for confirmation everywhere.

The Brain That Fills in the Blanks

Your pattern-seeking brain does something else remarkable: it completes incomplete information. Psychologists call this "closure" or "completion"—the brain's tendency to fill in gaps to create coherent wholes.

You've experienced this visually. When you see three Pac-Man shapes arranged in a triangle, you perceive a white triangle floating above them—even though no triangle actually exists. Your brain creates the triangle because it prefers complete patterns to incomplete fragments.

The same thing happens with language. If I write "Once upon a ____," your brain has already filled in "time" before you consciously think about it. You hear a song's opening notes, and your brain has predicted the melody before it plays. You see a friend frown, and your brain has already constructed what they're about to say.

This same process happens with life experiences.

You have a difficult conversation with your boss. Later, she passes you in the hallway without smiling. Your brain connects these two events—fills in the blank between them—and constructs a story: "She's still upset with me." That story may or may not be true. She may have been distracted, or having a difficult day, or thinking about a meeting she had just left. But your brain doesn't present it as "one possible interpretation." It presents the filled-in story as what happened.

This completion process is running constantly. Your brain takes fragments of information—a tone of voice, a facial expression, a coincidence of timing—and weaves them into coherent narratives. The narratives feel like observations of reality, but they're actually constructions. They're your brain doing what it evolved to do: making meaning out of incomplete data.

The question isn't whether your brain fills in blanks. It does. The question is whether the patterns it uses to fill them in are accurate—or whether they're based on old data from situations that no longer apply.

Born to Story: Why Humans Are Narrative Creatures

The pattern-recognition we've been discussing takes a specific form in humans that makes us unique among all species: we are storytelling animals. We don't just recognize patterns—we weave them into narratives with characters, motives, beginnings, middles, and ends.

This isn't a cultural accident. Anthropologists have found storytelling in every human society ever studied—from isolated tribes to modern civilizations, across every geography and every era of history. Story appears to be hardwired into human cognition.

Why? Because a story is how humans make meaning.

Raw information is just data. A sequence of events is just chronology. But a story—a narrative with cause and effect, with intention and consequence—creates meaning. It tells us not just what happened, but *why* it happened and *what it means.*

Our ancestors sat around fires and told stories to transmit crucial survival information: where the good hunting grounds were, which plants were poisonous, and how to navigate conflicts within the tribe. But they also told stories to answer deeper questions: Where did we come from? Why do we suffer? What happens when we die? What makes a good life?

Every culture developed creation myths, hero journeys, cautionary tales, and wisdom stories. The Greek myths. The Hindu epics. Indigenous Dreamtime Stories. Biblical narratives. Norse sagas. These weren't entertainment—they were operating systems for making sense of human experience. They taught people who they were, where they belonged, what mattered, and how to live.

Joseph Campbell spent his life studying myths across cultures and discovered what he called the "monomyth"—a universal story structure that appears everywhere. The hero's journey: an ordinary person receives a call to adventure, crosses into the unknown, faces trials, discovers something transformative, and returns home changed. This pattern appears in ancient myths and modern movies alike because it reflects a deep aspect of the human experience of growth and transformation.

Story became the primary vehicle for human understanding. It's how we learn, how we remember, how we make sense of our experience, and how we connect with each other. Research shows that information delivered in story form is up to twenty-two times more memorable than information delivered as facts alone. Our brains are literally structured to receive and retain narrative.

This is why you don't experience your life as a random sequence of events. You experience it as a story—*your* story—with you as the protagonist navigating challenges, learning lessons, and (hopefully) growing toward something meaningful.

But here's the crucial insight: you're not just living a story. You're also *telling* a story. And the story you tell shapes the life you live.

The Stories You Tell Yourself

Now we arrive at the heart of this chapter.

You have a narrator in your head. This narrator takes the raw material of your experience—the events, the interactions, the outcomes—and weaves them into ongoing stories about who you are and how life works.

Some of these stories are expansive:

"I'm someone who figures things out."

"Challenges help me grow."

"I can trust myself to handle what comes."

Some of these stories are limiting:

"I'm not the kind of person who..."

"Things never work out for me."

"I always end up..."

And here's what makes this so powerful: the stories don't just describe your life—they direct it. Your brain, that pattern-completing machine we discussed, will actively work to make your stories come true.

If your story is "I always get overlooked for promotions," your brain will filter for evidence that confirms this narrative. It will notice every time someone else gets recognized and minimize or explain away your own successes. It will interpret ambiguous situations through the "I get overlooked" lens. And it may even influence your behavior—causing you to hold back, not advocate for yourself, or subtly communicate that you don't expect to be chosen—in ways that make the story self-fulfilling.

This is not magical thinking. It's the documented phenomenon researchers call "confirmation bias" married to the brain's predictive processing system. Your stories become the predictions your brain expects to see confirmed. And a brain looking for confirmation is remarkably good at finding it.

The stories you tell yourself are not neutral descriptions of reality. They are creative acts with real consequences. They shape what you perceive, how you interpret what you perceive, and what actions seem possible or impossible in response.

A Story in Action: How It Forms and Spreads

Let me show you how a single story can form and then spread across an entire life. This connects directly to what you learned in Chapter 6 about filters and Chapter 7 about characters.

Imagine a boy named Michael. He's eight years old, and he loves to share his ideas. One day at dinner, he excitedly tells his family about something he learned at school. His father, stressed from work and not really listening, dismisses him: "That's not how it works, Michael. You've got it all wrong."

That's one experience. But watch what happens.

Michael's filters begin to form: sharing ideas becomes something risky. His biases begin to tilt: he scans for signs that people think he's wrong. His distortions begin to warp: "My ideas aren't valuable." A character steps onto the stage—maybe The Intellectual, who now over-prepares obsessively before speaking, or The Invisible One, who stops sharing ideas altogether.

And beneath all of this, a story takes root: "When I speak up, I get shot down."

Now Michael is fifteen, and he has an insight in history class. He starts to raise his hand, but the story whispers: *Remember what happens when you share your ideas.* His hand lowers. The teacher calls on someone else, who says something similar. Michael thinks, "See? Not that original, anyway." The story has just found confirmation.

Now Michael is twenty-eight, and he's in a meeting at work. He has a solution to a problem that the team has been struggling with. The story is running: *When I speak* up; *I get shot down.* He hesitates. Someone else voices a partial version of his idea. His boss loves it. Michael tells himself, "I should have spoken up," but the story adds, "Though they probably would have dismissed it coming from me."

Now Michael is forty-three. He's been passed over for leadership positions because he's perceived as "not assertive enough" and "not a big-picture thinker"—when in reality, he's full of big-picture ideas he's never voiced. His marriage is struggling because his wife feels like she doesn't really know him, as he holds back. He has a nagging sense that he's not living his real life, but he can't quite name why.

One story. Formed at eight. Running for thirty-five years. Expressed in relationships, career, self-expression, and even his sense of identity. And Michael has no idea the story is operating. He just thinks this is who he is: "I'm not really a speak-up kind of person."

This is how stories work. They don't announce themselves. They masquerade as identity. They feel like facts about who you are rather than interpretations that could be questioned.

How Stories Show Up Across Dimensions

Just like your characters from Chapter 7, your stories don't stay in one lane. They manifest across every dimension of your Life Code. Let's look at how a single story—"I have to do everything myself to make sure it's done right"—might show up in each dimension:

Biologically, this story lives in your body as chronic tension and exhaustion. You carry everything, so your shoulders carry everything. Your nervous system stays activated because you can't relax when you're the only one holding things together. You might experience headaches, insomnia, digestive issues—your body bearing the weight of a story that says you can't put anything down.

Neurologically, this story has carved deep grooves. Your brain is exceptionally good at scanning for tasks, anticipating what might go wrong, and planning how to handle it all. The neural pathways for vigilance and control are superhighways. The pathways for receiving help, trusting others, and letting go are overgrown trails you rarely travel.

Psychologically, the story manifests as a web of beliefs: "If I want it done right, I have to do it myself." "Other people always let me down." "Asking for help is a weakness." These beliefs feel like wisdom earned from experience—and in a sense, they are. But they're also self-fulfilling: when you don't trust others with tasks, they don't develop competence; when they fail, you have more evidence for your story.

Culturally, this story may have been reinforced at every turn. Perhaps your family of origin celebrated self-reliance and viewed asking for help as shameful. Perhaps your professional culture rewards individual achievement over collaboration. Perhaps the broader culture you grew up in glorified the "self-made" person who needs no one. These cultural messages didn't create your story, but they provided a supportive environment for it to thrive.

Relationally, the story creates a predictable dynamic. You become the over-functioner—the one who handles everything—and you attract or create under-functioners around you. Partners learn they don't need to step up because you'll handle it. Colleagues let you take the lead because you always do. Then you feel resentful and alone, which confirms another layer of the story: "No one is there for me." But they're not there for you partly because your story won't let them in.

Spiritually, this story blocks surrender. How can you trust a higher power, the universe, or the flow of life when your operating premise is that you alone can be relied upon? Practices that ask you to let go of control feel threatening. Faith—in anything beyond yourself—feels naïve. The story constructs a world in which you are fundamentally alone, and the spiritual dimension of connection to something larger is walled off.

One story. Six dimensions. Dozens of specific manifestations. And all of it operating largely beneath conscious awareness, showing up as "just how things are" rather than as a narrative that could be examined and revised.

The Recurring Patterns

If the same stories run through your narration, the same patterns will run through your life.

Consider: Is there a relationship dynamic that keeps showing up? A type of person you keep attracting or being attracted to? A way that partnerships unfold that feels frustratingly familiar?

Is there a pattern in your work life? A ceiling you keep hitting? A conflict that keeps recurring with different people? A point in projects where things fall apart?

Is there a pattern in how you relate to your own success? Do you sabotage right before breakthroughs? Discount accomplishments as soon as you achieve them? Move the goalpost so satisfaction is always just out of reach?

These patterns are not random. They're not bad luck. They're not proof that the universe is against you. They're the outward expression of inward stories—your internal narrative made visible in the events of your life.

And this is actually good news. Because if your patterns were random, you'd be helpless against them. But if they're connected to stories, and stories can be examined and revised, then your patterns can change.

Connecting the Dots

Most people experience their lives as a series of individual events. This happened, then that happened, then something else happened. When patterns are pointed out, they're often surprised: "I never noticed that before."

That's because connecting the dots requires stepping back from the events to see the larger picture they form—the way stepping back from a pointillist painting reveals an image that's invisible when you're examining individual dots.

Your cast of characters from Chapter 7 plays a role here. Often, the same character shows up across your patterns. The People Pleaser who can't say no in relationships is the same People Pleaser who over-commits at work and the same People Pleaser who feels resentful but won't address it. The pattern looks different in each context—relationship problems, work burnout, unspoken frustration—but the through-line is the same character running the same script.

A client I'll call Lorraine came to coaching describing three separate problems: a friendship that had quietly collapsed, a promotion she'd been passed over for twice, and a growing distance in her marriage. She presented them as unrelated — just a rough few years.

In our third session, I asked her to walk me through each situation in detail. As she talked, I noticed something. In every story, there was a moment where she had sensed something was wrong — a shift in the dynamic, a signal she'd caught — and had said nothing. In the friendship, she'd noticed her friend becoming distant months before the rupture, but told herself she was probably imagining it. At work, she'd felt undervalued long before the promotion decision, but hadn't raised it with her manager. In her marriage, she'd been feeling unseen for over a year but hadn't wanted to create conflict.

When I named the thread — the consistent pattern of noticing something and going quiet — Lorraine was silent for a long moment.

"I thought those were three different problems," she said finally.

"They might be three different stages of the same one," I said.

She sat back. "I've been doing this my whole life, haven't I?"

It wasn't a question. And it wasn't despair. It was the particular quality of recognition that comes when someone finally steps back far enough to see the whole painting.

From that session forward, we weren't working on a friendship, a career, or a marriage. We were working on one story: *I notice what I need, and I go quiet.* Everything else was downstream of that.

Your filters, biases, and distortions from Chapter 6 also connect the dots. The confirmation bias that expects rejection finds evidence for rejection everywhere—in the friend who canceled plans, the colleague who didn't respond to an email, the partner who seemed distracted. These separate events become connected by the filter through which you perceive them.

Connecting the dots means seeing these through-lines. It means asking: "What do these seemingly separate situations have in common? What story links them? What character might be at work across all of them?"

This isn't about finding something to blame—yourself or anyone else. It's about finding the leverage point. Because when you can see the thread connecting your patterns, you have somewhere to pull.

Stories About Stories

Here's where this work gets layered—and powerful.

Not only do you have stories running your life, but you also have stories *about* those stories. Meta-narratives that shape how you relate to your own patterns.

Some people tell themselves, "This is just who I am. I've always been this way. I'll always be this way." That story about the story creates a sense of permanence and helplessness. If the patterns are fixed features of identity, nothing can change.

Other people tell themselves, "There must be something wrong with me. Normal people don't struggle like this. I'm broken." That story about the story creates shame, making the patterns harder to look at directly and keeping them running in the dark.

Still others tell themselves: "These patterns are information. They developed for reasons. They can be understood. And with understanding comes choice." That story about the story creates curiosity rather than shame, agency rather than helplessness.

The story you tell about your stories matters. It determines whether you approach your patterns as a prosecutor building a case against yourself, or as a curious investigator seeking to understand what's been happening and why.

I invite you to adopt the investigator stance. Your patterns are not evidence of your brokenness. They're evidence of your brain doing exactly what brains do—seeking patterns, completing narratives, trying to make sense of experience with the data it has. The data might be outdated. The interpretations might need revision. But the mechanism works perfectly.

When You're in the Story vs. Seeing the Story

There's a crucial difference between being *inside* a story and *observing* a story—and this is where your witness from Chapter 4 becomes essential.

When you're inside a story, you don't know it's a story. It just feels like reality. The interpretations feel like facts. The conclusions feel like the truth. You're not telling yourself a narrative about what's happening; you're simply experiencing what's happening. The story is invisible because you're looking *through* it rather than *at* it.

When you're observing a story, everything shifts. You can see the narrative as a narrative. You can notice the interpretation as one possible interpretation. You can feel the emotional charge of the story without being completely hijacked by it. There's space between you and the pattern.

This is what your witness makes possible. It can notice: "Ah, the 'I always get rejected' story is running right now. That's why this minor disappointment feels so devastating—it's plugged into a much bigger narrative." That noticing doesn't make the feeling disappear, but it changes your relationship to it. You're no longer just the character living the story. You're also the awareness watching the story unfold.

The shift from inside to observing often happens in moments of recognition. Something clicks. You catch yourself mid-pattern and think, "Wait—I've been here before. This is that thing I do." That moment of recognition is profound. It's the instant when what was unconscious becomes conscious, when the automatic becomes available for examination.

These moments are breadcrumbs. They're your awareness trying to show you something. And every time you honor them—every time you pause and get curious instead of just continuing the pattern—you strengthen your capacity to see the stories rather than just live them.

Becoming the Author

You've been living inside stories you didn't consciously write. Stories that were constructed from childhood interpretations, cultural scripts, protective strategies, and the brain's automatic pattern-completion.

But you are not just a character in these stories. You can become the author.

This doesn't mean fabricating a false narrative or engaging in empty positive thinking. It means examining the stories you've been telling, questioning whether they're accurate and whether they're serving you, and consciously choosing which stories to continue and which to revise.

Some questions to start the examination:

What's the story? Can you name the narrative that runs through a particular pattern? Not just "I have bad luck with relationships" but the fuller story: "I give too much, don't get my needs met, become resentful, and eventually the relationship falls apart." Name it specifically.

Where did this story come from? Stories aren't born from nothing. They were constructed from experiences and interpretations. What early experiences might have seeded this narrative? What did you witness? What were you told? What did you conclude from what happened?

Is this story true? Not "does it feel true" (it will feel true; that's how stories work), but can you actually verify it? Is there evidence that contradicts it? Are there exceptions you've been minimizing?

Is this story serving you? Even if partially true, is this narrative helping you live the life you want? Is it opening possibilities or closing them?

What would a revised story sound like? Not the opposite extreme, but a more accurate, more nuanced, more empowering version? A story that accounts for the real challenges while leaving room for growth and change?

This is authorship. This is moving from being written to writing. It doesn't happen overnight—stories that have been running for decades don't dissolve with a single insight. But every time you catch a story in action, question it, and consciously choose your response, you're weakening the automatic pattern and strengthening your capacity to choose.

The Dots Are Breadcrumbs

Here's what I want you to see: the patterns in your life are not just problems to be solved. They're breadcrumbs.

Every recurring struggle points to something that wants to be healed. Every repeated pattern highlights a story that's ready to be examined. Every frustrating theme is an invitation to look beneath the surface at what's driving it.

Your patterns are not evidence that you're failing at life. They're evidence that your unconscious is trying to get your conscious attention. The same situation keeps arising because something in you keeps creating it—and that something is asking to be seen.

In this sense, your patterns are gifts. Not pleasant gifts, necessarily, but valuable ones. They're showing you exactly where the work is. They're connecting the dots for you, if you're willing to see the picture they form.

The question isn't "Why does this keep happening to me?" The question is, "What is this pattern trying to show me? What story is it revealing? What would shift if I really understood it?"

Pause and Reflect

Before moving to the next chapter, take a moment to sit with these questions. Let them work on you.

What story do you tell about yourself that you've never really questioned? Where did that story come from?

What's a pattern that keeps showing up in your life—in relationships, work, or how you treat yourself? If that pattern could speak, what would it say it's trying to protect or accomplish?

When your brain "fills in the blanks" in ambiguous situations, what does it typically fill in? Positive assumptions or negative ones? What does that reveal about the stories running in the background?

If you stepped back and looked at your life like a pointillist painting, what larger picture would emerge from the individual dots?

Can you recall a recent moment when you caught yourself inside a story—when you shifted from living it to seeing it? What made that shift possible?

What's one story you've been telling that might not be as true—or as permanent—as it feels?

The Breadcrumb

Each chapter closes with a single breadcrumb—a key insight to carry forward on your journey.

Your brain is a pattern-seeking, story-creating machine. It can't help itself—it will find patterns and weave narratives whether you ask it to or not. This is how it makes sense of the eleven million bits, how it fills in the blanks, how it transforms raw experience into coherent meaning. But the patterns it finds and the stories it tells are not neutral. They're shaped by old data, childhood conclusions, cultural scripts, and the protective strategies you developed long ago. These stories feel like the truth because you've been living inside them for so long. But they're not truth—they're interpretations. And interpretations can be re-examined. The recurring patterns in your life are not proof of your brokenness; they're invitations to look deeper. The threads connecting your experiences are not chains binding you to repetition; they're breadcrumbs showing you exactly where the work is. You've been a character in stories you didn't write. Now you can become the author. See the pattern. Question the story. Connect the dots. And begin to write something new.

Going Deeper: Your Digital Companion

The questions above are meant to stir something in you—to begin the inner conversation. But real integration happens when you take time to explore your responses more fully.

In your digital companion, you'll find the following exercises for Chapter 8:

Your Recurring Stories — A narrative analysis exercise to identify the stories you tell yourself repeatedly. What are the plotlines that run through your self-talk? How long have they been running?

Pattern Mapping — Identifying the recurring themes across different areas of your life—relationships, work, health, creativity. What shows up again and again? What connects the dots?

The Origin Story — For each major pattern or story, trace it back. Where did it begin? What experience seeded it? What interpretation did you form?

Story Across Dimensions — Taking one core story and mapping how it manifests biologically, neurologically, psychologically, culturally, relationally, and spiritually

Story Audit — Examining your core stories through three questions: Is it true? Is it the whole truth? Is it serving me?

The Revised Draft — Practice rewriting one limiting story. Not into its opposite, but into a more accurate, nuanced, and empowering version.

Mindset Mind Map Update: The Threads — Adding your recurring patterns and stories to the evolving map of your inner landscape

---

You've now seen both the cast and the scripts—the characters who've been running the show and the stories they've been performing. In Chapter 9, we'll explore what happens at the edges of your story—where you end, and others begin. We'll look at boundaries: how they form, how they get eroded, and how to reconstruct what protects your authentic self without building walls that keep life out. The territory is becoming clearer. Let's keep mapping.

CHAPTER NINE

TROUBLE AT THE BORDER

WHEN will you ever learn...that resistance is a signpost, not a stop sign?

"The cave you fear to enter holds the treasure you seek." — Joseph Campbell

"What we resist persists." — Carl Jung

IN CHAPTER 8, YOU discovered the stories and patterns running your life. These are the narratives you've lived inside without realizing they were narratives at all. You learned that your brain weaves these stories automatically. It fills in blanks and connects dots using old data and childhood conclusions.

But here's what happens when that awareness does its work: something pushes back.

This chapter is about that pushback—what happens when the unconscious material beneath your waterline rises, revealing the gap between how you've been operating and what is actually surfacing. It's the border between the conscious and unconscious, and the trouble that erupts when something tries to cross it.

Your system doesn't surrender its secrets easily. The 90% beneath the waterline didn't end up there by accident. It was placed there, piece by piece, by a protective system. This system decided this material was too threatening, too painful, or too dangerous to keep in conscious awareness. That same protective system fights to keep it buried.

Understanding this resistance isn't about defeating it. It's about recognizing it for what it is: a signpost pointing directly at the work that matters most.

The Waterline Is a Border

In Chapter 3, you met the iceberg—10% of yourself above the waterline, and 90% beneath it, driving nearly everything. That waterline isn't just a metaphor for the conscious and unconscious—it's a border, and like any border, it's patrolled.

Your unconscious material remained unconscious for a reason. Some beliefs felt too threatening to examine. Certain memories carried too much pain. Parts of yourself weren't acceptable to your family or culture. Some needs had gone unmet for so long that they felt unbearable to acknowledge. All of this was pushed below the waterline by a system designed to protect you from overwhelm.

That system is still active. And it has border guards.

When something from below starts to rise—when a buried truth begins to surface, when an old wound asks to be seen, when the gap between your story and reality becomes too obvious to ignore—the border guards mobilize. They don't want that material crossing into conscious awareness. Their job, as they understand it, is to keep you safe. And safety, to them, means keeping the border secure.

This is why insight isn't enough. This is why you can understand something intellectually and still feel completely stuck. This is why you can read all the right books, do all the exercises, know exactly what your patterns are—and still repeat them. The border guards are doing their job.

Beyond the Everyday Defenses

In Chapter 7, you met your cast of characters: the Perfectionist, the People Pleaser, the Controller, and the rest. These are your everyday defenses. They are the strategies you use to manage anxiety, maintain relationships, and navigate the world. They're always on stage, running their familiar scripts.

When something threatens to surface from the deep—when real awareness approaches—another level of defense activates. These aren't the everyday characters. They're emergency responders, deployed specifically to prevent breaches of the waterline.

Think of it as a two-tier system:

Tier One defenses are your cast of characters. They operate continuously, shaping how you move through the world. The Perfectionist keeps you safe from criticism. The People Pleaser keeps you safe from rejection. They're working all the time, often without your awareness, but they're managing day-to-day life.

Tier Two defenses activate when Tier One isn't enough—when something from the depths is rising and threatens to become conscious. These are the emergency protocols. The heavy artillery. The last line of defense before buried material breaks through into awareness.

You've experienced Tier Two defenses, even if you didn't recognize them as such. They're why, right before a breakthrough, everything suddenly gets foggy. You might be in an important conversation and suddenly feel exhausted, confused, or numb. Or you could be doing deep work on yourself, only to find yourself reorganizing a closet or picking a fight over something trivial.

Tier Two defenses are sneaky. They don't announce themselves. They disguise themselves as reasonable explanations, physical symptoms, external circumstances, or sudden changes in priority. Their job is to redirect your attention away from whatever is trying to surface—and they're remarkably good at it.

The Gap That Triggers the Guards

What actually triggers these emergency defenses? It's the gap—the growing awareness that something about how you've been operating doesn't match reality.

Maybe you've been telling yourself you're fine with your career, but something keeps whispering that you're not. Maybe you've constructed a story about your childhood as basically happy, but certain memories keep intruding that don't fit the narrative. Maybe you've built an identity around being strong and independent, but lately you've been feeling a desperate longing to be held and cared for.

This gap between your operating story and the emerging truth creates cognitive dissonance—a psychological discomfort that your system is highly motivated to resolve. And there are only two ways to resolve it: update the story to match reality or defend the story against reality's intrusion.

Guess which one your protective system prefers?

Updating the story requires dismantling what you've built. It means acknowledging that some of what you believed about yourself, your history, or your life isn't accurate. It means feeling the feelings you've been avoiding, sometimes for decades. It threatens your identity, your relationships, your sense of how the world works.

Defending the story only requires activating border guards—easier and more automatic than changing your beliefs.

This is why change is so hard. Not because you're weak or lazy or not trying hard enough. But because your system is designed to resist the very awareness that would set you free.

How the Border Guards Operate

Let's look at the specific tactics your system uses to keep material from surfacing. These operate largely outside your awareness—which is precisely what makes them effective. If you could easily see them, they wouldn't work.

Distraction and Redirection

Just as awareness approaches something important, your attention suddenly goes elsewhere. You were about to sit with a difficult feeling, and now you're scrolling through your phone. You were in the middle of journaling about something real, and now you're making a grocery list. You were on the verge of a conversation that matters, and now you're talking about logistics.

This isn't random. This is redirection (and misdirection) —your system pulling the fire alarm to clear the building before anyone sees what's actually burning.

Intellectualization Without Integration

You can talk about your patterns endlessly. You can analyze your childhood with precision. You can explain your defense mechanisms in sophisticated psychological language. But somehow, nothing changes.

This is intellectualization serving as a defense—the illusion of doing deep work while actually staying safely in your head. Real integration requires feeling, not just understanding. When you find yourself getting more and more analytical about an emotional topic, the border guards may be at work.

Sudden Fatigue or Fog

You're in a coaching session or a deep conversation, and suddenly you can barely keep your eyes open. Or your mind goes completely blank—you were just thinking something important, but now it's gone, like trying to remember a dream that slips away as you wake.

This isn't a coincidence. Fatigue and mental fog are classic Tier Two defenses. Your system is essentially saying, "If you fall asleep, you can't see what's surfacing. If you can't think clearly, you can't process what's emerging."

Physical Symptoms

The headache that arrives precisely when you're about to do inner work. The stomachache that shows up before a difficult conversation. The sudden illness that derails your retreat or therapy intensive.

Your body is not separate from your psychological defenses—it's deeply integrated with them. Sometimes, keeping material below the waterline requires a physical intervention. Not that all physical symptoms are psychosomatic, but the timing of certain symptoms is worth noticing.

Emotional Flooding

Sometimes the defense isn't numbness—it's the opposite. You're approaching something significant, and suddenly you're overwhelmed with emotion. So much feeling floods in that you can't possibly think clearly or stay present with what is emerging.

Paradoxically, flooding with emotion can be a way of avoiding emotion. When you're drowning, you're not processing. You're just surviving. The flood serves to wash away whatever was about to become conscious before you could actually see it.

Picking Fights and Creating Crises

You're in a period of real growth, doing meaningful work on yourself, and suddenly your relationship is in crisis. Or you have an explosive conflict with a family member. Or a drama erupts at work that demands all your attention.

Sometimes these are genuinely external events. But sometimes they're unconsciously created—or unconsciously amplified—as a way of redirecting energy away from internal work. It's hard to focus on your inner landscape when there's a fire to put out in your outer world.

The "I Already Know This" Defense

Perhaps the most sophisticated border guard of all: the sense that you already understand whatever is trying to emerge, so there's no need to look more deeply.

"Yes, I know I have abandonment issues." "Yes, I'm aware I seek approval." "Yes, I understand this comes from my relationship with my mother."

This knowing becomes a shield against actually feeling and transforming. It's like having a map of a territory and believing you've therefore traveled it. The "I already know" defense keeps awareness at the intellectual level, preventing the descent into the body and emotions where real change happens.

Resistance Across the Six Dimensions

Just as your characters and stories manifest across all six dimensions of your Life Code, so does your resistance. The border guards operate everywhere. Let's look at how this emergency defense system shows up in each dimension:

Biologically, resistance lives in your body as physical symptoms that conveniently interrupt deep work. Headaches, fatigue, illness, digestive distress, muscle tension that suddenly flares—your body has countless ways to pull attention away from psychological material and redirect it to physical concerns. You might notice that you always get sick during vacations when you might have time to reflect, or that certain physical symptoms mysteriously appear when certain topics arise.

Neurologically, resistance manifests as the brain's difficulty maintaining focus on threatening material. The fog, the forgetting, the sudden inability to think clearly—these are your neural circuitry protecting itself from information it's not sure it can handle. Your brain literally makes it harder to see what's surfacing by disrupting the cognitive processes required to see it. You might notice that you can think with perfect clarity about neutral topics but become strangely confused when certain subjects arise.

Psychologically, resistance shows up as the sophisticated defenses we've discussed: rationalization, intellectualization, projection, and denial. Your mind generates explanations, analyses, and narratives that all serve to keep the threatening material at bay. "I don't need to look at that because..." "That's not really the issue because..." "I've already dealt with that." The psychological dimension is where the border guards do much of their most skilled work.

Culturally, resistance gets reinforced by cultural norms that discourage deep self-examination. "Don't dwell on the past." "Just think positive." "What doesn't kill you makes you stronger." "Other people have real problems." Cultural messages that frame introspection as self-indulgent or as a sign of weakness become allies of your internal resistance. They give your border guards backup: "See? Normal people don't dig around in their psyche like this."

Relationally, resistance operates through the people around you—or more precisely, through your relationships with them. You might unconsciously choose relationships that support your defenses, surrounding yourself with people who won't challenge your stories or push you toward growth. Or you might sabotage relationships that are getting too intimate, too real, too close to your hidden material. Partners who see you as really threatening. Friendships that go deep get mysteriously dropped.

Spiritually, resistance manifests as disconnection from practices that might open you to deeper awareness. The meditation practice you can't seem to maintain. The prayer life has gone quiet. The sense of meaning or purpose has faded to gray. When spiritual practices are working, they surface material from below the waterline, which is exactly why your resistance might keep you from them. "I just can't find the time" becomes a cover story for "I can't find the safety."

Why This Isn't the Enemy

Now, here's where I need to say something important: your resistance isn't the enemy. It's not something to be conquered, defeated, or destroyed. It's a protection system that's trying to keep you safe.

Remember the core principle from Chapter 7: your defenses were solutions, not problems. The same is true for your Tier Two emergency defenses. They developed because, at some point, the material they were guarding genuinely became too much. The pain really was overwhelming. The awareness really would have destabilized a system that couldn't handle it. The border guards were protecting you from flooding that might have drowned you.

The question isn't whether your resistance was valid. It was. The question is whether it's still needed at the level it's operating. You are no longer the child who can't handle certain truths. You are no longer the young person without the resources to process certain pain. You now have capacities you didn't have then: a witness to observe without being overwhelmed, an understanding of how your system works, compassion for yourself and your history.

Your resistance doesn't know this yet. It's still running the old program, protecting you from dangers that may no longer exist in their original form. Part of your work is to update the program—to let the border guards know that times have changed.

Strategies for Working with Resistance

So how do you work with resistance rather than against it? How do you help the border guards stand down without forcing a breach that overwhelms your system?

Name It Without Shaming It

When you notice resistance arising, practice simply naming it. "Ah, resistance is here. Something must be trying to surface." This differs greatly from "What's wrong with me? Why can't I just deal with this?"

Naming without shaming keeps your witness engaged. It acknowledges what's happening without making it mean something terrible about you. And often, simply naming the resistance reduces its power—it's harder to operate unconsciously when consciousness is watching.

Get Curious About What's Being Protected

Instead of trying to push through resistance, get curious about it. What is this resistance protecting? What does it fear will happen if this material surfaces? What would be threatened if you really looked at whatever is trying to emerge?

This shifts you from an adversarial relationship with your resistance to a collaborative one. You're not fighting the border guards—you're asking them what they're guarding and why. Sometimes, just having that conversation changes everything.

A client I'll call Ellen had been in therapy for six years before she came to coaching. She was one of the most self-aware people I'd ever worked with

— articulate about her patterns, fluent in the language of psychology, able to trace almost every difficulty in her life back to its origin with impressive precision.

And nothing was changing.

She described it herself: "I understand everything. I just can't seem to move."

In one of our early sessions, I noticed that every time we approached anything emotionally charged, Ellen would shift into explanation mode. She'd slow down, become more analytical, and produce a beautifully organized account of why she felt what she felt and where it came from. By the end, the emotion had dissolved — not processed, dissolved. Filed neatly away.

I asked her if she'd noticed what happened in those moments.

She thought about it. "I get clear," she said. "Like the fog lifts."

"Or," I said gently, "as the fog arrives."

She was quiet for a long time. Then: "I've been using understanding as a way not to feel it."

Six years of sophisticated self-knowledge, and the border guard had been running the whole time — in the cleverest possible costume. Not denial. Not avoidance. Comprehension. The one thing that felt like progress was the very thing keeping her still.

Once she could see it, she could work with it. We began sitting with things instead of explaining them. It was uncomfortable. It was also, finally, movement.

Go Slow

Your protective system activates when it perceives a threat. The faster you push toward unconscious material, the more threatening it feels.

Going slow—approaching gently, taking breaks, respecting your system's pace—often allows you to go deeper than forcing ever could.

Think of it like approaching a wild animal. If you rush toward it, it flees. If you sit quietly near it, it may come closer over time. The material below your waterline works similarly. It will surface when it feels safe enough to do so.

Work with the Body

Because resistance operates across all dimensions, working at multiple levels simultaneously can help. If your mind is running sophisticated defenses, sometimes going through the body bypasses them. Breathwork, movement, and somatic practices can access material that intellectual approaches can't reach.

Your body holds what your mind can't yet acknowledge. Working with the body honors this truth and provides alternative pathways around the mental border guards.

Titration: Small Doses of Truth

You don't have to process everything at once. Titration means exposing yourself to small, manageable doses of the difficult material, then returning to safety. A little bit of truth, then rest. A little more, then integration.

This respects your system's limits while still making progress. It teaches your border guards that small amounts of this material can be tolerated, gradually increasing their tolerance for larger amounts.

Find Safe Relationship

Deep material often surfaces best in the presence of a safe relationship—a skilled coach, a trusted friend, a supportive group. The presence of a regulated other can help regulate your own system, making it safe enough to approach what you couldn't approach alone.

This isn't a weakness. This is how humans are designed. We are relational creatures, and our healing often requires relational support. The border guards relax when they sense that you're not alone.

The Breakthrough That Resistance Precedes

Here's the paradox: resistance is usually strongest right before a breakthrough. The border guards don't mobilize over irrelevant material. They mobilize for material that matters—the very material that holds the key to your liberation.

When you feel the most resistance, you're often closest to something important. The fog, the fatigue, the sudden urge to quit—these are signs you're approaching the waterline, that something significant is about to surface.

This doesn't mean you should push through recklessly. But it does mean you should pay attention. The places where you resist most strongly are often the places where the deepest treasure lies.

In the next chapter, we'll explore specific hiding places—the Denial Box and other containers where you've stored what you weren't ready to see. But for now, know this: the trouble at the border isn't a sign that something is wrong. It's a sign that something is trying to come home.

Pause and Reflect

Before moving to the next chapter, take a moment to sit with these questions. Let them work on you.

What Tier Two defenses do you recognize in yourself? Distraction, intellectualization, fatigue, physical symptoms, emotional flooding, or creating external crises?

When have you experienced sudden fog or forgetting right before you were about to do something important? What might have been trying to surface?

In which dimension does your resistance show up most strongly—in your body, your thinking, your relationships, your spiritual practice?

What topic or area of your life triggers the most defensive response when someone brings it up or when you try to explore it? What might the border guards be protecting?

Can you recall a time when resistance preceded a breakthrough—when pushing through (or gently persisting) led to genuine insight or change?

How might you work with your resistance rather than against it? What would it look like to collaborate with your border guards rather than fight them?

The Breadcrumb

Each chapter closes with a single breadcrumb—a key insight to carry forward on your journey.

Your unconscious material didn't end up below the waterline by accident. It was placed there by a protective system that judged it too threatening, too painful, or too dangerous to keep in awareness. That system is still active, still patrolling the border between conscious and unconscious, still ready to mobilize when something tries to surface. This is why insight alone doesn't change you—the border guards don't care what you understand intellectually. They care about keeping buried material buried. When you experience resistance—the fog, the fatigue, the sudden distraction, the convenient crisis—you're not failing. You're approaching the waterline. Something is trying to emerge, and your system is doing what it was designed to do: protect you. The question is whether that protection is still needed at the level where it's operating. You are not the child who couldn't handle certain truths. You are the adult with a witness, with understanding, with resources you didn't have then. Your work is not to defeat your resistance but to update it—to let the border guards know that times have changed, that you can handle more than you once could, that what lies below the waterline is not your enemy but your lost self, asking to come home. The trouble at the border is the beginning of the breakthrough. Resistance is a signpost, not a stop sign.

Going Deeper: Your Digital Companion

The questions above are meant to stir something in you—to begin the inner conversation. But real integration happens when you take time to explore your responses more fully.

In your digital companion, you'll find the following exercises for Chapter 9:

Mapping Your Resistance Patterns — Identifying which Tier Two defenses are most active in your system. When and where do they show up? What seems to trigger them?

The Fog Journal — Tracking moments when mental fog, sudden fatigue, or forgetting occur. What were you thinking about or approaching when the fog arrived?

Resistance Across Dimensions — Examining how your border guards operate in each dimension: biological symptoms, neural fog, psychological defenses, cultural reinforcement, relational sabotage, spiritual disconnection

What Are They Guarding? — For each major resistance pattern, exploring what material might be trying to surface. What is your system trying to protect you from?

The Gentle Approach — Practicing titration: approaching difficult material in small doses, then returning to safety. Building tolerance gradually.

Working with the Body — Somatic exercises for accessing what the mind's defenses won't allow. Breath, movement, and body awareness practices.

Mindset Mind Map Update: The Border Guards — Adding your resistance patterns to the evolving map of your inner landscape

---

You've now seen the border guards at work—the emergency defenses that mobilize when buried material threatens to surface. But where exactly is that material stored? In Chapter 10, we'll open the Denial Box and explore the other hiding places where you've stored what you weren't ready to see. The border guards patrol the waterline. The Denial Box is where the treasure is actually hidden. Let's find out what you've been keeping from yourself—and why it might be time to look.

CHAPTER TEN

THE DENIAL BOX AND OTHER HIDING PLACES

WHEN will you ever learn...that what you've hidden holds the key to what you seek?

"The only way out is through." — Robert Frost

"The dark does not destroy the light; it defines it. It's our fear of the dark that casts our joy into shadows." — Brene Brown

IN CHAPTER 9, YOU met the border guards—the emergency defenses that mobilize when buried material threatens to surface. You learned how resistance operates, why it exists, and how to work with it rather than against it.

But the border guards are just the patrol. This chapter is about what they're guarding.

Somewhere in the vast territory beneath your waterline, there are containers. Boxes you've sealed. Rooms you've locked. Closets you've closed and walked away from. Inside these containers is everything you couldn't look at, couldn't process, couldn't integrate at the time it happened—so you put it away. You told yourself you'd deal with it later. Or you told yourself it didn't matter. Or you simply forgot it was there.

This is human. This is how we survive what we can't yet handle. But those containers don't disappear just because we stop looking at them. They sit in the dark, taking up space, leaking into our lives in ways we don't recognize.

This chapter is about finding those hiding places. It's about understanding why you put what you put there, what it costs you to keep it hidden, and what becomes possible when you finally gather the courage to look.

The Denial Box

Let's start with the most common container: the Denial Box.

The Denial Box is where you've stored everything you're not ready to admit—to yourself or anyone else. It's not a physical place, of course. It's a psychological container, and everyone has one. Some are small and tidy. Others are overflowing, stuffed with decades of material that keeps threatening to spill out.

What goes in the Denial Box?

Truths about yourself you don't want to face. The ways you've contributed to your own problems. The patterns you keep repeating while blaming external circumstances. The gap between who you present yourself to be and who you actually are. The desires that don't fit your self-image. The parts of yourself you're ashamed of.

Truths about your relationships you don't want to see. The dysfunction you've normalized. The ways you've been complicit in your own mistreatment. The relationships that aren't working but that you keep pretending are fine. The love you're not receiving. The love you're not giving.

Truths about your life you don't want to acknowledge. The career that doesn't fit. The dreams you've abandoned. The compromises have cost too much. The way your life has drifted from what you actually wanted. There is a growing awareness that something fundamental needs to change.

The Denial Box is sealed with a particular kind of lock: the genuine belief that you're not in denial. That's what makes denial so effective. It doesn't feel like denial from the inside. It feels like an accurate assessment of reality. "My marriage is fine." "I'm happy with my career." "That doesn't really bother me." "I've dealt with that."

The border guards from Chapter 9 work hard to keep the Denial Box closed. When something inside threatens to surface—when reality keeps contradicting your story—they mobilize to push it back down, explain it away, redirect your attention elsewhere.

But the contents don't stay quiet forever. They knock. They leak. They find ways to make themselves known.

Other Hiding Places

The Denial Box isn't the only container. Your psyche has developed multiple hiding places, each with its own purpose and mechanism.

The Shadow Basement

In Chapter 3, we introduced Jung's concept of the shadow—the parts of yourself you've rejected, denied, or hidden because they weren't acceptable. Think of the shadow as a basement where you've stored everything that couldn't live in the well-lit rooms of your personality.

The shadow holds what was dangerous to express. Anger, if your family punished anger. Sexuality, if your culture shamed desire. Ambition, if you learned that wanting too much was selfish. Vulnerability, if showing weakness, invited attack. Power, if being strong, threatened someone who needed you small.

But the shadow also holds gifts. Creativity, you were told, was impractical. Joy that was too exuberant for your environment. Confidence that was labeled arrogance. Sensitivity that was called weakness. These golden qualities went into hiding too—not because they were bad, but because they weren't safe.

The shadow is a hiding place with a particular quality: you often can't see what's in it, but others can. It leaks out in projection—criticizing in others what you won't acknowledge in yourself. It leaks out in slips and dreams and the things you say when your guard is down. It leaks out in the very intensity of your insistence that you're "not like that."

The "Later" Drawer

This is where you've filed everything you've promised yourself you'll deal with—but not yet. The conversation you need to have. The decision you need to make. The grief you need to process. The change you need to implement.

The Later Drawer is seductive because it feels responsible. You're not ignoring these things—you're just waiting for the right time. When work calms down. When the kids are older. When you have more money, more energy, and more clarity. The right time never comes, of course, but the Later Drawer lets you feel like you're being prudent rather than avoidant.

Meanwhile, everything in the Later Drawer is still affecting you. Unprocessed grief doesn't wait patiently—it seeps into depression or numbness. Unmade decisions create a background anxiety that colors everything. The conversation you're not having is still shaping the relationship.

The "It Wasn't That Bad" Minimizer

Some things are hidden not in a box but in a reframe. You take experiences that were actually significant—sometimes even traumatic—and you minimize them into something manageable. Something that doesn't require attention.

"It wasn't that bad." "Other people had it worse." "It made me stronger." "I'm over it."

The Minimizer is particularly common around childhood experiences. You needed to survive your childhood, and one way to survive was to tell yourself that what happened was normal, wasn't damaging, didn't really affect you. That story helped you keep functioning. But it also hid the material from your own awareness, preventing the integration that would actually set you free.

The Body Vault

When the psyche can't hold something, the body often does. Memories, emotions, and unprocessed experiences get stored in muscle tissue, in chronic tension, in the nervous system's baseline settings.

The Body Vault is a hiding place you can't access through thinking alone. You can analyze your childhood endlessly and never touch the terror that lives in your tight shoulders, the grief stored in your chest; the rage locked in your jaw. The body remembers what the mind has forgotten—or never consciously knew.

This is why somatic approaches are so important in deep work. The body vault requires body-centered keys.

Projection: Hiding in Plain Sight

Sometimes we hide things by putting them somewhere we can see them—just not as ours. Projection takes the disowned material and attaches it to someone else.

The anger you won't acknowledge in yourself becomes your partner's anger problem. The ambition you've suppressed becomes your judgment of ambitious people. The fear you can't face becomes your perception that the world is full of frightened people.

Projection is a hiding place that's hidden by its very visibility. You're looking right at the material—but you're convinced it belongs to someone else.

What Gets Hidden Across the Six Dimensions

Just as your resistance operates across all dimensions, so do your hiding places. Let's look at what might be stored away in each dimension:

Biologically, you may have hidden your body's signals and needs. Hunger, you learned to ignore. Fatigue you pushed through until you couldn't feel it anymore. Pain you normalized. Pleasure you learned was dangerous to feel. The body's wisdom was speaking, but you learned not to listen—so those messages went into hiding, expressing themselves now as mysterious symptoms, chronic conditions, or a fundamental disconnection from physical sensation.

Neurologically, you may have hidden certain ways of thinking and processing. Perhaps you had a creative, divergent mind but learned to hide it in favor of linear, "acceptable" thinking. Perhaps you experienced the world intensely and learned to dampen your neural responses to fit in. The brain's natural patterns got pushed aside, and now you may not even remember that you once thought differently.

Psychologically, you've hidden beliefs, emotions, and parts of your identity that weren't welcome. The Denial Box is largely psychological—full of self-concepts you can't face, emotions you can't allow, truths about your inner life that threaten the story you tell about yourself. This dimension holds most of what we typically think of as "hidden material."

Culturally, you may have hidden parts of yourself that didn't fit your cultural context. Aspects of your identity that your culture shamed. Ways of being that your family or community didn't have room for. Values that contradicted what you were "supposed to" believe. Cultural hiding places are particularly insidious because the hiding feels like adaptation rather than suppression.

Relationally, you've hidden your authentic needs, desires, and responses to protect your connections. The need for more intimacy might scare a partner away. The anger at a parent that feels too dangerous to acknowledge. The ways you've betrayed yourself to maintain relationships. Relational hiding places are often guarded by the fear that if you reveal what's hidden, you'll end up alone.

Spiritually, you may have hidden your deepest longings and questions. The faith you lost and grieved. The experiences that didn't fit your spiritual framework. The questions you were told not to ask. The mystical or transcendent experiences you couldn't explain and learned to dismiss. Spiritual hiding places often hold both our deepest wounds and our most profound gifts.

The Payoffs of Staying Hidden: Secondary Gains

Here's the uncomfortable truth: you get something out of keeping things hidden. If you didn't, you wouldn't do it.

Psychologists call these "secondary gains"—the hidden benefits of maintaining a problem or keeping something out of awareness. Understanding your secondary gains isn't about blame. It's about seeing the whole picture of why change is hard.

The payoff of not facing your relationship problems: You don't have to risk the relationship ending. You don't have to have the terrifying conversations. You don't have to face being alone or starting over. Denial keeps you in a familiar pain rather than an unknown one.

The payoff of not acknowledging your career dissatisfaction: You don't have to make a scary change. You don't have to admit that years were spent on the wrong path. You don't have to face the uncertainty of what else you might do. Staying hidden keeps the current structure intact.

The payoff of not looking at your childhood wounds: You don't have to feel the pain you've been avoiding. You don't have to revise your story about your family. You don't have to grieve what you didn't get. The Later Drawer protects you from the weight of what's actually there.

The payoff of not owning your shadow qualities: You get to maintain your self-image. You get to be the "good one" while others carry the projections. You don't have to integrate parts of yourself that threaten your identity.

These payoffs are real. They're not trivial. The protection that hiding provides has genuine value—that's why you've been doing it. But every payoff has a cost, and usually the cost is your aliveness, your authenticity, your capacity for genuine connection, and your ability to live the life that's actually yours.

How Hidden Material Signals Its Presence

The things you've hidden want to be found. They haven't disappeared—they've just gone underground. And from underground, they send signals. Learning to read these signals is essential to finding what you've stored away.

Recurring Problems

When the same issue keeps showing up in different forms, in different relationships, in different contexts—that's a signal. The universe isn't conspiring against you. Your hidden material is trying to get your attention by creating situations that mirror what you won't look at directly.

Disproportionate Reactions

When your emotional response is bigger than the situation warrants, something is being triggered. You're not just reacting to what's happening now—you're reacting to what's stored in the hiding place that this situation has accidentally opened.

What You Judge in Others

Strong judgment often points to shadow material. The qualities you can't stand in others are frequently the qualities you've disowned in yourself. "I would never..." is often a cover for "I don't want to see that I could..."

Physical Symptoms

Chronic pain, mysterious illness, persistent tension—these can be the body's way of expressing what hasn't been processed psychologically. The body vault sends signals through symptoms.

Dreams

Your unconscious communicates through dreams. The strange scenarios, the impossible situations, the charged images—these are messages from the hiding places. You don't need to interpret them perfectly, but paying attention to them opens a channel.

What You Avoid

Notice what you won't talk about, won't think about, won't go near. The avoidance is a map. It shows you exactly where the hiding places are. Whatever you're most determined not to look at is probably what most needs to be seen.

The Courage to Open What's Sealed

At some point, if you want to reclaim your wholeness, you have to open the boxes.

This takes courage. Genuine courage—not the absence of fear, but the willingness to move forward with fear as a companion. What's in those hiding places got put there because it was overwhelming once. Approaching it again means being willing to feel what you've been avoiding, sometimes for decades.

But here's what I can tell you after forty years of accompanying people into their hidden places: you can handle it. The child who couldn't process the experience has grown into an adult with resources that didn't exist before. The person who sealed the box is not the same person who's opening it now.

You now have a witness—the observer you developed in Chapter 4 — who can watch without being overwhelmed. You have understanding—the framework from these chapters that makes sense of what you'll find. You have compassion, hopefully—or at least the beginning of it—for the self who needed to hide these things.

And you don't have to do it alone. In fact, you probably shouldn't. The deepest hidden material often surfaces best in a safe relationship—with a coach, a therapist, a trusted friend who can stay present while you explore.

Finding Treasure in What You've Avoided

Here's the paradox that transforms this work from excavation of pain to recovery of gifts: what you've hidden isn't just wounds. It's also a treasure.

The anger you suppressed holds your boundaries and your passion. The grief you avoided holds your capacity to love deeply. The fear you denied holds your accurate perception of real dangers. The parts of yourself you disowned hold qualities you desperately need.

Think of it this way: you didn't just hide what was too painful. You hid what was too much. And "too much" includes gifts that were too bright, needs that were too intense, capacities that were too threatening to those around you.

The person who reclaims their shadow doesn't just find darkness. They find exiled power, creativity, and aliveness. They find parts of themselves that have been waiting in the dark, still carrying the gifts they were born with.

A client I'll call Margaret had spent forty years being proud of one thing above all others: she was not an angry person. It was central to her identity. While others lost their tempers, she stayed calm. While others made scenes, she managed herself. Her family called it grace. Her colleagues called it professionalism. She called it the thing she was most sure of about herself.

What brought her to coaching was a marriage that had gone quiet. Not hostile — quiet. Two people moving through the same house as polite strangers. She described it carefully, analytically, without apparent emotion.

When I asked what she felt about it, she said: "I'm not angry. I've processed this."

I believed that she believed it.

Over several sessions, we approached what lived in her shadow basement. Not through confrontation, but through small invitations — noticing what she never said, what she smoothed over, what she described in language slightly too careful to be real.

One afternoon, she said, almost to herself: "I've never once told him when something hurt."

Not once. In twenty-two years.

The anger was there — had always been there. Decades of it. But anger had been in her family's denial box long before it was in hers. Her mother didn't get angry. Her grandmother didn't get angry. Anger was what ungracious women did. So Margaret had sealed it away so completely she genuinely couldn't feel it anymore.

When it finally came — quietly, in that session, more grief than rage — she said something that has stayed with me: "I thought it would make me someone I didn't want to be. But it's just me, asking to be treated well."

That was the treasure. Forty years in the dark, holding her voice, her boundaries, her rightful claim on her own life. Not a flaw to be managed. A self that had been waiting.

This is why the work of opening the hiding places isn't just a therapeutic necessity. It's the path to becoming whole. Every box you open has the potential to return something precious that was never supposed to be locked away.

Strategies for Opening the Hiding Places

So how do you actually do this work? How do you find and open containers you've hidden even from yourself?

Follow the Signals

Start with what's already knocking on the door. What's that recurring dream about? What does that physical symptom want to tell you? What's underneath that disproportionate reaction you had last week? The signals are breadcrumbs leading to the hiding places.

Invite, Don't Force

You can't crowbar the Denial Box open. Forcing just strengthens the defense. Instead, extend an invitation. Let the hidden material know you're willing to see it now. Create space—through journaling, through meditation, through quiet time—and see what wants to emerge.

Start with the Edges

You don't have to dive into the deepest, most terrifying material first. Start with the edges—the things that are almost conscious, the truths that are almost admitted. Each small opening builds capacity for larger ones.

Use Multiple Doorways

If thinking about it doesn't work, try moving it (somatic practices). If talking about it doesn't work, try making art about it. If the direct approach doesn't work, try approaching through dreams or metaphor. Different hiding places respond to different keys.

Get Support

Some boxes shouldn't be opened alone. If you sense that a hiding place contains material that was genuinely traumatic, please get professional support. A skilled coach or therapist can help you open containers without being re-traumatized, can hold space when the contents are overwhelming, and can help you integrate what you find.

Trust the Timing

Hidden material surfaces when you're ready for it. If something isn't opening despite your best efforts, it might not be time yet. Keep doing your work, keep building your capacity, and trust that what needs to emerge will emerge when you can handle it.

Completing the Education

With this chapter, we've completed the deep education of Part Three—Understanding the Territory. You now have a comprehensive map of your inner landscape:

Your **cast of characters** (Chapter 7)—the defense mechanisms that have been running the show, the protectors who can become collaborators when you take the director's chair.

Your **stories and patterns** (Chapter 8)—the narratives woven by your pattern-seeking brain, the scripts that have been shaping your life, and your capacity to become the author.

Your **border guards** (Chapter 9)—the Tier Two defenses that mobilize when buried material threatens to surface, and how to work with resistance rather than against it.

And now your **hiding places** (Chapter 10)—the Denial Box and other containers where you've stored what you couldn't face, the secondary gains that have kept things hidden, and the treasure waiting to be reclaimed.

This is the territory beneath your waterline. This is what's been driving the 90% while you were focused on the 10%. And now you can see it—not perfectly, not completely, but enough to begin working with it consciously.

In Part Four, we'll shift from understanding to action. From mapping the territory to actually walking the path. But the understanding you've built here is the foundation for everything that follows.

Pause and Reflect

Before moving to Part Four, take a moment to sit with these questions. Let them work on you.

What might be in your Denial Box—the truths about yourself, your relationships, or your life that you've been avoiding?

What qualities do you judge most harshly in others? Might any of these be shadow material—aspects of yourself you've disowned?

What have you put in the "Later" drawer, promising to deal with it when the time is right? What has that delay cost you?

Where does your body store what your mind won't process? What physical symptoms or chronic tension might be signals from the Body Vault?

What are the secondary gains of your primary hiding places? What do you get to avoid by keeping certain things hidden?

If you were to open one container—gently, with support—what might be in there that you're actually ready to see?

The Breadcrumb

Each chapter closes with a single breadcrumb—a key insight to carry forward on your journey.

You have hiding places. Everyone does. The Denial Box is stuffed with truths you're not ready to face. The shadow basement stores everything that wasn't acceptable to express. The Later drawer is full of things you've promised to deal with someday. The Body vault holds what the mind couldn't process. These containers exist because you needed them—because some material was too much to face when it first appeared. You did what you had to do to survive and function. But survival isn't the same as wholeness, and functioning isn't the same as living fully. What's hidden takes energy to keep hidden. It leaks into your life in ways you don't recognize. It creates patterns you can't explain. It keeps you from the aliveness and authenticity that's your birthright. The invitation now is to open *what's been sealed—not recklessly, not alone, but with courage and support and timing that respects your readiness. What you'll find isn't just pain, though there will be pain. You'll find parts of yourself that have been waiting in the dark. Gifts you forgot were yours. Capacities that were too much for your early environment but are exactly what your life needs now. The hiding places guard your wounds. They also guard your treasure. What you've avoided holds the key to what you seek.*

Going Deeper: Your Digital Companion

The questions above are meant to stir something in you—to begin the inner conversation. But real integration happens when you take time to explore your responses more fully.

In your digital companion, you'll find the following exercises for Chapter 10:

Inventory of Hiding Places — A guided exploration of your Denial Box, shadow basement, Later drawer, Body Vault, and projection patterns. What might be stored in each?

Signal Tracking — Documenting the recurring problems, disproportionate reactions, harsh judgments, and persistent symptoms that point to hidden material

Secondary Gains Audit — Examining the payoffs you receive from keeping things hidden. What do you get to avoid? What does denial protect?

Shadow Work Introduction — Beginning exercises for exploring the shadow: what you judge, what you deny, what you "would never."

The Edge Approach — Identifying material that's almost conscious—truths you almost admit, feelings you almost allow—and gently inviting them forward

Body Listening — Somatic exercises for accessing the Body Vault. What is your body holding that your mind hasn't acknowledged?

Mindset Mind Map Update: The Hidden Material — Adding what you've discovered about your hiding places to the evolving map of your inner landscape

---

You've now completed Part Three: Understanding the Territory. You've mapped your inner landscape—the characters running the show, the stories shaping your perception, the resistance that guards the waterline, and the hiding places where you've stored what you couldn't face. This is the territory below *the 10%. This is what's been driving your life from below the surface. In Part Four—Following the Trail—we'll move from understanding to action. You'll learn to rewrite your Life Code, make choices from wholeness rather than wounds, work with fear as a companion rather than an obstacle, and release the fallacy of perfection that keeps so many people paralyzed. The map is drawn. Now let's walk the path.*

Part IV: Following the Trail

The Active Journey Home

CHAPTER ELEVEN

REWRITING YOUR LIFE CODE

WHERE do you think you are...in your own transformation?

"We are what we repeatedly do. Excellence, then, is not an act, but a habit." — Aristotle

"The most common way people give up their power is by thinking they don't have any." — Alice Walker

WELCOME TO PART FOUR: Following the Trail.

Parts One through Three laid your foundation. You heard the call, uncovered the Life Code formed outside your will, and discovered the iceberg beneath awareness. You developed your witness, recognized breadcrumbs, and noticed perceptual biases. You met your inner cast, traced stories and patterns, saw how resistance guards the waterline, and explored where you've hidden what you couldn't face.

That was mapping the territory. This is walking it.

Part Four is where understanding becomes action. Where insight transforms into change. Where you stop being the person who was programmed and start becoming the programmer.

This chapter is about the actual mechanics of rewriting your Life Code—not as an abstract concept, but as a practical skill. Because here's what forty years of coaching has shown me: change is absolutely possible. Not easy, but possible. And it becomes far more achievable once you understand how change actually works and develop the clarity to see what needs to shift.

Let's begin with why change is so difficult—and then discover what makes it possible, anyway.

Why Change Is So Difficult

If you've ever tried to change a deeply ingrained pattern and failed, you might have concluded that something is wrong with you. That you lack willpower. That you're not committed enough. That change is possible for other people, but somehow not for you.

None of that is true. Change is difficult for everyone, and the difficulty has nothing to do with your character or commitment. It has to do with how your brain is designed.

Your brain's primary job is efficiency, not accuracy. Once it learns a pattern—any pattern—it wants to automate that pattern so it can free up resources for other tasks. This is why you can drive a familiar route while thinking about something else entirely. Your brain has encoded the driving pattern so thoroughly that it no longer requires conscious attention.

This efficiency is a gift when the patterns serve you. It becomes a problem when they don't—because your brain automates limiting patterns just as readily as helpful ones. The neural pathway for "I'm not good enough" gets just as efficiently encoded as the pathway for tying your shoes.

Neuroscientists describe this as the brain forming "ruts"—like wagon wheels wearing grooves into a dirt road. The more a pathway is traveled, the deeper the rut becomes, and the harder it is for the wagon to go anywhere else. Your thoughts, emotions, and behaviors follow these grooved pathways automatically, without your conscious participation.

Then there's homeostasis—your system's powerful drive to maintain equilibrium. Your body regulates temperature, blood sugar, and countless other variables within narrow ranges. Your psyche does the same thing with identity and patterns. When something threatens to disrupt the familiar equilibrium—even if that disruption would be beneficial—your system responds to restore the status quo.

This is why insight alone doesn't produce change. You can understand your patterns perfectly and still repeat them. Understanding happens in the conscious mind, but the patterns run in the automated systems below conscious awareness. It's like knowing intellectually that you should take a different route while your hands keep turning the steering wheel the familiar way.

Here's the paradox that keeps people stuck: the familiar feels safe even when it's harmful. Your nervous system doesn't evaluate patterns based on whether they're good for you. It evaluates them based on whether they're known. Known equals predictable. Predictable equals survivable. So, your system will fight to maintain patterns that are actively hurting you, simply because those patterns are familiar.

This is not a design flaw. This is your brain doing exactly what it evolved to do. But understanding this removes the shame from failed attempts at change. You weren't weak. You were facing the full force of biological systems designed to resist exactly what you were trying to do.

What Makes Change Possible

Now for the good news: change is absolutely possible. Your brain is not fixed. The ruts can be rerouted. New pathways can be built.

The scientific term is neuroplasticity—your brain's ability to reorganize itself by forming new neural connections throughout your entire life. This isn't wishful thinking; it's documented neuroscience. People recover from strokes by building new pathways around damaged areas. Musicians develop enlarged regions in the parts of their brains related to their instruments. London taxi drivers have measurably larger hippocampi from navigating complex spatial information.

Your brain is changing right now as you read these words. The question isn't whether it can change. The question is whether the changes are happening by default or by design.

Here's what makes intentional change possible:

Clarity comes first. You cannot change what you cannot see. The work you've done in Parts One through Three—developing your witness, recognizing your patterns, understanding your defenses—has been building the clarity that makes change possible. This is why I say change becomes achievable once clarity is achieved. You now see the code. Seeing is the prerequisite for rewriting.

Repetition builds new pathways. Just as old patterns get grooved through repetition, new patterns get established the same way. A single insight rarely changes anything permanently. But that same insight, revisited and reinforced consistently over time, gradually builds a new pathway that can eventually become as automatic as the old one.

Emotion accelerates encoding. Experiences with emotional charge create stronger neural connections than neutral experiences. This is why a single traumatic moment can create a lifelong pattern, while years of rational understanding might shift nothing. When you're working to install new patterns, connecting them to genuine emotion helps them encode more deeply.

Attention is the spotlight. What you pay attention to gets strengthened. When you notice yourself running old code and consciously redirect to new code, you're literally redirecting neural traffic. Each time you do this, you weaken the old pathway slightly and strengthen the new one. This is why your witness—that observing capacity you developed in Chapter 4—is essential for change.

Self-compassion mobilizes; **shame freezes.** Research by Kristin Neff and others has shown that self-compassion actually supports change more effectively than self-criticism. When you beat yourself up for falling into old patterns, you activate threat responses that make learning harder. When you meet yourself with compassion—acknowledging the difficulty while recommitting to the direction—you stay in a state where change remains possible.

Small and consistent beats dramatic and sporadic. Your system resists big disruptions but can adapt to gradual shifts. Small changes, maintained consistently, accumulate into transformation. This isn't as exciting as the fantasy of an overnight breakthrough, but it's how sustainable change actually happens.

Understanding Your Life Code as Actual Code

In Chapter 2, we introduced the concept of your Life Code—the operating system running beneath your conscious awareness, shaping your perceptions, reactions, and choices. Now let's look at that code more specifically, because understanding its structure helps you rewrite it.

Think of your mind as running programs—not in a technical sense, but in the sense that certain inputs reliably produce certain outputs. When a specific situation arises, a specific response runs. When a particular thought appears, a particular emotion follows. These aren't random. They're programmed responses, and they follow a kind of logic, even when that logic no longer serves you.

Source code is the original programming—the beliefs, interpretations, and strategies written during your formative years. This code was written before you had the capacity to evaluate it. A child can't say, "I notice my parent is anxious about money, but I'll choose not to internalize that as my own belief." The child simply absorbs: "There's never enough. Money is scary. Security is fragile." That becomes source code.

Legacy code is old programming that's still running even though the circumstances that created it no longer exist. The scarcity programming installed during a financially unstable childhood might still run decades later, even though your actual financial situation is now secure. Legacy code doesn't update automatically when circumstances change. It just keeps running the old program.

Runtime errors occur when the code produces results that don't work—when your programming generates outcomes that harm you or conflict with what you actually want. The people-pleasing code that helped you survive a volatile household produces runtime errors in adult relationships, preventing genuine intimacy.

Bugs are code glitches that cause unintended behavior. You might have code that says, "Be successful," and code that says, "Don't outshine others." These conflicting instructions create bugs—self-sabotage, inexplicable anxiety about achievement, success followed immediately by self-destruction.

The code runs automatically until you access it and edit it. That's what we're learning to do.

The Power of Language in Your Life Code

Here's something crucial: your Life Code is written in language. Not computer language, but human language—the words and phrases that run through your mind, often so automatically that you don't notice them.

These linguistic patterns are what I call behavioral statements—the actual lines of code that generate your experience. They're the specific sentences, running beneath conscious awareness, that tell your brain how to interpret situations, what to feel, and how to respond.

Language isn't just how you describe your experience. Language shapes your experience. The words running in your mind literally influence which neural pathways fire, which emotions arise, and which actions seem possible. Change the language, and you change the code.

Let's look at the types of behavioral statements running your Life Code:

"I am..." statements are an identity code. "I am not creative." "I am too sensitive." "I am bad with money." "I am the responsible one." These statements define who you believe yourself to be, and your brain works to maintain consistency with that identity. Whatever follows "I am" becomes a self-fulfilling instruction.

"I always/never..." statements are pattern code. "I always end up alone." "I never follow through." "I always attract the wrong people." "I never get what I want." These statements encode expectations, and expectations shape perception and behavior in their own direction.

"I can't..." statements are a form of limitation code. "I can't speak up for myself." "I can't handle conflict." "I can't change." These statements close doors before you even approach them. They feel like observations about reality, but they're actually instructions that prevent you from testing whether they're true.

"I should/must..." statements are obligation code. "I should always put others first." "I must be perfect to be loved." "I should never show weakness." These statements often carry someone else's voice—a parent, a culture, an authority—still running in your own mind, generating guilt and pressure.

"People are..." statements are relational code. "People can't be trusted." "People always leave." "People only care about themselves." These statements determine how you approach relationships before any specific person has done anything.

"The world is..." statements are reality code. "The world is dangerous." "Life is hard." "There's never enough." "Good things don't last." These statements create the lens through which you perceive everything.

Some of these statements you speak out loud. But the most powerful ones run silently, beneath conscious awareness—so automatic that they feel like reality rather than interpretation. Your work is to surface these silent statements, evaluate them, and decide whether to keep running them.

Collapsing Old Code

You can't simply delete old code. If you try to just remove a pattern without replacing it, your system will either restore the original programming or generate chaos in the vacuum. Old code has to be collapsed—acknowledged, released, and replaced with something new.

Here's the process:

Identify the specific statement or pattern. Be precise. Not "I have issues with relationships," but "I believe that if I show my real needs, people will leave." Not "I'm insecure," but "I constantly tell myself I'm not as smart as others in the room." The more specific you can name the code, the more effectively you can work with it.

Source where this code was installed. This isn't about blame—it's about understanding. When did this programming get written? What experiences taught your system this pattern? Understanding the origin often loosens the code's grip, because you can see that it was a response to specific circumstances, not an eternal truth.

Evaluate whether this code still serves you. Did it ever accurately reflect reality, or was it always a distortion? Even if it was once adaptive, does it still produce good results in your current life? Be honest. Some code was never accurate. Some code served you once but has since become legacy, causing runtime errors.

Acknowledge what the code was trying to do. This is crucial. Your old programming wasn't random—it was trying to protect you, help you belong, keep you safe. Before releasing it, acknowledge that intention. "This code was trying to protect me from rejection. It was doing its best with what it knew. And I no longer need this form of protection."

A client I'll call Thomas had spent his adult life running a piece of code he'd never examined: *Needing help means you're weak, and weakness gets you hurt.* He didn't say it in those words. He just never asked for help. Not at work, where he quietly shouldered things that should have been shared. Not at home, where his wife described feeling like a bystander in his life. Not even when he was genuinely struggling.

When we surfaced the code and traced it back, it led to a father who had treated any display of vulnerability as an invitation to criticize. The lesson had been written early and written clearly: handle it yourself or pay for it.

I asked Thomas to acknowledge what that code had been trying to do for him.

He resisted at first — it felt like making excuses. But I held the question.

Finally, quietly: "It kept me safe. It kept me from giving him something to use against me." He paused. "It probably kept me sane."

Something shifted in the room when he said it. Not sentimentality — recognition. He could feel, maybe for the first time, the difference between the code that had been running him and the child who had written it out of genuine necessity.

"Thank you," he said — to that part of himself, not to me. "You did your job."

That acknowledgment was the actual hinge. Without it, the new code — *I can receive help, and it makes me stronger, not weaker* — would have been a performance. With it, there was real space for something different to take root.

Release the code consciously. This isn't a onetime event but a practice. Each time the old code runs, notice it, name it, and consciously choose not to follow it. "There's the 'I'm not good enough' code again. I see you. I'm choosing differently now." Over time, with repetition, the old pathway weakens.

Installing New Patterns

Nature abhors a vacuum. You can't just collapse old code—you need to install new code in its place. And the new code needs to be written carefully if it's going to run effectively.

Effective new code is specific. Not "I want to be more confident" but "I speak up in meetings when I have something to contribute." Vague code produces vague results. Specific code gives your brain clear instructions.

Effective new code is present tense. Not "I will learn to trust myself" but "I trust my own judgment." Writing in the future tense keeps the new pattern perpetually in the future. Present tense installs it now.

Effective new code is positive. Your brain doesn't process negatives well. "I don't sabotage myself" keeps "sabotage" as the active instruction. "I support my own success" gives your brain something to move toward rather than away from.

Effective new code is believable. If your old code says, "I'm worthless," and your new code says, "I'm the most amazing person alive," your system will reject it as obviously false. New code needs to be a stretch, but not a fantasy. "I have worth that isn't dependent on others' approval" might be the bridge that eventually leads to deeper self-acceptance.

Effective new code connects to your authentic self. The best new code doesn't feel like something foreign being imposed. It feels like something true being remembered. It aligns with the values you've actually chosen, not inherited. It resonates with your Original Self, the one who was there before the programming.

Here's the installation process:

Write the new statement clearly. Get it down in words. Be specific. Let it take whatever form is most true for you.

Feel into it. Don't just think the new code—let yourself feel what it would be like if this were already true. Emotion helps encoding. If the statement is "I trust my own decisions," feel in your body what it feels like to trust yourself.

Repeat consistently. New code gets installed through repetition. This might mean daily affirmations, journaling, or simply noticing opportunities throughout the day to run the new code instead of the old one.

Act in alignment. Behavior reinforces belief. Each time you take an action consistent with your new code, you strengthen the installation. If your new code is "I speak up when I have something to contribute," actually speaking up—even when it's uncomfortable—reinforces the new pathway.

Celebrate small wins. When you successfully run new code, acknowledge it. Let yourself feel good about it. The positive emotion helps encode the new pattern. Your brain learns: "Running this code feels good. Let's do that again."

The Cascade Effect: Collapsing Code Across Dimensions

Here's something powerful I've observed in forty years of coaching: when you change code in one dimension, it often collapses code in others.

Remember the six layers of your Life Code from Chapter 2—biological, neurological, psychological, cultural, relational, and spiritual? These layers are interconnected. A shift in one ripples through the others.

A client changes her psychological code from "I must be perfect to be loved" to "I am worthy of love as I am." This psychological shift leads to relaxation in her body (biological)—the chronic tension in her shoulders that she'd carried for years begins to release. New neural pathways form (neurological). She stops needing cultural approval as her compass (cultural). Her relationships shift as she stops performing and starts being real (relational). She reconnects with a sense of meaning she'd lost (spiritual).

One piece of code, consciously collapsed and replaced, created a cascade.

This is why the work, while challenging, is so worthwhile. You're not just changing one thing. You're changing a system. And systems, once they begin to shift, can shift in ways that exceed what you consciously intended.

Learning to Observe Your Own Change Process

Here's something I want you to develop as you do this work: the capacity to observe your own process of change. Not just to change, but to notice how you're changing. This awareness becomes a skill you can use for life.

Pay attention to what works for you. What conditions support your growth? What time of day is best for this kind of work? What approaches make it easier to install new code? What triggers old code, and what helps you catch it faster?

Notice the sequence of your change. What happens first? What shifts lead to other shifts? Where do you tend to get stuck, and what helps you move through?

This observation serves two purposes. First, it accelerates your current change process by helping you do more of what works. Second, it builds a meta-skill—the ability to facilitate your own transformation—that you'll have for every future change you want to make.

You're not just rewriting code right now. You're learning how to rewrite code. And that learning is perhaps even more valuable than any specific change, because it makes you the author of your ongoing evolution.

The Mindset Mind Map: Seeing Your Whole System

In your digital companion, you can access a Mindset Mind Map—a visual tool that lets you see your entire system at once.

The Mind Map has HOME at its center, representing your authentic self and your wholeness. Radiating outward are rings corresponding to each part of this book and each chapter's work. As you've moved through the material, you've been adding to this map—building a visual representation of your inner landscape.

Now, as you enter Part Four, your Mind Map becomes a tool for tracking your reprogramming. You can see which old code is being released. You can visualize where new code is being installed. You can notice connections between different parts of your system that you might not have seen otherwise.

The map is a living document. It grows as you do. And having a visual representation of your system helps you see yourself as a whole—not as a collection of problems, but as an integrated being in the process of coming home.

You Are the Programmer Now

Let's name what has shifted.

When you began this book, your Life Code was running you. The programming installed in childhood, layered with cultural conditioning and relational patterns, was generating your experience while you thought you were making free choices. You were a character in a story someone else wrote, following a script you didn't know you were reading.

Now you can see the code. You understand how it got installed, what it's been doing, and why it's been so hard to change. You have tools to collapse old patterns and install new ones. You have a witness who can observe the code running and choose whether to follow it. You have a map of your whole system.

You are no longer the one being programmed. You are the programmer.

This doesn't mean the work is done. Rewriting your Life Code is an ongoing process, not a onetime event. Old patterns will reassert themselves. New patterns will take time to stabilize. There will be days when you feel like you're back at square one.

But you're not at square one. You can't be. Because now you can see. And once you've seen, you can't fully unsee. The awareness you've built is permanent. The skills you're developing will deepen with practice. The direction is set, even when the path gets difficult.

You are the author now. And the story you write from here forward is yours.

Pause and Reflect

Before moving to the next chapter, take a moment to sit with these questions. Let them work on you.

What behavioral statement have you been running that you're now ready to examine? Can you trace when and where that code was installed?

If you could write a new "I am..." statement for yourself—one that reflects who you're becoming rather than who you were programmed to be—what would it say?

In which of the six dimensions is old code most actively running your life? What would change if that code collapsed?

When you've successfully changed something in the past, what made that change possible? What conditions supported it? What can you learn from your own history of transformation?

What new code would you like to install? What's one small action you could take today that would begin running that new program?

How might you observe your own change process as you do this work? What would you want to notice and track?

The Breadcrumb

Each chapter closes with a single breadcrumb—a key insight to carry forward on your journey.

You didn't write the original code. It was installed by well-meaning parents, teachers, and a culture that was passing along its own programming. By the time you were old enough to evaluate what you believed, the beliefs were already encoded, running in the background, shaping your experience while feeling like simple reality. Change has been difficult, not because something is wrong with you, but because your brain is designed to maintain established patterns. It grooves neural pathways through repetition and then fights to keep the wagon wheels in those ruts. It prefers the familiar—even harmful—to the unknown. This is not a flaw. This is biology. And biology can be worked with. Neuroplasticity means your brain can change at any age. Clarity means you can see the code that's been running. And the skills you're building—identifying behavioral statements, collapsing old code, installing new patterns—mean you can actually do something about what you see. The language running in your mind shapes the life you live. "I am" becomes an instruction. "I always" becomes a prediction. "I can't" becomes prohibition. Change the language, and you change the code. Change the code in one dimension, and watch it cascade through others. You are no longer the child being programmed. You are the adult with your hands on the keyboard, able to access the source and decide what stays, what goes, and what gets written fresh. From here forward, you are the programmer. Write well.

Going Deeper: Your Digital Companion

The questions above are meant to stir something in you—to begin the inner conversation. But real integration happens when you take time to explore your responses more fully.

In your digital companion, you'll find the following exercises for Chapter 11:

Code Audit — Identifying specific behavioral statements across all six dimensions. What's running in your "I am," "I always/never," "I can't," "I should," "People are," and "The world is" code?

Source Tracing — For your most significant behavioral statements, tracing back to when and where they were installed. What experiences wrote this code?

The Collapse Process — A guided exercise for releasing one piece of old code. Moving through identification, sourcing, evaluation, acknowledgment, and release.

Writing New Code — Crafting replacement statements with proper architecture: specific, present tense, positive, believable, and connected to your authentic self.

Installation Protocol — A daily practice structure for encoding new patterns through repetition, emotion, action, and celebration.

Observing Your Change Process — A tracking tool for noticing what works in your personal transformation, building meta-skills for ongoing evolution.

Mindset Mind Map Update: The Reprogramming — Visualizing old code releasing and new code installing on your evolving map

---

You've learned to rewrite your Life Code—to collapse old programming and install patterns that actually serve you. But having new code isn't the same as running it in every moment. In Chapter 12, we'll explore the power of choice: the difference between operating on autopilot and making genuine decisions from a place of awareness. New code gives you options. Choice is how you exercise them. The programmer has tools now. Let's learn to use them in the moments that matter.

Chapter Twelve

The Power of Choice

WHERE do you think you are...when you're actually at choice?

"Life is the sum of all your choices." — Albert Camus

"Awareness is the greatest agent for change." — Eckhart Tolle

We believe we make thousands of choices every day: what to wear, what to eat, what to say, and how to respond. But is it true that we're really in charge—truly the ones deciding? This is the question at the heart of our exploration.

But here's the uncomfortable truth: most of what we call "choice" isn't choice at all—it's autopilot in action. Much of what we believe are decisions are actually conditioned responses, automatic routines shaped by old programming. We simply keep the illusion that we're the ones at the controls.

The difference between reacting and choosing is the difference between being run by your code and living from your authentic self. It's the difference between life happening to you and consciously creating your life.

In Chapter 11, you gained tools to rewrite your Life Code—to collapse old programming and install new patterns. But having new code isn't the same as running it. This chapter is about the moment of choice itself—the instant when you can either default to autopilot or consciously select a different response. Those moments, accumulated over a lifetime, determine who you become.

The Autopilot Life

Let's name what we're dealing with.

Autopilot is when your conditioned responses run without your conscious participation. It's when the stimulus arrives, and the response fires before awareness even registers that something happened. It's when you have said the thing, done the thing, felt the thing—and only afterward realize you had no say in it.

Your brain loves autopilot. In Chapter 11, the brain's primary job is efficiency. Once it learns a pattern, it wants to automate it to conserve resources. This is why you don't have to consciously think about walking, or speaking your native language, or recognizing faces. These have been automated so thoroughly that they require no conscious attention.

The problem is that your brain automates everything—not just neutral skills, but your reactions to conflict, your responses to stress, your patterns in relationships, your relationship with yourself. All of it gets automated. All of it runs on autopilot unless you consciously intervene.

And here's what makes this so insidious: autopilot feels normal. It feels like "just the way I am." When you've been running the same patterns for decades, you don't experience them as patterns. You experience them as identity. "I'm just not good at confrontation." "I always shut down when I'm criticized." "That's just how I react."

But those aren't facts about who you are. Those are descriptions of running autopilot programs. And programs can be interrupted.

The first step is the wake-up moment—the recognition that you've been on autopilot. This moment is often uncomfortable. It means seeing that much of what you thought was "you" making choices was actually conditioning, making choices while you watched from somewhere far away. But this discomfort is the doorway to freedom. You can't choose differently until you see that you haven't been choosing at all.

How Autopilot Manifests Across Dimensions

Autopilot doesn't just run in one area of your life. It runs everywhere. Let's look at how it shows up across all six dimensions of your Life Code:

Biologically, autopilot shows up as automatic physical responses that you hardly notice. Your shoulders tense when you hear your mother's voice, or your jaw clenches at certain topics at work. You reach for food when not hungry, override fatigue, and ignore your body—all on autopilot. Your nervous system activates stress responses to triggers you haven't examined. You hold your breath in unnoticed stressful situations. Your body runs programs written decades ago, unnoticed.

Neurologically, autopilot shows up as thought loops running without your permission. The same worries cycle through your mind, the same interpretations apply to new situations, and the same mental commentary narrates your experience. Your attention automatically goes where it's always gone—to threat, criticism, or what might go wrong—not because you chose to focus there but because neural pathways are deeply grooved. Familiar stimuli trigger predictable emotional sequences: a certain tone of voice elicits a feeling, which in turn triggers a cascade of thoughts. All automatic. All running before you're even aware it started.

Psychologically, autopilot runs your self-talk, default beliefs, and emotional reactions. When someone compliments you, the automatic response dismisses it before you even consider accepting it. A challenge appears, and the "I can't" program runs before you decide if it's true. Your identity reflexively defends, explains, and justifies—with no conscious choice. The stories you tell yourself about who you are and what's possible repeat endlessly, shaping your experience but seeming like objective facts.

Culturally, autopilot manifests as unexamined adherence to scripts you absorbed but never chose. You pursue what you're "supposed to" pursue. You value what your culture told you to value. You feel shame about things that violate cultural norms you've never consciously evaluated. You follow collective autopilot—doing what everyone does, thinking what everyone thinks—and experience it as making your own choices. The cultural programming runs so deep that questioning it doesn't even occur to you. It just feels like "how things are."

Relationally, autopilot shows up as patterned responses to certain people and situations. You play the same role you've always played in your family. You have scripted conversations in which everyone recites their familiar lines. You respond to your partner's tone the way you've always responded—defending, withdrawing, attacking—before you've made any conscious choice about how to engage. You attract the same types of relationships, create the same dynamics, and hit the same walls. The relational choreography runs automatically, partners moving through steps neither of them consciously chose.

Spiritually, autopilot manifests as going through the motions without presence. Practices that once connected you to something deeper become routine—meditation you do while planning your day, prayers you recite without feeling them, rituals performed by habit rather than intention. Your default meaning-making runs automatically: this is good, this is bad, this matters, this doesn't. Your relationship to the deeper questions of existence operates on old programming, and you've stopped genuinely inquiring. The spiritual dimension becomes another area where autopilot runs the show.

This is the autopilot life. It's not evil or broken—it's simply unconscious. And unconsciousness is the opposite of choice.

What True Choice Actually Looks Like

True choice is something different entirely.

True choice requires awareness—the witness you developed in Chapter 4. You can't choose consciously if you're not aware that a choice point exists. When you're fully identified with your reactions, fully merged with your conditioning, there's no "you" separate enough to choose. The witness creates that separation. It notices: "Something is happening. A response is arising. I could do X, or I could do Y."

True choice requires a pause—however brief—between stimulus and response. This is the space that holds our freedom. On autopilot, there is no pause. Stimulus leads directly to response with nothing in between. True choice inserts a moment of awareness into that gap—a moment where alternatives become visible.

True choice involves seeing options, not just the automatic one. When you're on autopilot, only one response exists: the conditioned one. It doesn't feel like you're choosing it; it feels like it's simply what's happening. True choice opens the field. You see the automatic response, and you see other possibilities. You recognize: "I could react the way I always react, or I could respond differently."

True choice is responsive rather than reactive. Reaction is automatic, driven by past conditioning. Response is conscious, informed by present reality. Reaction says, "This is what I always do." Response asks, "What does this situation actually call for?"

Remember: true choice doesn't always provide an obvious "right" answer. Sometimes you genuinely don't know what to do. That uncertainty is part of a conscious choice. On autopilot, there's false certainty; in true choice, you recognize you are selecting from options, and the outcome isn't guaranteed. It's uncomfortable, but that's what freedom feels like.

Genuine choice feels different from autopilot. There's presence—you're in the moment, not running old programs. There's often a sense of aliveness, and sometimes discomfort—because choosing consciously means accepting responsibility.

The Anatomy of a Choice Point

Let's slow down and look at what actually happens in the moment of choice—because these moments pass quickly, and understanding their structure helps you work with them.

First, there's a **trigger**—an external event or internal state. Someone says something, a situation arises, or a feeling appears, calling for a response.

Next, the **automatic response** rises—your conditioning activates, neural pathways fire, and habitual patterns start to run. This often happens before conscious awareness catches up.

Then—if you're aware enough—the **witness notices**. That observing capacity you've been developing recognizes: "Something is happening. A response is forming." This noticing is crucial. It's the moment where autopilot can be interrupted.

The witness creates a **pause**—maybe just a fraction of a second, but enough. This is the space between stimulus and response, the gap where choice lives. The automatic response is still there, ready to run, but it hasn't taken over yet.

In that pause, you can **see alternatives**. The automatic response is one option, but now you can glimpse others. "I could react with anger, like I always do. Or I could take a breath. Or I could ask a question. Or I could excuse myself for a moment." The field of possibilities opens.

Then comes the **conscious selection**—the actual choosing. You don't just let the automatic response run; you actively select a response. It might be the same as the automatic one, but now it's chosen rather than defaulted to. Or it might be different—an experiment with a new way of responding.

Finally, there's **action from choice rather than reaction**. You move forward with what you've selected, experiencing the reality of having genuinely chosen.

This entire sequence can happen in seconds. But those seconds changed everything. They're the difference between a life on autopilot and a life that's consciously lived.

Choosing from Wholeness vs. Choosing from Wounds

Here's a distinction that transforms the quality of your choices: you can choose from two fundamentally different sources—your wounds or your wholeness.

Choosing from wounds is fear-based, protective, and reactive. It's trying to avoid the pain you've experienced before. It's attempting to get unmet needs met through indirect means. It's letting old injuries run your current decisions. When you choose from wounds, your choices are essentially backward-looking—determined by what hurt you in the past rather than what's true in the present.

Signs you're choosing from wounds: There's a quality of desperation or urgency. Your body feels contracted, tight, defensive. You're focused on what you don't want rather than what you want. You're trying to control outcomes because the uncertainty feels unbearable. The choice reinforces your old stories: "See, I have to do this because people can't be trusted / I'm not good enough / the world is dangerous."

Choosing from wholeness is grounded in your authentic self. It's aligned with your genuine values—not inherited ones, but the ones you've consciously chosen. It responds to present reality rather than past programming. It's connected to what actually matters, not what your conditioning says should matter.

Signs you're choosing from wholeness: There's a quality of clarity rather than urgency. Your body feels more open, more grounded. You can hold uncertainty without being hijacked by it. You're oriented toward what you want to create rather than what you want to avoid. The choice aligns with who you're becoming, not just who you've been.

Here's what makes this tricky: the same external choice can be made from either place. You might set a boundary from wounds—as a wall to keep everyone out because you've been hurt before. Or you might set the same boundary from wholeness—as a genuine honoring of your needs and limits. The outer action looks similar. The inner source is completely different. And the results, over time, will be completely different too.

When you notice yourself about to make a choice, pause and ask: "Am I choosing this from fear and old protection? Or am I choosing this from clarity and my authentic self?" The answer isn't always obvious—wounds can disguise themselves as wisdom, and fear can masquerade as prudence. But asking the question reveals the source.

A client I'll call Nina had built a very successful consulting practice by being the person who never said no. She was good at everything, available for everything, and privately exhausted by everything. She came to coaching because she was burning out—but she described it as a time-management problem.

In one session, she mentioned that a long-standing client had asked her to take on a project she genuinely didn't have the capacity for. She'd already decided to say yes.

I asked her where that yes was coming from.

She thought about it. "He's been with me for seven years. I can't let him down."

"Is that a yes from your values," I asked, "or a yes from somewhere older than that?"

A long silence. Then: "My mother used to say that if you let people down, they leave." She paused. "I've never said no to him because I've always been afraid that would be the moment he decides I'm not worth keeping."

She looked at the yes she'd been about to give — and saw it clearly for the first time. Not a professional decision. Not a values-based choice. A seven-year-old's strategy for keeping people from leaving, running in a fifty-two-year-old's business.

She called him that afternoon — not to say no, but to say she needed two more weeks and a reduced scope. He said that was completely fine.

The yes she'd been ready to give hadn't been about him at all. It had been about the wound. The wholeness choice was smaller, more honest, and turned out to be more than enough.

How to Access Choice with So Much Running in the Background

Here's the honest truth: you can't stop all the background programming. You will never reach a state where conditioning isn't operating, where autopilot isn't ready to run, where your past doesn't influence your present. That's not how the human system works.

But you can create more moments of genuine choice. You can expand the percentage of your life that's consciously lived. Here's how:

Slow down. Speed is autopilot's best friend. When you're rushing, there's no time for awareness, no space for the witness, no gap where choice can live. Slowing down—even slightly—creates room for consciousness to enter. Before you respond to that email, pause. Before you react to that comment, breathe. Before you make that decision, wait. Speed serves automation. Presence requires pause.

Engage your witness. Use the phrase from Chapter 4: "I notice that I am..." When you catch yourself about to run a familiar program, name it. "I notice I'm about to defend myself the way I always do." "I notice I'm about to say yes when I want to say no." This naming creates space. It moves you from inside the reaction to observing the reaction—and observation is where choice lives.

Name the automatic response. Make the unconscious conscious. When you can specifically identify what your autopilot is about to do, it loses some of its power. "My automatic response right now is to withdraw and go silent." "My conditioning wants me to over-explain and seek approval." Naming the pattern interrupts it.

Ask the clarifying question. In the pause, ask yourself: "What would I choose if I weren't afraid?" Or: "What would I choose if I weren't trying to protect myself?" Or: "What would I choose if I trusted myself?" These questions bypass the conditioned response and access something deeper.

Check alignment. Ask: "Does this choice align with my values and who I'm becoming?" This isn't about perfection—it's about direction. You're not asking if the choice is flawless. You're asking whether it moves you toward the person you want to be or away from that person.

Start with low-stakes choices. Build the muscle of conscious choosing in moments that don't carry high pressure. Practice pausing before small decisions. Practice noticing autopilot in minor situations. The capacity you build in low-stakes moments will be available when the stakes are higher.

Small Choices, Profound Shifts

There's a myth that life is changed by big decisions—the dramatic turning points, the major crossroads, the life-altering moments. And those moments do matter. But here's what forty years of coaching has shown me: life is actually shaped by thousands of small choices, most of which we never recognize as significant.

Each small choice either reinforces old code or strengthens new code. Each conscious choice builds the muscle of choosing. Each moment where you catch yourself, pause, and select a different response adds another thread to the fabric of your transformed life.

Consider the compound effect: A single conscious choice might seem insignificant. But one conscious choice per day becomes 365 per year, which becomes thousands over a decade. Each one is weakening the autopilot pathways, strengthening the conscious pathways, and gradually shifting the balance from reaction to response.

Consider the "small" choices that reshape a life: How you respond when triggered—with your habitual reaction or with something new. What you say yes or no to—honoring your authentic desires or defaulting to people-pleasing. How you talk to yourself in difficult moments—with the old harsh criticism or with the compassion you're learning. Whether you honor or dismiss your own needs, reinforcing self-abandonment or practicing self-loyalty. How you show up in ordinary conversations—performing on autopilot or being genuinely present.

These aren't dramatic moments. There's no movie soundtrack, no visible crossroads. But they're the actual material of your life. And when they shift, everything shifts.

The macro follows the micro. You don't need to make one huge choice that changes everything. You need to make many small choices that change the pattern. Transform the small moments, and the big picture transforms itself.

Obstacles to Choice and Working with Them

Genuine choice isn't always accessible. Life throws obstacles in the way—conditions that make autopilot more likely and conscious choice harder to reach. Here's how to work with the most common ones:

Overwhelm occurs when too much happens too fast for conscious processing. Strategy: Pre-decide. Create default settings aligned with your values that run when you can't fully show up. If you know certain situations overwhelm you, decide in advance how you'll handle them. The choice happens before the moment, so when the moment comes, you don't have to rely on depleted capacity.

Powerful emotions hijack the system. When fear, anger, or grief is intense, the automatic responses are incredibly powerful. Strategy: STOP. Stop what you're doing. Take a breath—or several. Observe what's happening in your body and mind. Proceed only when you've created some space. You don't have to suppress the emotion. You just have to pause before you act on it.

Fatigue depletes the resources needed for conscious choice. When you're tired, the brain defaults to automation because it doesn't have the energy for anything else. Strategy: Design your environment to support good choices when willpower is low. Make the conscious choice the easy choice by setting up systems, removing friction from healthy options, and adding friction to unhealthy ones.

Social pressure activates relational autopilot. When others expect the old you, when the surrounding system is configured for your old patterns, choosing differently can feel impossible. Strategy: Prepare for pushback. Know that systems resist when a part changes. Connect to your why—the reason you're making different choices. Remind yourself that temporary discomfort is the price of lasting change.

The familiar pull is perhaps the subtlest obstacle. Autopilot just feels easier. It's known. It doesn't require effort or presence. The temptation is to let it run because choosing consciously is work. Strategy: Remember the cost. Remember what the autopilot life has cost you. Connect to the vision of who you're becoming. Let that vision pull you forward through the resistance.

The Crossroads Moment

Life presents obvious crossroads—moments where you clearly know a significant choice is being made. The job offer. The relationship decision.

The major life transition. These announce themselves. They say: "This is important. Choose carefully."

But there are also a thousand invisible crossroads every day—choice points that don't announce themselves, moments where you could choose consciously but let autopilot run because you didn't recognize the moment as a crossroads at all.

Learning to see these invisible crossroads is part of the work. The moment when you're about to respond to criticism—that's a crossroads. The moment when you feel the urge to distract yourself from an uncomfortable emotion—that's a crossroads. The moment when you're about to say yes to something you don't want—that's a crossroads.

Every moment you're aware enough to notice is a crossroads. Every moment your witness activates is an opportunity to choose.

You're not waiting for your life to change. You're changing it one choice at a time, one crossroads at a time, one moment of awareness at a time. The crossroads don't have to be dramatic to be significant. They just have to be conscious.

Freedom Isn't the Absence of Conditioning

Let me offer a final reframe of what all this means.

You will never be free of conditioning. You will never eliminate autopilot entirely. You will never reach a state where your past doesn't influence your present, where old programming doesn't arise, where you're choosing purely from some unconditioned space.

That's not what freedom is.

Freedom is the ability to see the conditioning and choose anyway. Freedom is having autopilot arise and not being captured by it. Freedom is noticing the old response forming and consciously selecting something different—or even selecting the same thing, but doing so consciously rather than automatically.

This is what it means to be the author of your life. Not that you control everything—you don't. Not that you're free from influence—you're not. But in more and more moments, you're the one choosing. You're awake at the wheel. You're responding to life rather than just reacting to it.

The witness you developed in Chapter 4. The rewritten code from Chapter 11. The conscious choice you're learning now. Together, these create genuine agency—the ability to participate in your own life rather than just be carried along by it.

You can't choose what conditioning you carry. But you can choose what you do with it. And that—that ability to choose—is the greatest power you have.

Pause and Reflect

Before moving to the next chapter, take a moment to sit with these questions. Let them work on you.

Where in your life are you most clearly on autopilot? What would change if you brought genuine choice to that area?

In which of the six dimensions does autopilot run most strongly for you—biologically, neurologically, psychologically, culturally, relationally, or spiritually?

When you make decisions, are you more often choosing from wounds (fear, protection, avoidance) or from wholeness (values, authenticity, presence)? How can you tell the difference?

What's one recurring situation where you could practice pausing before your automatic response? What might you choose differently?

What small choice could you make today—right now—that would align with who you're becoming rather than who you've been?

What obstacles most often hijack your ability to choose consciously? What strategy from this chapter might help?

The Breadcrumb

Each chapter closes with a single breadcrumb—a key insight to carry forward on your journey.

Most of what you've called "choice" has been autopilot—conditioning running you while you believed you were in charge. Your brain loves automation, and it has automated not just neutral skills but also your reactions to stress, your relationship patterns, and your relationship with yourself. All of it runs automatically unless you consciously intervene. True choice is different. It requires awareness, a pause between stimulus and response, and the willingness to see options beyond the automatic one. You can choose from wounds—from fear and old protection and the desperate attempt to avoid pain—or you can choose from wholeness, grounded in your authentic self and aligned with what actually matters. The same outer choice, made from different sources, produces completely different lives. You won't eliminate all the background programming. But you can slow down, engage your witness, name the automatic response, and ask what you'd choose if you weren't afraid. You can build the muscle of conscious choosing in small moments until it's available in large ones. Life isn't shaped by a few big decisions. It's shaped by thousands of small choices, each one either reinforcing the old code or strengthening the new. Freedom isn't the absence of conditioning. Freedom is seeing the conditioning and choosing anyway. Every moment you're aware enough to notice is a crossroads. What will you choose?

Going Deeper: Your Digital Companion

The questions above are meant to stir something in you—to begin the inner conversation. But real integration happens when you take time to explore your responses more fully.

In your digital companion, you'll find the following exercises for Chapter 12:

Autopilot Inventory — Identifying where autopilot runs most strongly in each of the six dimensions of your life

The Pause Practice — Building the muscle of creating space between stimulus and response through daily exercises

Wounds vs. Wholeness Check — A self-assessment tool for recognizing which source you're choosing from in key decisions

Small Choice Tracking — Recording conscious choices for one week to observe the compound effect of choosing differently

Obstacle Strategies — Developing personalized approaches to your specific obstacles to conscious choice

Crossroads Recognition — Learning to see the invisible choice points in everyday moments

Mindset Mind Map Update: The Crossroads — Mapping areas of autopilot and emerging conscious choice on your evolving map

---

You've learned to rewrite your code and to choose consciously in the moments that matter. But there's an obstacle we haven't fully addressed—one that derails more choices than any other. Fear. When fear arises, we often surrender our power to choose, letting the fear decide for us. In Chapter 13, we'll explore how to feel fear fully without letting it run the show—how to follow the breadcrumbs even when every part of you wants to turn back. The path home isn't fearless. It's fear-felt-and-followed-anyway.

CHAPTER THIRTEEN

FEEL THE FEAR AND FOLLOW ANYWAY

HOW are you going to make it...when fear stands in your path?

"Fear is not the enemy. Waiting to stop feeling afraid is." —
Marie Forleo

"Fear is a natural reaction to moving closer to the truth." —
Pema Chödrön

FEAR HAS THE WORST reputation of any emotion.

We've been taught to conquer it, overcome it, push through it, and eliminate it. The message is everywhere: "Don't be afraid." "Be brave." "Face your fears." Clearly, fear is the enemy, and the goal is to defeat it.

But what if we've misunderstood fear entirely? Consider another possibility: what if fear isn't the enemy at all, but a messenger carrying important information? If so, our war against fear may actually be part of the problem.

In this chapter, then, we're going to reframe your relationship with fear. Not so you can eliminate it—that's neither possible nor desirable. Instead, you'll learn how to understand it, work with it, and move forward even when it's present. This is essential because the path home isn't fearless. It's fear-felt-and-followed-anyway.

Fear's Noble Purpose

Fear is one of the oldest survival mechanisms—millions of years old, refined by evolution, and passed down through generations. It's part of your inheritance as a human being.

The biology is elegant in its simplicity. Your amygdala—two almond-shaped structures deep in your brain—constantly scans for threats. When danger is detected, they trigger a cascade of responses: adrenaline floods your system, your heart rate increases, blood flows to your muscles, and your senses sharpen. This is the fight-flight-freeze response, and it's designed to keep you alive.

Fear kept your ancestors alive long enough to become your ancestors. The ones who didn't feel fear—who didn't run from predators, who didn't avoid dangerous situations—didn't survive to pass on their genes. You are descended from a long line of people who felt fear and responded to it. Fear is literally part of why you exist.

Fear is designed to alert you to danger, mobilize your resources, and prepare you to act. It's an early warning system that operates faster than conscious thought. By the time you're aware you're afraid, your body is already preparing to protect you.

Here's the crucial reframe: fear is information, not instruction. It tells you that something matters, that there's something at stake, that your system has detected a potential threat. But it doesn't tell you what to do about it. That's your job.

The problem isn't fear itself. Rather, the problem is our relationship with fear—treating it as an enemy instead of a messenger, trying to eliminate it instead of understanding it, letting it make our decisions instead of allowing it to inform them.

Why Fear Gets a Bad Rap

From earliest childhood, we receive messages about fear that distort our relationship with it.

"Don't be a scaredy-cat." "Big girls don't cry." "There's nothing to be afraid of." "Be brave." These messages, however well-intentioned, teach us that fear is shameful, that feeling afraid means something is wrong with us, and that the goal is to not feel fear at all.

We've pathologized a completely normal human experience. We treat fear as if it's a character flaw, a weakness to be overcome, evidence of inadequacy. This creates a secondary problem: fear of fear itself. We become anxious about our anxiety, afraid of our fear. Now we're fighting on two fronts.

And here's the paradox: fighting fear makes it stronger. What we resist persists. When you try to push fear away, deny it, or defeat it, you're actually giving it more power. You're telling your system that the fear is indeed dangerous—so dangerous that you can't even allow yourself to feel it.

Fear is often a compass pointing to what matters most. We don't feel afraid of things that are irrelevant to us. We feel afraid of things that carry significance - our dreams, our relationships, our growth, our authentic expression. As Joseph Campbell said, the cave you fear often holds the treasure you seek.

What if fear isn't marking danger but marking significance? What if the presence of fear means you're approaching something that actually matters?

When Fear Becomes Toxic

Having said all that, let's be honest: fear can become toxic. It can stop being a helpful messenger and start being a prison guard.

Fear was designed for acute threats—the tiger in the bush, the cliff edge, the immediate physical danger. These situations require a burst of response, and then the threat passes. The system activates, does its job, and returns to baseline.

Modern life doesn't work that way. We face chronic stressors that don't resolve: financial pressure, relationship tension, work demands, and global uncertainty. The fear response activates, but has nowhere to go. The tiger never goes away. The nervous system stays mobilized, always prepared for danger that never quite arrives and never quite leaves.

This is when fear becomes toxic:

When it stops you from living—when you organize your life around avoiding anything that could trigger anxiety. When the goal becomes not feeling afraid, your world shrinks smaller and smaller.

Fear is toxic when it runs your decisions long after the danger has passed. An experience from twenty years ago can still dictate your choices today. Old fears control present possibilities.

When it generalizes from one experience to everything—when a single failure becomes evidence that you should never try again, when one betrayal becomes proof that no one can be trusted.

When fear keeps you small, safety becomes a cage, costing you the life you want.

The difference between healthy fear and toxic fear is the difference between fear as a signal and fear as a dictator. Healthy fear informs your choices. Toxic fear makes your choices for you.

If trauma locks fear into your system, know there's help. Trauma is real; its effects are real, and healing is possible—often requiring more than a book. Be gentle and seek support.

Fear Across the Six Dimensions

Fear appears in all six dimensions of your being. Knowing where and how fear shows up lets you work with it effectively.

Biologically, fear lives in your body. Racing heart, shallow breath, tight muscles, churning stomach, sweating palms—these are the physical preparations for danger. Your body is readying itself to fight, flee, or freeze. When fear becomes chronic, these physical manifestations become chronic too: persistent muscle tension, digestive issues, sleep problems, and immune suppression. Learning to recognize fear's body signature is the first step in working with it. Where does fear show up in your body? What's your personal physical pattern when you're afraid?

Neurologically, fear hijacks your brain. When the amygdala detects a threat, it essentially takes over, bypassing the slower, rational thinking centers. This is why you can't "think" your way out of fear at the moment—the thinking brain isn't fully online. Fear also creates tunnel vision, literally narrowing what you can see and process. Complex situations become black and white. Nuance disappears. The negativity bias—our brain's tendency to notice and remember threats more than safety—means fear gets extra neural real estate. Your brain is wired to look for what's wrong.

Psychologically, fear generates beliefs and stories: "I'm not safe." "I can't handle it." "Something bad will happen." "I'm not strong enough." These fear-based beliefs feel like truth and don't announce themselves as interpretations. Fear often fuels catastrophic thinking, making us imagine worst-case scenarios and treat them as likely. The stories we tell about what we're afraid of often create more suffering than the reality would.

Culturally, fear gets passed down through generations. Your family carried fears about money, success, visibility, difference—and those fears were transmitted to you, often without words. Culture uses fear as a control mechanism, teaching you what to be afraid of and who gets permission to feel afraid. Collective fears—about outsiders, about change, about the unknown—shape what feels possible.

Relationally, fear shapes how you connect with others. Fear of abandonment might make you cling. Fear of engulfment might make you keep your distance. Fear of rejection might make you hide your authentic self. Fear of intimacy might make you sabotage a connection just as it deepens. Many relationship patterns that seem mysterious become clear when traced back to underlying fears.

Spiritually, fear touches the deepest questions. Fear of meaninglessness. Fear of death. Fear of the unknown, the unknowable, the infinite. But also fear of the sacred—fear of what we might become, fear of our own potential, fear of the transformation that real spiritual opening might require. Sometimes we resist our own growth because becoming who we're meant to be is terrifying.

The Chemistry of Fear and How to Work with It

Understanding what's actually happening in your body when fear arises helps you work with it rather than against it.

When your amygdala detects a threat, it triggers the release of stress hormones—primarily adrenaline and cortisol. These chemicals create the physical sensations you experience as fear: the racing heart, the heightened alertness, the energy surge. This cascade happens in milliseconds, before your conscious mind even knows what's happening.

Here's what's crucial to understand: you cannot "think" your way out of this response. The chemicals are already in your bloodstream. The body has already mobilized. Trying to use logic to talk yourself out of fear while the chemistry is active is like trying to think yourself sober—the substance is in your system and needs to run its course or be actively processed.

This is why the body needs to be involved in fear regulation. Movement helps—the stress chemicals were released to fuel physical action, so physical action helps metabolize them. Deep breathing activates the parasympathetic nervous system, sending signals of safety. Human connection co-regulates the nervous system; a calm presence literally helps calm your system.

Here's something liberating: the actual lifespan of an emotion, if you simply let it move through you without fighting it or feeding it, is roughly ninety seconds. Ninety seconds from arising to dissipation—if you don't resist it, don't add stories to it, don't fight it. The sustained fear we experience isn't usually a single wave; it's wave after wave, often triggered by our thoughts about the fear itself.

Working with fear means working with your nervous system, not against it. It means letting the wave move through rather than bracing against it. It means using breath, movement, and connection to help your system return to a state of regulation. It means understanding that the intensity will pass if you can simply stay present with it.

Threshold Sickness: The Fear at the Edge

There's a specific fear that deserves its own attention: threshold sickness. This is the intense fear that arises at the moment of no return—the edge where decision becomes action.

Picture the skydiving scenario. You've signed up. You've trained. You've gotten on the plane. You've ascended to altitude. You've gone through all the preparation. And now the door opens, and you're standing at the edge, looking at the vast emptiness below.

This is when threshold sickness hits. The fear is intense—perhaps the most intense fear of the entire experience. Every part of you screams to step back, to abort, to stay in the safety of the plane.

But here's what's crucial to understand about threshold sickness: by the time you're at the threshold, you've already seen it.

You've imagined the jump countless times. You've visualized falling through the air. You've thought about the parachute deploying, the landing, all of it. You've processed this experience mentally and emotionally. You've decided to do it.

The fear you're feeling at the threshold isn't about the unknown. The unknown has already been made known in your imagination. You've already seen what's on the other side. There's nothing new to fear—only the doing of what's already been decided.

Threshold sickness is the gap between decision and action. It's the last gasp of resistance before transformation. It's your system running one final check: "Are you sure? Are you really sure?"

A client I'll call Rachel had spent three years writing a memoir. Not dabbling — genuinely writing, revising, showing up at the page. She was good. People who'd read sections told her so. Her coach told her so. She knew it herself on the days she was honest.

She came to a session in a state she described as "completely falling apart." She had a manuscript. She had a literary agent who'd expressed interest. She had everything she'd said she wanted. And she was about to email the agent to ask for more time.

"I'm not ready," she said. "I can see everything that's wrong with it."

I asked her when she'd started seeing everything that was wrong.

She thought about it. "After I emailed to say I was almost done."

I asked her whether she'd seen those same problems the week before she sent that email.

A long pause. "No."

"What changed?"

Another pause. Longer. "It became real."

That was threshold sickness. Not new problems with the manuscript — the same manuscript, now standing at the edge of becoming visible to the world. The fear wasn't telling her that the work wasn't ready. It was telling her she was at the threshold. She'd already decided. She'd already done the work. She'd already imagined this moment hundreds of times. There was nothing new to fear — only the crossing.

She sent the pages that week. The agent loved them. The fear didn't disappear before she hit send. She hit send with the fear fully present, her hands shaking a little, which is exactly how threshold moments are supposed to feel.

This insight changes everything. When you recognize threshold sickness for what it is—not a signal that you shouldn't proceed, but the natural intensity that arises at the edge of any significant action—you can name it, acknowledge it, and take the step anyway.

And on the other side of the threshold sickness? Relief. Aliveness. Expansion. The discovery that you could, that you did, that you can. The fear that felt so insurmountable moments ago dissolves into exhilaration.

Where in your life are you standing at the threshold? What have you already seen, already decided, already processed—but haven't yet done? The fear you feel isn't about the unknown. It's about the crossing.

What Your Fear Is Protecting

Every fear is guarding something. Understanding what your fear is trying to protect reveals both its logic and its limitations.

Ask yourself, when fear arises: "What is this fear trying to protect me from?"

Sometimes, fear protects you from failure and humiliation. The fear of public speaking, for instance, is often the fear of being seen as incompetent, of being judged, of the social death of embarrassment. The protection makes sense—social belonging has been crucial to human survival. But the cost of this protection might be a lifetime of silence when you have something important to say.

Sometimes fear is protecting you from success and its consequences. This sounds paradoxical, but success brings its own threats: increased visibility, higher expectations, potential envy from others, and the responsibility that comes with achievement. Fear of success often masks a fear of exposure or fear of not being able to sustain what you've built.

Sometimes fear is protecting you from being truly seen. If people really knew you—your thoughts, your desires, your imperfections—they might reject you. The fear of authenticity is often the fear of abandonment in disguise.

Sometimes fear is protecting you from loss and grief. We avoid attachment to avoid the pain of losing what we love. We keep relationships at arm's length to avoid the devastation of their ending. This protection keeps us from the very connection that makes life meaningful.

Sometimes fear is protecting you from change itself. Even positive change threatens the familiar. Your system knows how to survive the current situation—it doesn't know if it can survive the new one. Fear of the unknown is often the system saying, "Better the devil you know."

Here's the key question for each fear: Is the danger it's protecting you from still real, or has it become outdated? Some fears are accurate warnings about genuine risks worth considering. Others are legacy fears—programs from the past still running long after the original threat has passed.

Discernment is the practice of distinguishing between fear as a warning and fear as a wall. Sometimes your fear is telling you something important about actual danger. Sometimes it's keeping you imprisoned in a cell whose door was unlocked years ago.

Moving Through Fear Without Waiting for It to Leave

Here's the myth that keeps people stuck: "I'll do it when I'm not afraid anymore."

People wait for fear to leave before taking action. They believe courage means not feeling fear, so they wait for the fear to subside before moving forward. They're still waiting.

The truth is this: fear rarely leaves until after you've acted. It's the action that transforms the fear, not the other way around. Waiting for fear to leave first is like waiting to feel confident before you do the thing that would build your confidence. The sequence is backward.

Courage isn't the absence of fear. Courage is action in the presence of fear. It's feeling the full weight of your fear and moving anyway—not recklessly, not in denial, but consciously, deliberately, with fear as your companion rather than your master.

Here's a practical process for moving through fear:

Acknowledge the fear. Don't pretend it's not there. Name it: "I'm afraid." This simple acknowledgment shifts you from being possessed by fear to being aware of fear.

Name what you're afraid of specifically. Not "I'm anxious" but "I'm afraid that if I speak up, people will think I'm stupid." Specificity reduces fear's power. Vague fears feel overwhelming; specific fears can be addressed.

Feel it in your body. Where is the fear? What does it feel like? Locate it, describe it, breathe with it. This keeps you present rather than spiraling into catastrophic thinking.

Ask what it's protecting. Honor the intention behind the fear. "This fear is trying to protect me from rejection. Thank you for trying to keep me safe."

Assess the actual risk. Is the danger real or imagined? What's the worst that could actually happen? Could you survive that? Often, the imagined consequences far exceed the likely ones.

Take the smallest step. You don't have to leap. You can step. Find the tiniest action that moves you toward what you fear and do that. Then the next smallest step. Momentum builds.

Act with fear as a companion. The fear can come along. It doesn't have to leave for you to move. Let it walk beside you rather than block your path.

Fear walks with you—it doesn't have to walk ahead of you. You can lead. You can choose the direction. Fear gets a voice, not a veto.

Fear as Breadcrumb

Here's perhaps the most important reframe of all: your fear is often a breadcrumb pointing toward what matters most.

Think about it. You don't feel fear about things that are irrelevant. You don't lie awake anxious about outcomes you don't care about. Fear marks significance. It shows up where the stakes are real, where something important is on the line.

The places you most fear to go often hold what you most need to find. The conversation you're most afraid to have might be the one that transforms your relationship. The creative expression you're most afraid to share might be the truest thing you've made. The change you're most afraid to make might be the one your soul has been waiting for.

This is the paradox: avoiding fear keeps you stuck. Following fear—not blindly, but wisely—leads to freedom. Your authentic self often lies on the other side of your deepest fears, waiting for you to find the courage to cross.

Use fear as a compass. Ask yourself: "What am I most afraid to do that I know I need to do?" That question will point you in the right direction every time.

The fears that keep recurring, that won't leave you alone, that show up again and again despite your best efforts to ignore them—these are breadcrumbs. They're marking something significant. They're pointing home.

The Other Side of Fear

What actually happens when you move through fear?

On the other side is expansion. Every fear you face increases your capacity. Your comfort zone literally grows. What terrified you before becomes manageable. What seemed impossible becomes merely challenging. You discover that you're bigger than you thought, more capable than you believed.

On the other side is aliveness. Fear suppressed creates numbness—we often can't selectively dampen emotions, so avoiding fear means dampening everything. When you allow yourself to feel fear and move through it, you recover access to the full spectrum of your emotional life. Aliveness returns.

On the other side is confidence—not the arrogant kind that pretends fear doesn't exist, but the earned kind that knows you can feel fear and act, anyway. This confidence isn't about the absence of fear; it's about the proven ability to handle fear.

Each fear faced teaches you something irreplaceable: that you can. That you did. That you will again. This accumulated evidence becomes a foundation. You don't become fearless—you become fear-capable. You know from experience that fear isn't the end of the story.

This is the freedom that comes from a transformed relationship with fear: not that you never feel it, but that you're no longer controlled by it. You feel the fear and follow anyway. You let fear inform you without letting it decide for you. You walk the path home with fear as a companion—neither enemy nor master, just part of the journey.

The path home isn't fearless. It never was. It's fear-felt-and-followed-anyway. And you're more ready for that journey than you know.

Pause and Reflect

Before moving to the next chapter, take a moment to sit with these questions. Let them work on you.

What fear has been standing in your path? What has it cost you to let fear make that decision?

When you feel fear in your body, where does it show up? What's your physical fear signature?

What might your persistent fear be trying to protect you from? Is that protection still needed, or has it become a prison?

Can you recall a time you experienced threshold sickness—that intense fear right at the edge of action? What happened when you moved through it?

What would you do if you weren't waiting for fear to leave first? What action has been waiting for your courage?

Where might fear be serving as a breadcrumb—pointing at something that actually matters deeply to your authentic self?

The Breadcrumb

Each chapter closes with a single breadcrumb—a key insight to carry forward on your journey.

Fear isn't your enemy—it's a messenger carrying important information. It was designed to protect you, and it has done its job well for millions of years. But fear was built for acute dangers, for tigers and cliffs and immediate physical threats—not for running your entire life. When fear becomes the decision-maker, you stop living and start merely surviving. You shrink your world to fit inside fear's boundaries. The secret isn't to eliminate fear—that's neither possible nor desirable. The secret is to change your relationship with it. Feel it fully. Acknowledge what it's trying to protect. Assess whether the danger is real or imagined, current or outdated. And then move anyway—with fear as a companion *rather than* a dictator. *At the threshold—that moment of maximum fear before the leap—remember this: you've already seen what's on the other side. You've imagined it, processed it, and decided. There's nothing new to fear, only the doing of what's already been decided. The fear you feel at the threshold isn't about the unknown; it's about the crossing. And you can cross. The path home isn't fearless. It's fear-felt-and-followed-anyway. Every fear you face expands your capacity. Every threshold you cross teaches you that you can cross thresholds. And often, what fear has been guarding most fiercely is exactly what your soul most needs to reclaim.*

Going Deeper: Your Digital Companion

The questions above are meant to stir something in you—to begin the inner conversation. But real integration happens when you take time to explore your responses more fully.

<u>In your digital companion, you'll find the following exercises for Chapter 13:</u>

Fear Inventory — Mapping your fears across the six dimensions: biological, neurological, psychological, cultural, relational, and spiritual

Fear Body Mapping — Identifying where and how fear shows up in your physical body—your personal fear signature

What Is It Protecting? — For each major fear, exploring what it's trying to guard you from and whether that protection is still needed

The 90-Second Practice — Learning to let fear move through rather than getting stuck—riding the wave

Threshold Recognition — Identifying places in your life where you're at the threshold, ready to move but frozen at the edge

Fear as Breadcrumb — Examining your fears for clues about what actually matters most to your authentic self

Mindset Mind Map Update: The Resistance — Mapping your fears, what they're protecting, and how you're learning to move through them

---

You've learned to feel fear and follow anyway—to let fear inform you without letting it control you. But fear has a favorite disguise, one that keeps countless people paralyzed while believing they're being responsible. That disguise is perfectionism. In Chapter 14, we'll explore the fallacy of perfection—why demanding flawless execution before you act is just fear wearing a reasonable mask. We'll discover why mistakes are breadcrumbs too, why learning is the point rather than the obstacle, and how releasing the need to be perfect might be the most liberating thing you ever do.

Chapter Fourteen

The Fallacy of Perfection

WHEN will you ever learn...that your humanness is the point?

"The expert in anything was once a beginner." — Helen Hayes

"Failure is simply the opportunity to begin again, this time more intelligently." — Henry Ford

In the last chapter, you learned to feel fear and follow anyway. You discovered that courage isn't the absence of fear, but action in its presence. You learned that fear is a messenger, not a master.

But fear has a favorite disguise—one so socially acceptable that we rarely recognize it for what it is. It looks like responsibility. It sounds like high standards. It feels like conscientiousness and commitment to excellence.

It's perfectionism.

The Perfectionist, whom you met in Chapter 7, makes a compelling promise: "If I do it perfectly, no one can criticize me." But beneath that promise lies a deeper, more desperate one: "If I'm perfect, I'll finally be safe. Finally, be worthy. Finally, be enough."

This chapter will reveal perfectionism as the very obstacle that blocks your best life. Through forty years of coaching, I've seen perfectionism act not as a path to a fulfilled existence but as the wall that keeps you from it. When you set an impossible standard and refuse to release it, you trade real growth for unattainable ideals. What changes when you expose perfectionism for what it is? You open the door to possibilities. To understand how perfectionism works, let's examine where this myth comes from.

The Perfection Myth

Let's start with a fundamental truth: perfection doesn't exist.

Perfection is a moving target that retreats as you approach. When you reach your standard, new flaws become visible. It's not a destination, but a mirage that keeps receding.

Consider nature. Nothing in nature is "perfect" in the mathematical, flawless sense—and yet nature is magnificent. Trees grow asymmetrically. Rivers meander. No two snowflakes are identical, and none of them are geometrically precise. The coastline is fractal and irregular. And all of it is beautiful beyond description.

The myth of perfectionism is that if you try hard enough, work long enough, and care deeply enough, perfection is achievable. In reality, perfection is only a concept—it cannot be reached. Pursuing an unattainable ideal leads inevitably to exhaustion and despair.

We've confused two very different things: excellence and perfection. Excellence is achievable; it means bringing your full attention, care, and skill to what you do. Excellence is satisfying—you can feel when you've done excellent work. In contrast, perfection demands flawlessness, which is impossible. Perfection is never satisfying because there's always something more to fix, improve, or polish.

And here's the cost that's rarely counted: while you're chasing perfection, life passes unlived. While you're polishing what could have been shared, you miss a connection. While you're waiting until it's perfect to begin, the opportunity closes. Perfectionism doesn't protect you from failure. It guarantees a different kind of failure—the failure to fully live.

How Perfectionism Develops

Perfectionism isn't a character trait you were born with. It's a protective strategy that developed for good reason.

Like all the characters you met in Chapter 7, the Perfectionist emerged from early environments where this strategy served a purpose. Perhaps love and approval in your family were conditional on performance. Perhaps mistakes were punished, shamed, or met with withdrawal of affection. Perhaps "good enough" was never good enough—there was always a way you could have done better. Perhaps being the best was the only acceptable outcome, and anything less than first place was treated as a failure.

The child in that environment learned something: my worth depends on flawless execution. If I perform perfectly, I'll be safe. If I achieve without error, I'll be loved. If I never give them anything to criticize, I'll belong.

This was an intelligent adaptation. The child couldn't change the environment, so the child changed the strategy. And it worked—at least enough to survive.

But here's what happens: the adult still operates from that childhood code, long after the original environment has changed. You're no longer that child. The people whose approval you needed may no longer be in your life, or their opinions may no longer carry the same weight. The circumstances are entirely different. But the Perfectionist is still running the old program: "Perform flawlessly or face rejection."

This is the crucial insight: perfectionism isn't about high standards—many people have those. Instead, it's the belief that your self-worth depends on flawless performance: that you're only as valuable as your last achievement, and that one mistake could expose you as a fraud.

Perfectionism Across the Six Dimensions

Like fear, perfectionism doesn't stay in one lane. It manifests across every dimension of your being.

Biologically, perfectionism creates chronic stress. Your body stays braced for the criticism that might come, the flaw that might be discovered, the failure that might be exposed. This isn't occasional stress but ongoing tension—a system that never fully relaxes because "done" never arrives. The physical toll accumulates exhaustion, immune suppression, tension headaches, and digestive issues. The body pays the price for the impossible standard.

Neurologically, perfectionism rewires your brain to detect flaws. Your neural pathways become grooved toward noticing what's wrong rather than what's working. The negativity bias—already present in all human brains—gets amplified. Your internal quality control becomes hypervigilant, scanning every output for defects. And the reward system gets hijacked: only perfection counts, so the satisfaction of good enough work becomes inaccessible. Nothing ever feels like enough.

Psychologically, perfectionism generates relentless inner criticism. The voice in your head evaluates everything and finds it wanting. Self-worth becomes entirely contingent on achievement—and since perfect achievement is impossible, self-worth becomes perpetually unstable. All-or-nothing thinking dominates: if it's not perfect, it's worthless. This leads to procrastination (if I don't start, I can't fail) and paralysis (if I can't do it perfectly, I won't do it at all).

Culturally, perfectionism finds endless fuel. Social media presents curated highlight reels that look like everyday life. Everyone else seems to have it figured out while you struggle behind the scenes. Cultural messages equate worth with accomplishment, appearance with value, and optimization with virtue. The comparison trap is everywhere—and the comparison is always to an airbrushed, filtered, carefully staged fiction.

Relationally, perfectionism damages connections. You apply impossible standards to others, criticizing what doesn't measure up. Or you hide your imperfect parts, preventing real intimacy because you can't let anyone see the mess. Relationships stay shallow because vulnerability—the gateway to deep connection—requires showing up as you actually are. When criticism comes, you defend rather than receive, because any feedback feels like confirmation that you're not enough.

Spiritually, perfectionism creates distance from the sacred. You believe you must earn your place, earn your worth, earn your right to exist. You feel unworthy of belonging to something greater because you know all the ways you fall short. Perfectionism becomes a substitute for genuine meaning—achievement filling the void where purpose should be, accomplishment providing the sense of worth that could come from simply being.

The Imagination Thief

Here's something crucial that perfectionism steals, often without our realizing: imagination.

Imagination—the ability to conceive of what doesn't yet exist—is one of humanity's most extraordinary gifts. It's how we create art, solve problems, envision better futures, and connect across differences. Imagination is the birthplace of everything that ever was new.

But imagination requires something that perfectionism cannot tolerate: play. Exploration. The willingness to try things that might not work. The freedom to be messy, awkward, and wrong.

Perfectionism demands safety, certainty, and guaranteed outcomes. It wants to know that what you create will be good before you create it. It wants assurance that you won't embarrass yourself before you take the risk.

You cannot imagine freely while simultaneously evaluating whether each thought is "good enough." The creative and critical impulses are opposites.

The inner critic and the creative muse cannot occupy the same space at the same time.

Think about how children create. They draw without worrying about proportion. They make up stories without concern for plot structure. They dance without choreography, sing without worrying about pitch, and build without architectural plans. Their imagination is free because it hasn't yet been colonized by the demand for perfection.

How many ideas have died unborn because they weren't "ready"? How many creative projects have been strangled in their cradles by the demand that they be perfect before they're allowed to exist? How much imagination has been sacrificed on the altar of perfectionism?

Imagination is one of your most valuable assets as a human being. It's not a luxury or an indulgence—it's essential to who you are and what you can contribute. When perfectionism steals your imagination, it steals something sacred.

Humanly Divine and Divinely Human

Here's what perfectionism misses entirely: your humanness is not a flaw to be overcome. It's not an obstacle on the path to worthiness. It's not the problem that needs to be solved.

Your humanness is the point.

You are humanly divine, carrying something sacred, something infinite, something transcendent within a physical, limited, gloriously imperfect form. The light doesn't shine despite the cracks; the cracks are how the light gets in. Your limitations aren't failures of divinity; they're the particular shape divinity takes in you.

And you are divinely human—the infinite expressing itself through the finite, the universal manifesting as the particular, the timeless showing up in time. Spirit didn't make a mistake by becoming embodied in all this messy, complicated, imperfect humanity. This is how spirit experiences itself. This is how love moves in the world—through hands that tremble, hearts that break, minds that doubt, lives that stumble and fall and get back up.

The divine doesn't demand perfection from you. That demand comes from somewhere much smaller—from fear, from wounds, from a child's desperate attempt to be worthy of love. The sacred doesn't require your perfection. It delights in your becoming. It celebrates your trying. It holds your failing with infinite tenderness.

Spirituality isn't about escaping your humanity. It's about fully inhabiting it. It's about bringing consciousness and love to the whole human experience—the beauty and the struggle, the triumph and the failure, the moments of clarity and the seasons of confusion.

You don't have to be perfect to be worthy. You don't have to be perfect to be loved. You don't have to be perfect to belong to something greater than yourself. You are worthy because you exist. You are loved because you are. You belong because belonging is your birthright, not something you must earn.

The Significance of Being Human

Being human is significant. Not despite the imperfections—including them. Not despite the mess—through it.

Consider what you are:

You have imagination—the ability to conceive of what doesn't yet exist, to envision possibilities that have never been, to dream worlds into being. No other creature we know of does this the way you do. This is extraordinary.

You have creativity—the capacity to bring something new into existence, to take what is and reshape it into what could be, to leave something in the world that wasn't here before you arrived. This is profound.

You have the capacity for growth—the ability to learn, to change, to evolve, to become more than you were. You are not fixed. You are not finished. You are always in the process of becoming. This is remarkable.

You have the capacity for connection—the ability to truly see another being and to be truly seen, to love and be loved, to create relationships that transcend isolation. This is transcendent.

You have consciousness itself—the miracle of awareness aware of itself; the universe looking back at itself through your eyes, experiencing itself through your senses. This is sacred beyond measure.

These are not obstacles to your significance. These ARE your significance. This makes human life precious. Not perfection—presence. Not flawlessness—aliveness. Not getting it right—showing up and trying.

You didn't come here to be perfect. You came here to be human. And being human—fully, messily, gloriously human—is a sacred act. It's enough. More than enough. It's everything.

Mistakes as Breadcrumbs

Here's a reframe that changes everything: your mistakes are breadcrumbs too.

Every mistake you've made has taught you something. Every failure carries information. Every "wrong turn" has shown you something about what doesn't work, which is essential knowledge on the way to what does.

Mistakes aren't detours from the path home. They're part of the path itself.

Consider how everything comes into being. Evolution works through trial and error—countless "failures" that gradually reveal what survives and thrives. Science advances through failed hypotheses—each disproven idea narrowing the field of possibilities. Art emerges from countless discarded drafts, abandoned paintings, crumpled pages—the "mistakes" that teach the artist what they're actually trying to create. Every success story is built on a foundation of failures that made success possible.

Your mistakes haven't disqualified you from the journey home. They've been shaping it. The relationship that didn't work taught you what you actually need. The career path that dead-ended taught you what doesn't fit. The choices you regret taught you what you actually value. The failures you're ashamed of taught you something about who you don't want to be.

What if you treated each "failure" as information rather than an indictment? What if, instead of evidence that something is wrong with you, your mistakes were evidence that you're learning, growing, finding your way? What if the things you got wrong were as much a part of the breadcrumb trail as the things you got right?

Learning as the Point, Not the Obstacle

Perfectionism treats learning as the embarrassing part before competence—the awkward phase to rush through as quickly as possible so you can arrive at knowing.

But what if learning is the point?

Life is continuous learning. There is no arrival at "knowing everything." There is no point at which you've figured it all out and can stop growing. The learning never ends—and that's not a problem to be solved. That's the adventure.

Psychologist Carol Dweck's research on mindset beautifully illuminates this. A growth mindset believes that abilities can be developed through dedication and effort. A fixed mindset believes that abilities are static—you either have talent, or you don't; you're either smart, or you're not, and your job is to prove yourself over and over.

Perfectionism is a fixed mindset in disguise. It's the belief that you must perform perfectly because imperfect performance reveals inadequate ability. It's protecting the image of competence rather than actually developing competence. It's managing how you appear rather than genuinely growing.

A growth mindset liberates you from this trap. If abilities can be developed, then mistakes are part of development, not evidence of deficiency. If learning is the goal, then not-knowing-yet is a stage to be embraced, not a shame to be hidden. If growing is the point, then every challenge becomes an opportunity rather than a threat.

What if being a learner was the goal, not the obstacle to the goal? What if your willingness not to know was as valuable as your knowledge? What if "I'm still learning" was a badge of honor rather than an admission of failure?

The Willingness to Be a Beginner

Beginners make mistakes. Beginners look awkward. Beginners don't know what they're doing.

And beginners are the only ones who grow.

Perfectionism refuses to be a beginner. The vulnerability is too great. What if someone sees you struggling? What if you look foolish? What if you fail publicly? Better to stay in the zones where you're already competent, where you can maintain the image of someone who has it together.

But refusing to be a beginner means refusing to learn anything new. It means limiting yourself to what you already know how to do. It means a shrinking life, a narrowing world, an increasingly rigid identity that can't flex, grow, or surprise itself.

Every master was once a disaster. Every expert was once clueless. Every professional was once an amateur. The people you admire for their skill were once terrible at the very things they now excel at. They became excellent by being willing to be bad first.

Your willingness to be bad at something is the doorway to becoming good at it. Your willingness not to know is the gateway to learning. Your willingness to look foolish is the entrance fee to growth.

Permission to be a beginner—at any age, in any domain, at any stage of life—is one of the greatest freedoms you can give yourself. It means you're never too old to start something new. It means no area of life is closed to you just because you don't know how yet. It means your potential isn't limited to what you've already mastered.

Releasing the Performance

Much of perfectionism is performance—the management of how others perceive you. It's curating an image, controlling a narrative, and presenting a carefully edited version of yourself that can withstand scrutiny.

But the performance is exhausting. It requires constant vigilance, constant effort, and constant monitoring of how you're being received. You can never relax because the mask might slip. You can never be spontaneous because unscripted moments might reveal something imperfect.

And here's the thing: the performance doesn't even work. Not really. People don't connect with your perfection. They connect with your humanity. The polished surface doesn't create intimacy—it prevents it. What draws people in, what makes them feel safe with you, what creates a real relationship is your willingness to be real.

A client I'll call Diane had been part of a professional women's group for four years. She was known in that group as the one who had it together — always composed, always prepared, always with the right answer or the right encouragement. She was proud of it. She was also privately exhausted by it.

She came to coaching describing the group as "supportive but somehow lonely." She couldn't quite explain it. These were good women. They liked her. And she never felt fully met.

In one session, I asked her what she'd never said in that room.

She thought for a long time. Then: "That I'm terrified I've made the wrong choices. That I perform with confidence, I don't feel. That I have no idea what I'm doing half the time."

I asked what would happen if she said those things.

"They'd think less of me."

The following month, something in her shifted. Not because of strategy — because she was simply tired. At the group meeting, someone asked how she was doing, and instead of the usual answer, she told the truth. That she was struggling. That she didn't have it figured out. That she was scared.

The room went quiet. And then, one by one, every woman in that circle said some version of: "Me too. I thought I was the only one."

Four years of polished performance had created a group of women who all believed they were the only ones struggling. One honest moment undid it. The connection that followed was unlike anything they'd built in the four years before.

The performance hadn't protected her. It had been keeping her alone.

Your struggles, your growth edges, your mess—these are what make you relatable. When you pretend to have it all figured out, you inadvertently communicate that others should have it figured out too. When you're honest about your imperfections, you give others permission to be honest about theirs.

Releasing the performance doesn't mean not caring. It doesn't mean being careless, sloppy, or indifferent to quality. It means caring about what actually matters—genuine connection over managed impression, real growth over performed competence, authentic presence over curated image.

You don't have to perform your worth. You don't have to earn your place through flawless execution. You already belong. You can show up as you actually are—imperfect, still learning, in process—and that is enough. More than enough.

The Permission

This chapter is titled "The Fallacy of Perfection." But on your Mindset Mind Map, the layer for this chapter is called "The Permission."

Because ultimately, what you need isn't another strategy to manage your perfectionism. What you need is permission to be imperfect.

So here it is. Consider this your permission slip:

Permission to start before you're ready. You will never feel ready. Readiness comes from starting, not before it.

Permission to share before it's polished. Done is better than perfect. Out in the world beats hidden in your drawer.

Permission to try before you know how. You'll learn by doing. You'll figure it out as you go.

Permission to fail publicly. Your failures are not the end of your story. They're chapters that lead to what comes next.

Permission to be a work in progress. You are not finished. You will never be finished. And that's beautiful.

Permission to be human. Messy, imperfect, still learning, sometimes struggling human. This is not a problem to be solved. This is what you came here to be.

You don't need anyone else to grant you this permission. You can grant it to yourself. In fact, only you can. No external authority can give you what you withhold from yourself.

So, grant it. Give yourself the permission you've been waiting for. Stop waiting for the day when you'll be perfect enough to live fully. That day will never come, because perfection is a mirage. Today—imperfect, uncertain, messy today—is the only day you get.

What will you do with your permission?

Pause and Reflect

Before moving to the next chapter, take a moment to sit with these questions. Let them work on you.

Where has perfectionism been running your life? What has it cost you—in unlived experiences, unshared creativity, unreached connections?

In which dimension does perfectionism show up most strongly for you—biologically, neurologically, psychologically, culturally, relationally, or spiritually?

What creative ideas or projects have you abandoned (or never started) because they couldn't be perfect? What has the imagination thief stolen from you?

What does "humanly divine and divinely human" mean to you? How might fully embracing your humanness change how you live?

What mistake from your past turned out to be a breadcrumb—teaching you something essential for your journey home?

What would you begin, try, or share if you gave yourself full permission to be imperfect?

The Breadcrumb

Each chapter closes with a single breadcrumb—a key insight to carry forward on your journey.

Perfectionism isn't high standards—it's fear wearing a responsible mask. It promises that if you execute flawlessly, you'll finally be safe, worthy, and enough. But perfection is a mirage that retreats as you approach. While you chase it, life passes unlived, creativity dies unborn, and connection stays shallow because you can't let anyone see the imperfect parts. Here's what perfectionism misses entirely: your humanness is not a flaw to be overcome. You are humanly divine, carrying something sacred in an imperfect form. You are divinely human—the infinite expressing itself through the particular, the messy, the real. Your imagination, your creativity, your capacity to learn and fail and grow—these are not obstacles to your significance. They ARE your significance. Mistakes aren't detours; they're breadcrumbs, teaching you what doesn't work so you can find what does. Learning isn't the embarrassing phase before competence; learning is the point. And your willingness to be a beginner—awkward, uncertain, not yet good—is the doorway to everything you've been afraid to try. You don't have to be perfect to be worthy. You don't have to perform your place in the world. You already belong. What you need isn't a better strategy to manage perfectionism. What you need is permission. Permission to start before you're ready, to share before it's polished, to try before you know how, to fail publicly, to be gloriously, messily human. Consider this chapter your permission slip. Now: what will you do with it?

Going Deeper: Your Digital Companion

The questions above are meant to stir something in you—to begin the inner conversation. But real integration happens when you take time to explore your responses more fully.

In your digital companion, you'll find the following exercises for Chapter 14:

Perfectionism Inventory — Mapping where and how perfectionism shows up across the six dimensions of your life

The Cost Accounting — Honestly assessing what perfectionism has cost you in unlived life, unshared creativity, and unreached connection.

The Mistake Museum — Reviewing your "failures" and finding the breadcrumbs they left—what each one taught you

The Imagination Reclamation — Exercises to reconnect with playful, judgment-free creativity

Beginner's Mind Practice — Deliberately trying something new with full permission to be bad at it

The Permission Slip — Writing yourself explicit permission for specific imperfect actions you've been avoiding

Mindset Mind Map Update: The Permission — Mapping perfectionism patterns you're releasing and permissions you're claiming

---

With fear felt and followed, with perfectionism released, with permission granted to be fully human, you're ready for the final movement of this journey. You've followed the breadcrumbs through understanding, through seeing, through engaging, through acting. Part Five awaits: Coming Home. In Chapter 15, we'll explore what home actually is—not a place you arrive at but a remembering, not a destination but an integration, not perfection but wholeness. The longing that brought you here is about to be fulfilled. You've been finding your way home this whole time. Now it's time to arrive.

PART V: COMING HOME

Integration and Wholeness

CHAPTER FIFTEEN

GOING HOME...THE LONGING FULFILLED

WHY are you here...and where have you been trying to get to all along?

"Home is not where you live but where they understand you." — Christian Morgenstern

"We shall not cease from exploration, and the end of all our exploring will be to arrive where we started and know the place for the first time." — T.S. Eliot

WELCOME TO PART FIVE: Coming Home.

You've traveled far to arrive here. In Part One, you realized you were in the woods—heard the call, recognized the fragmentation, saw the iceberg beneath your life. In Part Two, you learned to see the breadcrumbs—developed your witness, recognized the signals from your authentic self, and understood how your filters shaped what you could perceive. In Part Three, you mapped the territory—met your cast of characters, traced your stories and patterns, encountered your resistance, and explored your hiding places. In Part Four, you followed the trail—learned to rewrite your code, discovered the power of choice, felt fear and followed anyway, and released the fallacy of perfection.

And now, here you are.

The longing that brought you here—hiraeth, that unnamed ache for your own soul—is about to find its answer. Yet, not in the way you might have imagined. Home isn't somewhere you finally arrive through struggle. It is a sudden recognition, a flash of remembering, a gentle return to what you never truly lost.

What Home Actually Is

Home is not a destination you arrive at. It's a remembering.

It's not an award for effort, healing, or transformation. It's a breath, an awakening—a state of being wholly you that was always quietly present, hidden beneath layers of forgetting. Always there. Always waiting.

This is the core truth of the journey: home was never lost. YOU wandered away. Breadcrumbs marked the path back—signals from your authentic self. Home never moved. Wholeness waited, patient and permanent, beneath all conditioning and years spent being who you thought you had to be.

Home is when you are whole again: every part welcomed, nothing left in exile. It is the sacred reunion inside you, where what you concealed and what you revealed recognize one another, merging as beloved kin into the one true self you have always been.

Home is alignment: your inner truth and outer life in harmony. What you feel matches how you live. The gap between authenticity and pretending closes—not through more pretending, but through truth.

Home is recognition: the day you meet your own eyes in the mirror and know, with an ache of joy, that you are truly seen. It's the sacred instant when your choices ring with your own cadence. The moment you breathe in and feel that you belong to your own life again.

Home is what the breadcrumbs led you toward—not a new destination, but the integrated, whole self you left behind when life asked you to be smaller, quieter, more acceptable. Home is the you waiting for you to remember the way back.

Home as Feeling

Before we define home intellectually, let's feel it. Because home is a feeling before it's a concept. You know home not by understanding it but by recognizing it in your body, in your heart, in the quiet settling that happens when you're finally where you belong.

Peace. Home is peace—the inner stillness that comes when you're no longer fighting yourself. When the internal war between who you are and who you think you should be finally quiets. When you can simply be, without the exhausting effort of managing, controlling, and performing. Peace isn't the absence of challenges; it's the presence of alignment. You can face difficulties from home without losing yourself in them.

Safety. Home is safety—not the external kind reliant on circumstances, but the internal kind from trusting yourself. Knowing you can meet whatever comes. Being your own ally, advocate, ground. This safety doesn't mean that nothing bad happens. It means you belong to yourself, no matter what.

Comfort. Home is comfort—the ease of being yourself without the performance. The rest comes when you don't have to maintain an image. The deep relaxation of being known, especially by yourself. Comfort isn't complacency; it's the natural state of a self that doesn't have to pretend.

Rest. Home is rest—the exhale after years of holding your breath. The release of burdens you didn't know you carried. The permission to stop striving and simply be. Not lazy, not passive, but restored. Rest from which authentic action can arise.

Belonging. Home is the aching, fierce belonging you feel in your own bones—a place found not by reshaping yourself but by finally stopping the struggle. Here, you are woven into your own life, the larger story, with a presence that asks for nothing but your being. Not won by pleasing, but claimed by being true.

Recognition. Home is recognition—seeing yourself fully and being consumed by another's gaze. The moment you dare to meet your own reflection and refuse to look away. The moment you confess the truth and feel it echo. The moment you come back to yourself in your own life, after years wandering like a stranger there.

This is what home feels like. Not a concept to be understood, but an experience to be recognized. Somewhere within you, you already know this feeling. You've glimpsed it, felt it in moments. The journey home is learning to live there.

Home Across the Six Dimensions

Home isn't found in one dimension. It lives in all. Let's explore what coming home looks and feels like across the six dimensions of your Life Code.

Biologically, home is a regulated nervous system. It's a body that's no longer perpetually braced for threat, no longer living in chronic fight-flight-freeze. When you come home biologically, the tension you've carried for years begins to release. Your shoulders drop. Your jaw unclenches. Sleep comes easier because your system finally trusts that it's safe to rest. Energy that was consumed by constant vigilance becomes available for living. Home in the body is safety felt in the cells, ease experienced in the muscles, breath that flows freely without you having to think about it.

Neurologically, home is a brain that works with you rather than against you. The old programming has been examined, the destructive patterns have been collapsed, and new pathways have been installed. Your mind is no longer running legacy code that sabotages your intentions. The neural ruts that kept you trapped have been redirected. Your brain has become a partner in your becoming—supporting your growth, reinforcing your choices, creating new grooves that serve who you're becoming rather than who you were conditioned to be.

Psychologically, home is peace with yourself. The inner critic quiets, replaced by the compassionate witness you have developed. It's self-acceptance without needing perfection—being worthy as you are. Stories are rewritten; patterns recognized. You now choose responses, not just react from old wounds. Home is a self no longer at war.

Culturally, home means freedom from programming you didn't choose. It's living by values you've chosen, not inherited. Your definition of success is yours, not your culture's. Your worth isn't tied to others' checklists. You belong not by conforming but by claiming your own way of being. Home is living by your own code.

Relationally, home is showing up as your real self. Boundaries protect integrity without isolating you. Intimacy comes from being seen—you're no longer hiding. Connection arises from wholeness, not need. Home means belonging to yourself, so you can be with others without losing yourself.

Spiritually, home is a connection to something larger without losing your own center. It means that it doesn't depend on external achievement—a sense of purpose that arises from being, not just doing. It's the felt sense of being held by life even in difficulty, of having a place in the larger story, of your existence mattering not because of what you accomplish but because you are. Home spiritually is knowing you belong to the universe, and the universe belongs to you.

The Practical Home

Home isn't only a spiritual or internal feeling. It shows in the way you live. Inner and outer homes want to align.

Consider your living space. Does it reflect who you are or who you think you should be? Does walking through your door feel like entering a sanctuary, or like stepping onto a stage where you must perform? Your space expresses your inner world. When you reconnect with yourself, you often seek to do the same in your environment—clearing what doesn't fit, creating spaces that nourish, and keeping what truly matters.

Consider your daily rhythms. Do they honor your true energy, needs, and nature? Or are they shaped by "should," obligation, and what others do? Coming home means aligning days with your real self—not fantasy, but sustainable ways that respect your limits and nature.

Consider your work. Is it aligned with your purpose, or are you performing for a paycheck while your soul slowly starves? This isn't about quitting your job tomorrow—it's about honest acknowledgment of the gap between what you do and who you are and beginning to close that gap however you can. Coming home to work means bringing more of yourself to what you do and doing more of what brings you to life.

Consider your relationships. Do they allow you to be yourself, or do they require you to fragment—to show certain parts and hide others, to perform a version of yourself that isn't quite true? Coming home relationally means gradually shifting toward connections that honor your wholeness—and that may mean renegotiating some relationships, releasing others, and deepening the ones where you can be real.

Consider your choices. Are they coming from autopilot—from conditioning, from habit, from what everyone expects? Or are they coming from a genuine decision, from conscious selection, from the integrated you that knows what it actually wants? Coming home in choice means living from the inside out rather than the outside in.

When inner home and outer home align, life stops feeling performed and starts feeling true. This isn't about perfection—it's about congruence. The outer becomes an expression of the inner. Life becomes a reflection of the self.

You Are the One You've Been Looking For

The search that brought you here—what was it really searching for?

Perhaps you thought you were looking for answers. Solutions to your problems, strategies for your challenges, frameworks to make sense of your confusion. Perhaps you thought this book would give you something you didn't have—some insight or technique that would finally fix what felt broken.

Perhaps you thought you were looking for someone else to tell you what to do. An expert with authority, a guide with all the answers, a voice more trustworthy than your own.

Here's the profound truth you've been circling around this entire journey: you are the one you've been looking for.

The wholeness you've been seeking isn't outside you. It isn't in another book, another program, another expert's opinion. The wholeness you've been seeking IS you. It's the you who existed before conditioning told you who to be, the you who's been patiently waiting beneath the roles and expectations, the you where nothing is fragmented, performing, or left behind.

You didn't need to become someone else. You needed to remember who you already are.

The guide you needed was your own witness—that observing capacity you developed in Chapter 4, which sees you without judgment and holds space for your becoming. The wisdom you sought was your own knowing—the breadcrumbs you've been leaving yourself all along, pointing toward what was true even when you couldn't consciously see it. The home you longed for was your own integrated self—the wholeness that was never actually lost, only forgotten.

Not that the journey hasn't mattered. The tools you've gained, the awareness you've developed, the patterns you've recognized—these have all been essential. But they weren't adding something that wasn't there. They were removing what obscured what was always there. Like Michelangelo chipping away everything that wasn't David, you've been revealing what was waiting inside you all along.

The you who's been waiting for you to remember the way back—you've found them. They were never far. They were you.

Integration: Welcoming Back Every Exiled Part

Integration is the core of coming home. It's what makes the difference between understanding wholeness intellectually and actually living it.

Throughout your life, parts of you were exiled. Not dramatically, not all at once, but piece by piece, as you learned what was acceptable and what wasn't, what was safe and what was dangerous, what earned love and what threatened it.

Parts that weren't acceptable to your family—the emotions they couldn't handle, the needs they couldn't meet, the traits that threatened their stability. These parts learned to hide.

Parts that didn't fit cultural expectations—the dreams that didn't match the plan, the preferences that raised eyebrows, the ways of being that didn't fit the mold. These parts learned to disappear.

Parts that carried too much pain—the grief that was too overwhelming, the fear that was too intense, the wounds that couldn't be processed at the time. These parts were pushed below the waterline.

Parts that were too wild, too sensitive, too powerful—the bigness that scared people, the intensity that was "too much," the gifts that provoked envy instead of celebration. These parts learned to shrink.

But these parts didn't disappear. They went underground. They've been living in the 90% beneath your waterline, shaping your experience from the shadows, waiting to be welcomed home.

Coming home means welcoming them back. The dreams you abandoned. The creativity you silenced. The needs you denied. The emotions you suppressed. The truth you swallowed. The parts of you that you decided were too much, not enough, or simply not allowed.

Integration isn't fixing broken parts—it's recognizing that nothing was ever truly broken. Those parts weren't defective. They were just exiled. And now they can return.

Imagine the prodigal parts coming home. The self that loves to dance, even badly. The self that feels deeply, even when it's inconvenient. The self that dreams audaciously, even when it's impractical. The self that takes up space, even when it makes others uncomfortable. All of them were welcomed back. All of them honored. All of them were included in the whole.

This is integration. This is coming home.

Wholeness Isn't Perfection—It's Inclusion

Here's a distinction that changes everything: wholeness is not perfection.

Perfection demands flawlessness. It says: only the parts that measure up can be included. Only what's polished, presentable, and problem-free belongs. Everything else must be hidden, fixed, or eliminated.

Wholeness says something entirely different. Wholeness welcomes everything. It includes the full spectrum of who you are—the light and the shadow, the strength and the weakness, the triumph and the failure, the parts you're proud of and the parts you'd rather forget.

You don't become whole by eliminating your shadow. You become whole by integrating it. You don't achieve wholeness by perfecting yourself. You recognize wholeness by accepting yourself—all of yourself, without conditions.

This is radical acceptance. Not passive resignation to the idea that nothing can change. No approval of harmful behaviors. But active inclusion of all that you are, which paradoxically becomes the foundation for genuine transformation.

You can only transform what you first accept. You can only change what you first include. The parts you exile don't disappear—they just operate from the shadows, outside your awareness and beyond your conscious choice. Integration brings them into the light, where they can finally be worked with, understood, and transformed.

Wholeness includes your contradictions. You can be both strong and vulnerable. Both confident and uncertain. Both growing and struggling. These aren't failures of integration—they're the nature of being human.

You are whole not when you've fixed everything, but when you've welcomed everything. Not when you've become perfect, but when you've become complete. And completeness doesn't mean finished—it means nothing is left out.

What the Fragmented Pieces Look Like Coming Together

Integration isn't just a concept—it has a felt experience. When the fragmented pieces actually come together, something shifts. Life feels different.

The war inside quiets. When you're no longer fighting yourself, when the different parts of you are working together instead of against each other, there's a stillness that wasn't there before. You stop second-guessing every decision, stop arguing with your own desires, stop sabotaging what you're trying to build.

Energy becomes available. So much of your energy was going into internal conflict—to managing the exiled parts, maintaining the performance, keeping the fragmentation hidden. When integration happens, that energy is released. You have resources you didn't know you had, simply because they're no longer being consumed by the effort of staying divided.

Decisions become clearer. When you're whole, you know what you actually want. The confusion caused by different parts pulling in different directions is resolved. Your yes is yes, and your no is no. Choice becomes simpler—not always easy, but clearer.

Authenticity becomes natural. You stop performing without having to think about it. The mask you wore for so long becomes uncomfortable rather than comfortable. Being real feels like relief rather than risk.

Relationships deepen. When you can be truly present to yourself, you can be truly present to others. When you're not hiding parts of yourself, you can be truly seen. Intimacy becomes possible in ways it wasn't before.

Meaning arises naturally. You don't have to chase meaning when you embody it. Purpose isn't something you need to find externally when you're living from your whole self. Significance stops being about achievement and starts being about alignment.

This is what living from true choice looks like. Not perfect choices—there's no such thing. But YOUR choices. Choices made from clarity, not conditioning. Choices made from wholeness, not from wounds. Choices that reflect who you actually are rather than who you were programmed to be.

The Bridge Between Dimensions

Throughout this book, we've explored six dimensions of your being: biological, neurological, psychological, cultural, relational, and spiritual. Coming home means bridging them—experiencing them not as separate layers but as one integrated life.

When you're home, the body's wisdom informs your choices. You don't override what your system is telling you; you listen, you trust, you respond. The biological and the psychological work together.

When you're home, the new neural pathways support your intentions. The brain that used to sabotage now reinforces. The neurological changes enable the relational shifts—you can show up differently in relationships because your patterns have genuinely changed.

When you're home, your chosen values shape your relationships. The cultural liberation—living by your own code rather than inherited programming—shows up in how you connect with others. You attract and nurture relationships that align with who you actually are.

When you're home, your relationships are grounded in your sense of purpose. The relational and the spiritual inform each other. You connect from a place of meaning, and your connections contribute to your sense of meaning.

When you're home, your spiritual connection expresses through daily action. The transcendence doesn't stay abstract; it shows up in practical choices, in how you spend your time, in what you do with your one precious life.

Home isn't found in one dimension. It's the harmony of all dimensions aligned. When they bridge, when they flow into each other, when they work together rather than against each other—that's home. That's integration. That's the wholeness you've been seeking.

The Longing Fulfilled

Remember where we began? Hiraeth. The Welsh word for a longing for a home your soul remembers, but your mind has forgotten. Homesickness for yourself.

That longing brought you here. It was the first breadcrumb, the original signal from your authentic self, saying: " This isn't quite right. Something is missing. There's more.

That longing wasn't a problem to be solved. It wasn't evidence of ingratitude or chronic dissatisfaction. It was a call. An invitation. A guide that wouldn't let you settle for a life that was too small for your soul.

And now, having followed the breadcrumbs through all five parts of this journey, you can feel what that longing was reaching for.

It was reaching for this. For the integrated you. For the whole you. For the you who was always there beneath the fragmentation, waiting patiently for you to remember the way back.

A client I'll call Anna had been doing this work for almost two years. She'd been thorough and honest, and sometimes difficult to sit with, because she was the kind of person who didn't let herself off the hook. She'd traced her patterns, named her characters, and opened several things she'd spent decades keeping closed. She was changed. She knew it. She just didn't feel it yet — not the way she thought she was supposed to.

She came to one of our final sessions and said something I've heard in different forms many times: "I don't know if I've arrived. I thought it would feel bigger."

I asked her to tell me about the previous week.

She thought about it. There was a moment, she said — a Tuesday morning, unremarkable in every way. She was sitting with her coffee before anyone else in her house was up. She wasn't meditating. She wasn't journaling. She was just sitting. And she noticed that she wasn't braced for anything. Wasn't rehearsing anything. Wasn't managing her inner weather, or monitoring her mood, or preparing for whatever the day might require of her.

She was just there. In her kitchen. In her life. In herself.

"It lasted maybe ten minutes," she said. "And then the kids woke up, and it was over."

She told me this as if it were a small thing. I told her it was the whole thing.

That Tuesday morning was home. Not the ten minutes — the capacity for it. The fact that it was possible now in a way it had never been before. That peace had become available to her, even briefly, even ordinarily, in the middle of an unremarkable Tuesday.

She started to cry a little. "I've been looking for something bigger," she said.

"I know," I said. "That's what made it so easy to miss."

The longing fulfilled isn't a dramatic arrival with trumpets and fanfare. It's a quiet recognition. A gentle landing. A soft exhale of finally.

Oh. This. This is what I was looking for. This is who I've been all along.

The longing doesn't disappear entirely. It transforms. What was once homesickness becomes gratitude. Gratitude for the call that wouldn't let you stay lost. Gratitude for the breadcrumbs that marked the way. Gratitude for yourself—for having the courage to follow them home.

The longing that ached now rests. Not because everything is perfect, but because you're finally where you belong. In yourself.

The Arrival

You have arrived.

Not at perfection—that was never the destination. Not having it all figured out—that's not a place anyone gets to. Not at a final finish line where nothing ever changes and no challenges ever arise.

You have arrived at yourself.

At the home you never truly left, even when you wandered far and forgot the way back. At the wholeness that was waiting, patient and permanent, beneath all the years of fragmentation. At the integration of everything you are—light and shadow, strength and struggle, all of it welcomed, all of it included, all of it you.

The work isn't over. Life will continue to present challenges. Old patterns will occasionally resurface. The world will continue to invite fragmentation. The journey of staying home is its own adventure.

But the orientation has changed. You're no longer searching for home. You're living from it. You're no longer trying to find yourself. You're being yourself. The seeking has transformed into the being.

You are the one you've been looking for. You've found yourself. And from this place—from home—everything is different. Not because the external world has changed, but because the internal world has realigned. You're living from the inside out now. And that changes everything.

Welcome home.

Pause and Reflect

Before moving to the next chapter, take a moment to sit with these questions. Let them work on you.

When you imagine "home" as a feeling rather than a place, what does it feel like in your body? Where do you feel it?

In which of the six dimensions do you feel most "at home" right now? Where do you still feel like a stranger to yourself?

What exiled parts of yourself are ready to be welcomed back? What would integration look like for you?

How does the idea that "you are the one you've been looking for" land in you? What does it stir?

What would your life look like if your outer choices fully reflected your inner truth—if inner home and outer home were aligned?

The longing that brought you here—can you feel it transforming? What is it becoming?

The Breadcrumb

Each chapter closes with a single breadcrumb—a key insight to carry forward on your journey.

Home is not a destination you arrive at but a remembering of who you've always been beneath the conditioning. It's not a place you reach after enough work—it's a state you recognize when the fragmented pieces finally come together. Home is peace, safety, comfort, rest, belonging, and recognition. It's the exhale after holding your breath for years. It lives in every dimension of your being—in a body that can finally relax, a mind that works with you, a psyche at peace, values that are your own, relationships where you can be real, and a connection to something larger that holds it all. Home is also practical—your space, your rhythms, your work, your choices reflecting who you actually are. Integration is the core of coming home: welcoming back every exiled part, every abandoned dream, every suppressed truth. You don't have to fix what was never truly broken. You just have to welcome it home. Wholeness isn't perfection—it's inclusion. It's not eliminating what doesn't measure up; it's embracing the full spectrum of who you are. Light and dark, strength and struggle, triumph and failure—all of it, held together, is you. The longing that brought you here—hiraeth, homesickness for yourself—was the first breadcrumb. And you followed it. You followed them all. And now you're here. Not at the end of the journey, but at the center of yourself. Welcome home.

Going Deeper: Your Digital Companion

The questions above are meant to stir something in you—to begin the inner conversation. But real integration happens when you take time to explore your responses more fully.

In your digital companion, you'll find the following exercises for Chapter 15:

The Feeling of Home — A guided meditation to access what home feels like in your body, independent of any physical location

Home Across Dimensions — Assessing your sense of "home" in each of the six dimensions: where you're settled and where you're still settling

The Exiled Parts Inventory — Identifying which parts of yourself were sent away and are ready to be welcomed back.

Integration Ritual — A ceremonial practice for welcoming exiled parts home

Inner/Outer Home Alignment — Assessing where your outer life reflects your inner truth and where it still doesn't

The Longing Transformed — A reflective writing exercise on what your original longing has become

Mindset Mind Map Update: The Arrival — Completing the center of your map: your definition of home, the exiled parts returning, what wholeness feels like

---

You have arrived home. But arrival isn't the end—it's a new beginning. Coming home is profound, but the real question becomes: how do you LIVE from home? How do you maintain alignment between your inner truth and outer life? How do you make choices from wholeness in a world that constantly invites fragmentation? In Chapter 16, we'll explore what it means to live from home—to let your daily life become an expression of your integrated self. The journey doesn't end; it transforms. And living from home is where the adventure truly begins.

CHAPTER SIXTEEN

LIVING FROM HOME

WHY are you here...and how will you live now that you know?

"How we spend our days is, of course, how we spend our lives."
— Annie Dillard

IN CHAPTER 15, YOU came home. You felt at ease with yourself, as if you had set aside old habits and memories that hid your true nature. The emptiness you once felt was filled; the aspects of yourself you had ignored now felt present. You recognized who you are and have been.

But arrival is just a moment. The rest—living—is what comes next.

The question now isn't "How do I find home?" You've found it. The new question is, "How do I LIVE from home?" How do you take this inner arrival and bring it into the ordinary moments of your days? How do you maintain alignment between your inner truth and your outer life in a world that invites fragmentation?

Coming home was profound. Living from home is the practice.

This chapter is about wholeness in action. Authenticity as a daily habit. Alignment is an ongoing choice. It's about making home not just where you arrive, but where you live FROM—the ground beneath your feet as you move through your one precious life.

The Texture of Living from Home

Before we explore what living from home looks like in each dimension of your life, let's feel what it's like. Because living from home isn't primarily a set of practices or strategies—it's a way of being. A quality of presence. A texture to your days that's different from anything you've known before.

Living from home feels like finally fitting inside your own skin. That subtle sense of wrongness—of wearing a coat that almost fits but never quite keeps you warm—dissolves. You're not performing yourself anymore. You're simply being yourself. And being yourself, it turns out, is the most natural thing in the world. It's everything else that was exhausting.

Living from home feels like exhaling. Not once, at the moment of arrival, but continuously. An ongoing release of tension you didn't know you were holding. The breath flows more easily. The shoulders stay soft. The jaw unclenches without you having to remind it. Your body finally trusts that it's safe to relax—not because the world has become safe, but because you've come home to yourself.

Living from home feels like opening a window. The fog lifts. You notice what you want—not always, not perfectly, but more than before. Choices that once took hours now come faster. Life hasn't become simple, but you understand yourself better. When you're home, you can hear your own voice above the noise.

Living from home feels like presence. You're actually HERE for your life—not rehearsing the future, not rehashing the past. You inhabit this moment, this conversation, this ordinary Tuesday afternoon. The present feels spacious instead of something to rush through on the way elsewhere.

Living from home feels like permission. Permission to take up space. Permission to have needs. Permission to say no. Permission to want what you want without having to justify it. Permission to be human—gloriously, messily, imperfectly human. And to know that's enough. More than enough.

Living from home feels like a connection. Connection to yourself, first—all the parts welcomed, nothing exiled. And from that wholeness, connection to others becomes possible in ways it wasn't before. When you're not hiding yourself, you can truly meet another person. When you're not performing, you can truly be seen.

Living from home feels meaningful. Not a meaning you chase or manufacture, but one that arises naturally from living aligned with who you are. The search for significance quiets. You're no longer looking for it outside yourself. You ARE significant. Your life, fully inhabited, IS the meaning.

This is what you're stepping into—not rules to follow, but a way to be; not a destination to maintain, but a home to live in. The following practices aren't the point—just support. The point: you, living fully present, fully yourself, fully home.

The Difference Between Visiting and Residing

You've visited home before. You've glimpsed it throughout your life—when everything aligned, when you felt yourself, when performance dropped, and something real appeared. These weren't accidents. They were visits, brief returns to a place you always knew existed, even if you couldn't stay.

The difference now is the residence. You're not visiting home anymore. You're living there.

Visitors come and go; they don't unpack or rearrange the furniture, experiencing a place without inhabiting it. Residents stay, settle in, and make the space their own.

Living from home means making decisions FROM your integrated self, not toward it. It's a subtle but profound shift. When you're searching for home, every choice is about getting closer to wholeness. When you're living from home, every choice expresses the wholeness you already have.

Your wholeness is now your operating system, not just your aspiration. Your authenticity is the default, not the goal. You're no longer trying to become yourself—you ARE yourself, living from that truth.

This is the shift from working toward something to simply living. From traveling to arriving. From searching for a home to settling into it.

You've done the work of finding home. Now comes the adventure of living there.

Living from Home Biologically

Your body is where you live first from home. It's the most immediate, tangible expression of your wholeness—or your fragmentation.

When you live biologically from home, you trust your body's signals rather than overriding them. You rest when you're tired instead of pushing through. You eat when you're hungry, not when you're following external rules. You move when you're stagnant, rather than forcing yourself to stay productive. Your body becomes a partner in your life, not an obstacle to be managed or an enemy to be conquered.

Self-care transforms from a self-improvement project into an expression of self-respect. You care for your body not to fix what's wrong but to honor what's right. You honor your energy rhythms rather than fighting them—working with your natural patterns of alertness and rest rather than demanding constant output.

Boundaries become physical and emotional. You develop discernment about what depletes you and what nourishes you—foods, environments, activities, people. You protect your physical well-being not from fear but from self-love.

Living from home biologically might include a morning body check-in—asking "What does my body need today?" and actually listening to the answer. It might mean noticing tension as information rather than treating it as an enemy to be eliminated. Movement becomes a celebration rather than a punishment. Sleep becomes a non-negotiable foundation rather than an optional luxury.

When you live biologically from home, your body is your ally. You're no longer at war with your physical self. You're inhabiting it fully, caring for it tenderly, trusting its wisdom.

Living from Home Neurologically

Your brain, once the source of so much automatic sabotage, can now work with you rather than against you.

Living from home neurologically means catching old patterns before they complete their familiar circuits. You notice the trigger, feel the pull of the conditioned response, and in that gap—the space between stimulus and reaction that you've been developing throughout this book—you choose something different. Not always. Not perfectly. But more and more often.

The neural pathways you've been building now support rather than sabotage your intentions. The grooves that once led you automatically into old reactions are being redirected. New paths have been worn by conscious choice, and they're becoming easier to travel.

There's less mental static now. More clarity. Your thoughts become something you can observe rather than something that possesses you. The witness you developed in Chapter 4 is always available—that calm, watching presence that can see what's happening without being swept away by it.

Living neurologically from home might include celebrating when you notice yourself forming a new pattern rather than an old one—this reinforces the new neural grooves. It might mean regular mindfulness practices that strengthen your capacity to witness your own mind. It might mean practicing cognitive flexibility—the ability to hold multiple perspectives, to see situations from different angles, to avoid the rigidity that characterized your old programming.

When you live neurologically from home, your mind serves your intentions. The brain that once ran programs against your interests now supports who you're becoming.

Living from Home Psychologically

Inner peace becomes your default rather than a distant destination.

Psychologically, living from home means the inner critic has finally quieted. Not disappeared entirely—that voice may always show up from time to time—but it's no longer running the show. In its place is the compassionate witness: the part of you that can see your struggles without condemning you for them, that can acknowledge your imperfections without using them as evidence of your inadequacy.

Self-acceptance no longer requires perfection. You can be a work in progress and still be at peace with yourself. You can have growth edges and still belong to yourself. The war inside—the constant battle between who you are and who you think you should be—has ended. Not because you became perfect, but because you stopped requiring perfection as the price of self-acceptance.

Emotions are felt fully without ruling you. You can experience the full intensity of what arises—grief, anger, fear, joy—without being swept away by it. Feelings move through rather than getting stuck. You've learned that emotions are information and energy, not commands to be obeyed or threats to be suppressed.

Your needs are acknowledged and expressed rather than denied or hidden. You know what you need, and you can ask for it—not demanding, not manipulating, but clearly, simply, as someone who has a right to need things.

Psychologically, living from home might include practicing self-compassion in moments of struggle—treating yourself as you would a loved one. It might mean emotional naming: "I notice I'm feeling anxious" rather than being swallowed by the anxiety. It might mean regular check-ins: "What do I actually need right now?"

When you live psychologically from home, you're on your own side. Your inner world is a place of peace rather than warfare.

Living from Home Culturally

Freedom from programming you never chose becomes the foundation of how you live.

Living from home culturally means your values are consciously chosen rather than unconsciously inherited. You've examined what you were taught to believe, to want, to pursue—and you've decided for yourself what actually matters. Some inherited values you've kept because they genuinely fit. Others you've released because they were never yours to begin with.

Success is defined on your own terms now. The cultural scripts about what a good life looks like, what achievement means, what you should want by this age or that stage—you can see them for what they are. You can appreciate them as one perspective without being enslaved by them. Your definition of a life well-lived is yours.

You have permission to want what you actually want, even if it doesn't match what you're supposed to want. Even if it confuses people. Even if it doesn't fit the mold. Your desires are valid not because culture validates them, but because they're yours.

Belonging no longer requires conforming. You can be part of communities, contribute to collective life, honor your cultural roots—without sacrificing your authenticity as the price of admission. You belong not by fitting in but by showing up as yourself.

Living culturally from home might include noticing when "should" appears in your thinking and questioning its source. It might mean choosing your inputs intentionally—what media you consume, what messages you absorb, and what influences you allow into your mental space. It might mean surrounding yourself with people who support your authentic self rather than those who require your performance.

When you live culturally from home, you're writing your own code. Culture informs you without controlling you.

Living from Home Relationally

Showing up as your real self with others becomes possible in ways it never was before.

Living from home relationally means authenticity is the foundation of your connections. You bring your whole self to relationships—not a curated version, not a performance designed to be acceptable, but the actual you. This is vulnerable and sometimes scary. It's also the only way to experience real connection.

Boundaries protect without isolating. You can say no without a lengthy justification. You can protect your time, energy, and emotional resources without guilt. Boundaries aren't walls that keep people out—they're gates that allow you to regulate what comes in and what goes out.

Intimacy becomes possible because you can actually be seen. When you're not hiding parts of yourself, when you're not managing an image, when you're not performing a role—then someone can truly know you. And being truly known is the deepest human longing.

Your relationships nourish rather than deplete you. You give from overflow rather than obligation. You receive without guilt, knowing that accepting love isn't weakness but wisdom. The relationships that remain in your life as you become more whole are the ones that can hold your wholeness.

Some relationships will deepen as you become more real. These are the connections that were always waiting for you to show up fully. Some relationships will shift or even release as you stop performing. These changes, though sometimes painful, are part of living from home. You cannot maintain connections that require your fragmentation and live from wholeness at the same time.

Living relationally from home might include truth-telling with kindness, checking in with yourself during interactions to ask, "Am I performing or being real right now?", honoring your limits without over-explaining, and reaching out from genuine desire rather than duty.

When you live relationally from home, you connect from a place of wholeness. Your relationships become expressions of who you are rather than substitutes for who you're not.

Living from Home Spiritually

Connection to something larger is expressed through daily life rather than remaining abstract.

Spiritual living from home means that meaning doesn't depend on achievement. You don't have to earn significance through accomplishment. Your life matters not because of what you produce, but because of what you are. Being is enough. Presence is enough. You are enough.

Purpose weaves through ordinary moments rather than waiting for grand occasions. The sacred isn't somewhere else, reserved for special rituals or peak experiences. The sacred is here, in this conversation, in this meal, in this quiet moment of attention. Every act performed with presence becomes a spiritual act.

Gratitude becomes your orientation rather than an occasional exercise. You notice what's already here, already given, already present. Not to avoid difficulty, but to stay connected to the fullness of life, even in difficulty.

Trust in the unfolding develops—even when you can't see where it leads. This isn't passive resignation or blind optimism. It's the deep knowing that comes from having followed the breadcrumbs home: life can be trusted. The path reveals itself as you walk it. You don't have to figure everything out in advance.

Living spiritually from home might include moments of stillness throughout your day—not to achieve anything, but simply to connect with what is. It might mean gratitude practice: beginning or ending each day by noticing what's already here. It might mean service that arises naturally from overflow rather than obligation.

When you live spiritually from home, the sacred is everywhere, in everything. Your daily life becomes your spiritual practice.

Daily Life as Spiritual Practice

This is the integration of all six dimensions into ordinary moments.

Spirituality isn't separate from daily life. It IS daily life, lived consciously. The mundane becomes sacred when approached with presence. Doing the dishes, driving to work, having a conversation with a colleague, waiting in line—all of it can be practice. All of it can be an expression of living from home.

How you do anything is how you do everything. The attention you bring to small moments reflects the attention you bring to large ones. The presence you cultivate in ordinary tasks becomes the presence you have available for extraordinary ones.

Daily life as a spiritual practice means full attention to what's in front of you. It means ordinary tasks done with presence rather than impatience—not rushing through them to get to something "better" but recognizing that this moment is the only one you're ever actually living. It means each interaction is an opportunity for genuine connection, each task is an opportunity for presence, and each moment is an opportunity to be fully here.

Work becomes an expression of purpose rather than just a paycheck. Rest becomes sacred rather than lazy. Play becomes essential rather than indulgent. Everything shifts when you approach your life as the spiritual practice it is.

You don't need to escape daily life to be spiritual. You don't need special circumstances or extraordinary experiences. You need to fully inhabit the life you already have. The path home runs right through the middle of your ordinary days.

Alignment: When Inner and Outer Match

Alignment is the felt experience of living from home. It's what happens when your outer life reflects your inner truth.

When you're aligned, your choices arise from clarity rather than conditioning. Your relationships honor who you actually are rather than who you're pretending to be. Your work expresses your gifts rather than suppressing them. Your environment reflects your values rather than contradicting them. Your daily rhythms support your authentic self rather than working against it.

The Alignment Audit is a practice of honest assessment across key life areas. Where do you feel aligned—where your inner truth and outer life match? Where do you feel misaligned—where there's a gap between who you are inside and how you're living outside?

Consider your relationships: Do they allow you to be real, or do they require performance? Consider your work: Does it express your gifts and values, or does it demand that you suppress them? Consider your health:

Are you caring for yourself with love, or neglecting yourself with indifference? Consider your creativity: Are you expressing yourself, or have you silenced your creative voice? Consider your sense of meaning: Do you feel connected to a purpose, or are you just going through the motions? Consider your environment: Does your space reflect who you are, or who you think you should be?

Alignment isn't perfection. You will never achieve complete congruence between the inner and outer life for it is too dynamic, too complex for that. The goal isn't perfection, but progress. The goal is to increase alignment over time, closing the gaps where you can and accepting the ones that remain for now.

Misalignment is information, not an indictment. When you notice a gap between inner truth and outer life, that's not evidence that you've failed. It's awareness—and awareness is the first step to choice. You cannot change what you cannot see. Now you see. Now you can choose.

Work That Expresses Your Purpose

For many people, work is where the biggest misalignment lives. You spend most of your waking hours engaged in work—it matters whether that work aligns with who you are.

Living from home at work means bringing your authentic self, not just your productive self. It means finding purpose in what you do—or finding work that better fits your purpose. It means boundaries that protect your energy and integrity. It means a contribution that feels meaningful, not just profitable.

This doesn't mean quitting everything tomorrow and following your bliss into financial ruin. Living from home is practical, not reckless. But it does mean bringing more of yourself to what you currently do. It means gradually moving toward work that expresses more of who you are. It means refusing to accept permanent misalignment just because change is hard.

Even in imperfect circumstances—and most circumstances are imperfect—you can practice being real. You can bring presence to tasks that feel meaningless. You can find moments of genuine connection with colleagues. You can protect small spaces of authenticity even in environments that don't fully support it.

And over time, step by step, choice by choice, you can move toward greater alignment. Work that expresses your purpose rarely arrives in a single dramatic leap. It develops through a thousand small choices to bring more of yourself to what you do.

When Living from Home Gets Hard

Living from home isn't always comfortable. Let's be honest about that.

The world still invites fragmentation. Culture still pushes you toward performance. Old patterns still exert a gravitational pull. Some relationships may not adapt to your wholeness. Some work environments may not make space for your authenticity. The forces that originally caused you to fragment haven't disappeared just because you've come home.

Some days you'll forget you're home. You'll fall back into old patterns without noticing. You'll perform when you mean to be real. You'll react when you meant to choose. You'll find yourself far from home and wonder how you got there.

This isn't a failure. This is being human.

A client I'll call Grace had done deep work over the past 18 months. She'd changed in ways she could feel and that the people closest to her could see. And then, at a family gathering over the holidays, she disappeared.

Not physically. She was there the whole time. But somewhere in the first hour — in the familiar dynamics, the old roles, the unspoken expectations that her family of origin ran like weather — she quietly became someone she recognized from years ago. Smaller. More careful. Agreeing with things she didn't believe. Laughing at things that weren't funny. Managing everyone's comfort and abandoning her own.

She came to coaching in January, describing it with the old familiar language: "I don't know why I do this. What is wrong with me?"

I asked her what she would have said to a close friend who'd had the same experience.

She thought about it. "I'd probably say that being around family is hard. Those old patterns have deep roots. That slipping doesn't erase all the work."

"So say that to yourself."

A long pause.

"I forgot I was home," she said finally. "And then I remembered. And I came back."

That was it. That was the whole practice. Not that she hadn't wandered — she had. But she'd noticed. She'd named it without destroying herself over it. And she'd returned.

The wandering hadn't erased eighteen months of work. It had just been a visit to an old address. Home was still there, waiting, exactly where she'd left it.

The practice isn't to wander. The practice is to notice when you've wandered and gently return. To meet yourself with compassion rather than criticism when you find yourself off the path. To remember that home doesn't disappear when you forget—you just step away for a bit. The path back is always there.

When it's hard, return to the body. Ground in what's here, what's physical, what's immediate. Feel your feet on the floor. Take a breath. This is the simplest path back to presence.

When it's hard, remember that this is practice, not performance. You're not being graded. You're not supposed to do it perfectly. You're supposed to do it humanly—with all the forgetting and remembering, wandering and returning, that being human involves.

When it's hard, remember that the witness is always available. That calm, observing presence you developed—it's still there, even when you forget to access it. You can always return to watching, noticing, observing without judgment.

The goal isn't to struggle. It's struggling from home rather than from exile. To meet difficulties from your wholeness rather than your fragmentation. To face challenges as your integrated self rather than a scattered collection of reactions.

The Daily Path

Your Mind Map layer for this chapter is "The Daily Path." Because living from home is walked, one day at a time.

It's not a destination you reach once and then stay at forever. It's a practice you return to. A path you walk each morning when you wake and continue walking until you sleep. Some days you walk it well. Some days you wander. Every day, you can begin again.

The daily path might begin in the morning with intention. Before you check your phone, before you start your to-do list, before the world rushes in—a moment of asking yourself: "How do I want to show up today? What does living from home look like for me today?"

The daily path continues throughout your day with awareness. Checking in periodically: "Am I living from home right now, or have I wandered? Am I being real, or am I performing? Am I present, or have I left?" These aren't judgments—they're noticing. And noticing is always the first step to choice.

The daily path might end in the evening with reflection. A few moments before sleep to review: "Where was I real today? Where did I forget? What can I celebrate? What can I release? What do I want to remember for tomorrow?"

The path is made by walking it. There is no perfect map, no guaranteed route, no way to do it that ensures you'll never lose your way. There is only the walking. One day at a time. One choice at a time. One moment of presence at a time.

This is how we spend our lives. Day by day. And how we spend our days, as Annie Dillard reminds us, is how we spend our lives.

So, how will you spend today? And tomorrow? And the day after that? What will living from home look like for you, in the particular circumstances of your life, with the particular gifts and challenges that are yours?

No one else can walk your path. No one else can live your life. But you can live it—fully, presently, authentically. You can live it from home.

Pause and Reflect

Before moving to the next chapter, take a moment to sit with these questions. Let them work on you.

In which of the six dimensions do you most naturally live from home? Where is it still a stretch?

What does your daily life look like when you're living from home versus when you've wandered away? How can you tell the difference?

Where is the biggest misalignment between your inner truth and your outer life? What would closing that gap look like?

Which relationships in your life support your authentic self? Which ones require you to perform or fragment?

How might your relationship with work shift if you brought more of your whole self to it?

What daily practices would help you remember to live from home? What could your morning intention, daytime awareness, and evening reflection look like?

The Breadcrumb

Each chapter closes with a single breadcrumb—a key insight to carry forward on your journey.

Coming home was the moment of arrival—recognizing yourself, welcoming back the exiled parts, feeling the longing fulfilled. Living from home is everything that comes after. It's wholeness in action, authenticity as a daily habit, alignment as an ongoing choice. Living from home shows up in every dimension of your being: in a body you trust and care for, in a mind that serves your intentions, in a psyche at peace with itself, in values you've consciously chosen, in relationships where you can be real, in a spiritual connection that infuses ordinary moments with meaning. It shows up in how you work, how you rest, how you connect, how you spend your one precious life. Alignment is the felt experience of living from home—when your outer life reflects your inner truth, when choices come from clarity rather than conditioning. But living from home isn't always comfortable. The world still invites fragmentation. Old patterns still pull. Some days you'll forget. That's not failure—that's being human. The practice is noticing when you've wandered and gently returning. Home doesn't disappear when you forget; you just step away for a bit. The path back is always there. Living from home is walked one day at a time, one choice at a time, one moment of presence at a time. This is how we spend our days. And how we spend our days is how we spend our lives.

Going Deeper: Your Digital Companion

The questions above are meant to stir something in you—to begin the inner conversation. But real integration happens when you take time to explore your responses more fully.

In your digital companion, you'll find the following exercises for Chapter 16:

Living from Home: Six Dimensions Inventory — Assessing how fully you're living from home in each dimension and identifying where you want to grow

The Alignment Audit — A comprehensive assessment of alignment between your inner truth and outer life across key life areas

Daily Practices Design — Creating personalized morning intention, daytime awareness, and evening reflection practices

Relationship Reality Check — Evaluating which relationships support your authentic self and where adjustments might be needed

Work Alignment Exploration — Assessing where your work expresses your purpose and where there's room for greater congruence

The Wandering and Returning Practice — A self-compassion practice for when you've forgotten and need to find your way back

Mindset Mind Map Update: The Daily Path — Mapping your daily practices, alignment areas, and commitments to living from home

---

Living from home naturally raises a deeper question. When you're no longer lost, when you're no longer searching for yourself, when you're actually inhab-

iting your life fully—a question emerges: Why am I here? Not just "What do I do with my days?" but "What is my life FOR?" Living from home creates the foundation for purpose to emerge. Your wholeness wants to contribute. Your authentic self has gifts to give. In Chapter 17, we'll explore purpose, meaning, and the soul's invitation—and discover that your journey home doesn't just change your life. It ripples outward. Your healing heals others. Your wholeness contributes to a world that desperately needs more people living from home.

Chapter Seventeen

Why You're Really Here

WHY are you here...and what is your life actually for?

"The meaning of life is to find your gift. The purpose of life is to give it away." — Pablo Picasso

"Don't ask what the world needs. Ask what makes you come alive, and go do it. Because what the world needs is people who have come alive." — Howard Thurman

You've come home. You're learning to live from home. Now, as you settle in, a deeper question emerges.

Not "How do I fix myself?" That question has been answered. You were never broken—you were fragmented, and you've been gathering the pieces back together.

Not "How do I find myself?" That question has been answered, too. You've been leaving breadcrumbs all along, and you've learned to follow them home.

The question now is different. When you're no longer lost, no longer searching, no longer at war with yourself, a new question emerges. It's a question that arises from wholeness rather than fragmentation: *Why am I here? What is my life actually for?*

This isn't an intellectual puzzle to solve. It's not a riddle with a clever answer hidden somewhere. It's an invitation to be lived—a question you answer not once but continuously, through how you spend your days, what you give your attention to, and who you become in the process.

Purpose isn't something you find and then have, like a possession you can put on a shelf. It's something you discover and then express, day by day, choice by choice, for the rest of your life. And the clues to that purpose have been with you all along.

The Purpose Paradox: God Has a Plan But Forgot the Manual

We've all heard some version of it: "God has a plan for your life." "You were put here for a reason." "There's something only you can do." "Your life has a purpose."

Beautiful ideas. Comforting ideas. Ideas that suggest our existence matters, that we're not just random accidents in an indifferent universe, that there's meaning woven into the fabric of our being.

One problem: nobody gave us the user's manual.

We're told we have a purpose, but not what it is. We're told we're here for a reason, but not what that might be. We're told there's a plan, but nobody hands us the blueprint. It's like getting a treasure map with no markings. You know the treasure exists, but you do not know where to dig.

This creates a unique spiritual frustration. You sense you're meant for something and feel a pull toward significance. Deep down, you know your life should matter. But the specifics are maddeningly unclear. You wander, trying different paths, and wonder if this is it, if this is what you're supposed to do, or if you missed a memo that others received.

Here's what I want you to know: the manual exists. It's written in your life. It's encoded in your breadcrumbs.

Purpose isn't hidden in some cosmic vault waiting to be unlocked by the right prayer, the right meditation, or the right spiritual breakthrough. It's been expressing itself through you your entire life. You just haven't known how to read the language.

The breadcrumbs that led you home are the same breadcrumbs that point to your purpose. The clues have always been there. Now you can see them.

What Purpose Actually Is

Before we go further, let's clarify what purpose is—and what it isn't.

Purpose is not a job title. It's not a role you play or a position you hold. You can change jobs many times while living the same purpose. You can have the "perfect" job and be completely disconnected from your purpose.

Purpose is not a single grand mission. It's not necessarily a dramatic calling to change the world in some visible, measurable way. The mythology of purpose as world-changing heroism leaves most people feeling inadequate, as though their ordinary lives couldn't possibly be purposeful.

Purpose is more like a through-line—a consistent quality of being and contribution that runs through everything you do. It's the "why" beneath the "what." It's the essence of how you show up, regardless of the specific circumstances.

Purpose is less about WHAT you do and more about HOW and WHY you do it.

Two people can have the same job. One is living their purpose; the other is just earning a paycheck. The difference isn't in the work itself—it's in the relationship between the person and the work.

Purpose shows up in the teacher who stays late because something in her comes alive when a student finally understands. It's not the teaching that's her purpose—it's the awakening, the illumination, the moment of breakthrough. She could express that purpose in a hundred different ways.

Purpose shows up in the accountant who loves bringing order to chaos, helping people feel financially safe and clear. Accounting is the vehicle; the purpose is the order, the safety, the clarity it brings.

Purpose shows up in the parent who pours conscious intention of raising human beings who will contribute rather than just consume. Parenting is the context; the purpose is the cultivation of consciousness.

Your purpose is already expressing through you. The question isn't whether you have a purpose—you do. The question is whether you're conscious of it.

Purpose as Organizing Principle

When you know your purpose—when you can name it, feel it, orient toward it—it becomes an organizing principle for your entire life.

Decisions become clearer. Instead of weighing endless pros and cons, you have a filter: Does this opportunity align with why I'm here? Does this relationship support my deeper contribution? Does this use of my time express what I'm meant to express? Purpose doesn't make decisions for you, but it makes deciding easier.

Without purpose, you're reactive. You respond to whatever shows up—the opportunity that lands in your lap, the demand that screams loudest, the path of least resistance. You say yes to things that don't fit because you don't have a clear sense of what fits.

With purpose, you're directive. You choose from a center. You organize your life around what matters most. You can say no to good things because you're saving your yes for the right things.

Purpose gives coherence to the random events of your life. Looking backward, you can see how experiences that seemed disconnected were actually preparation. Looking forward, you can sense which possibilities are invitations and which are distractions. Purpose transforms "things that happened to me" into "chapters in a meaningful story."

Purpose doesn't eliminate difficulty. You'll still face challenges, setbacks, and pain. But purpose gives difficulty meaning. Suffering without meaning breaks us. Suffering in the service of purpose transforms us. The hard things become part of the path rather than obstacles to the path.

Think of purpose as a North Star—not a rigid set of rules that dictates your every move, but a consistent point of orientation that helps you navigate when the terrain gets confusing. You can take many routes, encounter many conditions, and still be heading in the right direction.

How Purpose Shows Up in the Dimensions

Purpose isn't just a mental concept. It expresses through every dimension of your being—and paying attention to each dimension reveals clues.

Biologically, purpose shows up in what gives you energy versus what drains you. Your body knows when you're aligned—there's a vitality, an aliveness that no amount of caffeine can replicate. And it knows when you're out of alignment—there's a fatigue that rest doesn't fix, because it's not physical tiredness but soul-weariness. Pay attention to what makes your body feel alive. That's the purpose speaking through your cells.

Neurologically, purpose shows up in what naturally captures your attention, without effort. Your brain lights up around certain topics, problems, and possibilities. You find yourself reading about, thinking about, and being drawn to certain things. Flow states—those experiences where time disappears, and you're fully absorbed in what you're doing—are neurological signatures of purpose. What were you doing the last time you lost track of time? There's a clue there.

Psychologically, purpose appears meaningful rather than empty. Some achievements leave you full; others leave you hollow even when you succeed. The hollowness isn't ingratitude—it's your psyche telling you that what you achieved wasn't aligned with why you're here. Meaning isn't added to life from outside; it arises from inside when you're living your purpose.

Culturally, purpose shows up—or gets buried—in the messages you received about what you should do with your life. Culture hands you scripts about what success looks like, what a good life involves, and what's worth pursuing. Some of those scripts may align with your actual purpose. Many don't. Part of finding purpose is distinguishing your calling from culture's expectations—hearing your own voice beneath the noise of what everyone says you should want.

Relationally, purpose shows up in how you naturally contribute in relationships. Are you the one who listens? Who organizes? Who brings humor? Who asks the hard questions? Who creates beauty? Who holds space? Your relational gifts point to your purpose. And purpose finds its fullest expression in contribution to others—not in isolation but in connection.

Spiritually, purpose connects you to something larger than yourself. It's your unique way of participating in the unfolding of life. Purpose gives you a role in the cosmic story—not as ego-inflation but as sacred responsibility. You're here for a reason, and that reason connects to the whole. Your purpose isn't just about you; it's about what flows through you to the world.

The Breadcrumbs That Point to Purpose

The same breadcrumbs that led you home point to your purpose. They've been there all along—you just didn't know what you were looking at.

What makes you come alive—not what you're good at, not what pays well, not what earns approval, but what lights you up from inside. This is purpose knocking. When you feel fully engaged, fully present, fully yourself—that's alignment with purpose.

The quiet longings—the desires that don't go away, no matter how much you achieve, no matter how thoroughly you try to ignore them. These persistent whispers point to unmet purpose, to something that's asking to be expressed through you.

The inexplicable tears—when you're moved by someone else living their purpose, when a movie or a story touches something deep, your own purpose resonates. What moves you reveals what you're meant to move toward.

The recurring themes—what shows up again and again in your interests, your conversations, your concerns. What do you keep coming back to? What problems do you keep wanting to solve? What topics do you never tire of? Patterns across time are purposely trying to get your attention.

The childhood dreams—before culture told you what was practical, before you learned what was realistic, what did you want to be? Not necessarily the specific job, but the quality of being. The child who wanted to be a firefighter might have been expressing a purpose to protect, to rush toward danger when others run away, and to help. The dream evolves; the essence often remains.

What you do naturally that others find remarkable—your gifts are so natural to you that you assume everyone has them. They don't. Your ease is someone else's struggle. What comes effortlessly to you, the thing you do without thinking that others notice and appreciate—that ease points to purpose.

Purpose Hidden in Your Life Stories

Your life stories aren't random. They're data.

In Chapter 8, you explored how patterns and stories shape your life. Now we look at those same stories differently—not as evidence of your conditioning, but as clues to your purpose.

The themes that run across your life experiences point to what you're here to learn, to heal, and to contribute. Your biography contains your purpose—encoded in the narrative, waiting to be read.

Look for the thread. What connects your most meaningful experiences? What were you doing in those moments when you felt most fully yourself? Who were you being? What impact were you having? The thread that connects your peak moments often reveals purpose.

Look for the pattern. What challenges keep showing up in your life? What have you had to learn again and again? What themes recur across different relationships, different jobs, different phases? Often our greatest wounds become our greatest gifts—our purpose is shaped by what we've had to overcome.

Look for the moments. When did you feel most fully yourself? Most alive? Most aligned? Those moments aren't accidents. They're purpose expressing. They're you living what you're meant to live, even if you didn't have words for it at the time.

The story of your life, when viewed with the right eyes, reveals the purpose running through it. Not imposed from outside, but emerging from within. Not a destiny that was forced on you, but an essence that was always trying to express.

The Wound That Becomes the Gift

There's a mysterious relationship between our deepest wounds and our highest purpose.

Often, what we give to the world is precisely what we had to learn to give ourselves. The medicine we needed becomes the medicine we offer.

The person who lacks unconditional love becomes the one who offers it—because they know what it's like to live without it, they can recognize when others are starving for it.

The person who felt unseen becomes the one who truly sees others—because they know the pain of invisibility, they offer the gift of being witnessed.

The person who struggled to find their voice becomes the advocate—because they know the cost of silence, they speak for those who can't yet speak for themselves.

The person who had to find their own way home becomes the guide—because they know what it's like to be lost, they can help others find the path.

This isn't about glorifying suffering. It's not suggesting that pain is good or necessary. But it is recognizing that nothing is wasted. Your pain, when processed and integrated, becomes medicine for others. Your struggle, when you've come through it, becomes a map for those still struggling.

The breadcrumbs that led you home can become the breadcrumbs you leave for others. What you had to learn becomes what you can teach. What you had to heal becomes what you can help others heal.

A client I'll call Caroline had spent most of her adult life managing what she called "the sensitivity problem." She cried easily. She picked up on emotional undercurrents in rooms before anyone else noticed them. She felt things — other people's things — as if they were her own. She'd spent thirty years treating this as a defect. Therapy, strategies, mantras about being stronger. A long, earnest effort to become less of what she was.

She came to coaching because she was burning out in a job that required her to stay detached.

Several sessions in, I asked her to describe the moments in her career when she felt most useful — most herself.

She thought for a while. "When I'm in the room with someone who's falling apart," she said slowly, "and I don't panic. I just — stay. I can feel what they're feeling, and I don't go under. Something in me knows it's survivable."

I asked where she thought that came from.

Another pause. Longer. "I grew up in that room," she said finally. "My mother. The unpredictability. I learned to read everything. I learned to stay steady when the weather was bad." She stopped. "I thought that was damage."

"What if it were training?"

She was quiet for a long time. And then something shifted in her face — not dramatic, just a settling. The settling that happens when something that has always been true finally gets spoken out loud.

The sensitivity she had been trying to correct for thirty years was the very thing that made her extraordinary. She didn't need to become less of it. She needed to stop apologizing for it and point it in a specific direction.

Your wounds don't disqualify you from your purpose. Often, they qualify you. They give you credibility, compassion, and capacity that you couldn't have gained any other way.

Purpose Isn't Always Grand

We've been sold a mythology of purpose as grand, dramatic, world changing. Purpose means founding a movement, curing a disease, or leading a revolution. Purpose means your name in lights, your biography written, your impact measurable and massive.

This mythology leaves most people feeling inadequate. If purpose has to be grand, then my ordinary life couldn't possibly be purposeful. If purpose requires changing the world, then I must not have a real purpose.

But most purpose is expressed quietly, daily, in the ordinary moments that no one applauds.

The purpose of the mother who raises conscious children with love and intention is to shape human beings who, in turn, will shape other human beings across generations.

The purpose of the craftsman who makes beautiful things with care—bringing more quality, more attention, more presence into a world of mass production and carelessness.

The purpose of the friend who shows up consistently when it matters—offering presence, listening, bearing witness to another's life.

The purpose of the worker who brings integrity to whatever they do—doing the right thing even when no one is watching, raising the standard just by showing up.

Not everyone will be Martin Luther King Jr. or Mother Teresa. Not everyone needs to be. The world doesn't only need dramatic revolutionaries. It needs ordinary people living with intention, bringing their full selves to their daily lives, expressing their purpose in a thousand small ways that ripple outward invisibly but powerfully.

Your purpose might be expressed in how you interact with the person at the checkout counter. In the attention you bring to your work. In the quality of presence, you offer your children. In the way you treat people who can do nothing for you.

A grand purpose is not better than a quiet purpose. It's just louder. The question isn't whether your purpose is big enough. The question is whether you're living it.

Your Wholeness Ripples Outward

Here's what changes when you live from purpose: it affects far more than just you.

Wholeness is contagious. When you live from your integrated self and express your purpose authentically, you give others permission to do the same. You become evidence that it's possible. You become a model of what living from home looks like.

Your healing heals others—not because you fix them, not because you tell them what to do, but because you show them what's possible. A person who has come home and is living their purpose shifts the energy of every room they enter. They don't have to say anything. Their presence says it.

This is the collective witness. Just as you needed witnesses on your journey home—people who saw you, believed in you, held space for your becoming—you become a witness for others on their journeys. You don't have to teach, coach, or preach. You just have to BE who you've become.

One person coming home helps others find their way. One person living their purpose gives others courage to seek their own. One person telling the truth makes it safer for others to tell theirs.

This is the ripple effect. It's not dramatic. You probably won't see most of it. But it's real. The life you live echoes outward in ways you'll never trace. The impact you have extends far beyond what you'll ever measure.

Your journey was never just about you. It was always about what would flow through you once you found your way home.

Legacy: What You Leave by Who You Become

Legacy isn't what you leave when you die. It's what you leave in every interaction while you live.

Every person you meet is changed, however subtly, by encountering you. They walk away with something—an impression, a feeling, an experience of having been in your presence. What is that something?

When you live from purpose, your legacy takes care of itself. You don't have to strategize about significance or manufacture meaning. You just have to be fully yourself, fully present, fully expressed. The impact flows naturally.

Legacy is created daily through the accumulation of moments when you showed up as yourself. In the countless small interactions where you were present or absent, kind or distracted, real or performing. These moments compound. They create a life. They leave a mark.

What imprint are you leaving? What do people experience when they're with you? What do they walk away with after encountering you? These questions aren't about ego or impression management. They're about alignment. When you're living your purpose, the imprint takes care of itself.

A life lived with purpose leaves an impact that continues long after you're gone. Not necessarily in monuments or achievements—though it might include those. But certainly, in the people whose lives you touched, who then touch others, who then touch others still.

You are a link in a chain that extends backward to those who shaped you and forward to those you will shape. Your purpose is not just about your life. It's about what flows through your life into lives you'll never know.

Living Your Purpose

Purpose isn't a destination you arrive at. It's a way you travel.

You don't "find" your purpose once and then have it forever, like a certificate you can frame and hang on the wall. You discover it, live it, refine it, and deepen it across your lifetime. Purpose evolves as you evolve. It expresses differently in different seasons.

Some people live the same purpose through many different expressions. Their purpose remains constant while its vehicle changes—different careers, different relationships, different life stages, all expressing the same underlying through-line.

Others discover that purpose itself evolves as they evolve. What they were here for in their twenties deepens and transforms by their fifties. The essence remains, but the expression matures.

The key isn't having your purpose perfectly defined. The key is alignment—living in a way that expresses why you're here, as best you understand it. Every choice is an opportunity to express purpose or to abandon it. Every day is a chance to live what you're here to live.

You don't need to know your purpose with certainty before you start living it. Clarity comes through action, not just reflection. You discover purpose by paying attention to what makes you come alive, then doing more of it. By noticing what feels meaningful, then orienting toward it. By following the breadcrumbs one at a time.

The path to purpose is the path you've been walking all along. You just see it differently now.

The Purpose

Your Mind Map layer for this chapter is "The Purpose." Not THE purpose—as if there's one right answer that you either get or miss. But YOUR purpose, as you understand it now.

It may be a single word: Healing. Connection. Beauty. Truth. Justice. Service. Creation.

It may be a phrase: Helping others find their voice. Bringing order to chaos. Creating beauty that awakens. Holding space for transformation.

It may be a quality of being: I'm here to love fiercely. I'm here to see what others miss. I'm here to ask the questions no one wants to ask.

It doesn't have to be final. It doesn't have to be perfect. It just has to be true for now, as best you can sense it.

What do you know about why you're here?

What do the breadcrumbs point toward?

What is asking to be expressed through you?

This is sacred territory. Approach it with reverence. But also, with trust—you've been preparing for this question your whole life. Every experience, every struggle, every joy, every loss has been preparation. You know more than you think you do.

Your purpose is encoded in your life. And now you can read it.

Pause and Reflect

Before moving to the next chapter, take a moment to sit with these questions. Let them work on you.

If you knew you were "put here for a reason" but no one told you what it was, how would you discover it? What clues have been there all along?

What makes you come alive—not what you're good at or what pays well, but what lights you up from inside?

What themes run across your most meaningful life experiences? What connects your peak moments?

How might your deepest wound be connected to your highest purpose? What have you had to learn that you could now offer to others?

If your purpose isn't grand or dramatic, where might it be expressed quietly, daily, in ordinary moments?

What do you know right now about why you're here? What words or phrases come closest to naming it?

The Breadcrumb

Each chapter closes with a single breadcrumb—a key insight to carry forward on your journey.

You were told there was a plan for your life, but no one gave you the manual. The truth is, the manual exists—it's written in your breadcrumbs. Your purpose has been expressed through you your entire life; you just didn't know how to read the language. Purpose isn't a job title or a single grand mission. It's a through-line—a consistent quality of being and contribution that runs through all you do. When you know your purpose, it becomes an organizing principle: decisions become clearer, difficulty gains meaning, and random events reveal themselves as chapters in a coherent story. Purpose shows up in every dimension: in what gives your body energy, in what captures your attention, in what feels meaningful, in how you naturally contribute to others, and in how you connect to something larger than yourself. The breadcrumbs that led you home are the same breadcrumbs that point to your purpose: what makes you come alive, the quiet longings, the inexplicable tears, the recurring themes, the childhood dreams, the gifts you don't even recognize as gifts. Often, your deepest wound becomes your greatest offering—what you had to learn to give yourself becomes what you can give to others. Purpose doesn't have to be grand to be real. Most purpose is expressed quietly, daily, in ordinary moments of presence and contribution. And when you live your purpose, it ripples outward. Your wholeness gives others permission to seek their own. Your healing becomes medicine. Your journey home becomes a trail others can follow. Legacy isn't what you leave when you die—it's what you leave in every moment you live from your integrated self. You are here for a reason. The reason is encoded in your life. And now you can read it.

Going Deeper: Your Digital Companion

The questions above are meant to stir something in you—to begin the inner conversation. But real integration happens when you take time to explore your responses more fully.

In your digital companion, you'll find the following exercises for Chapter 17:

Purpose Breadcrumbs Inventory — Gathering the clues: what makes you come alive, quiet longings, inexplicable tears, recurring themes, childhood dreams, natural gifts

Life Story Themes — Mapping the threads that run across your most meaningful experiences to reveal purpose patterns

The Wound and the Gift — Exploring how your deepest challenges connect to your highest contribution

Purpose Across Dimensions — How purpose is expressed in each of the six dimensions of your life

Living Purpose Daily — Identifying small, practical ways to express purpose in ordinary moments

The Ripple Effect — Considering how your wholeness and purpose contribute to others

Mindset Mind Map Update: The Purpose — Articulating your sense of purpose as you understand it now

---

With purpose discovered and beginning to be lived, you might think the journey is complete. You've come home. You're living from home. You've found your purpose. What more could there be? But home isn't a destination—it's a way of traveling. And the journey doesn't end; it transforms. In the final chapter, we'll explore what it means to continue this journey for the rest of your life. You will wander again—that's not failure, it's being human. The breadcrumbs never stop. You'll learn to become your own witness, to leave breadcrumbs for your future self, and to trust that the path home is always available, no matter how far you wander. The journey continues.

Chapter Eighteen

The Journey Continues

WHEN will you ever learn...that learning never ends?

"You can never go home again, but the truth is you can never leave home, so it's all right." — Maya Angelou

"What you seek is seeking you." — Rumi

You've arrived. And yet... your heart knows the journey isn't over.

This isn't a contradiction. It's the nature of being human.

Coming home wasn't the end. It was the start of a new life. The trail doesn't end—it transforms. What was sought becomes deepened. The path to home becomes the path from home, taking your wholeness into the world.

This final chapter isn't a conclusion. It's a commencement. A sending forth. The closing of one book and the opening of the rest of your life.

Bookending the Journey: From Hiraeth to Home

Remember where we began?

Hiraeth. That Welsh word for homesickness for a place you've never been—or perhaps, for who you've always been beneath it all. A longing that couldn't quite be named. A sense that, despite everything you'd achieved, something essential was missing.

You picked up this book because something was calling. A quiet dissonance beneath the surface of your life. A whisper wondering if this was really all there was. You were successful, perhaps. You'd checked the boxes, met the expectations, built something that looked—from the outside—like a life worth envying. And yet.

You weren't broken. You were fragmented. And you'd been leaving breadcrumbs all along.

Now look at where you are.

In Part One, you realized you were in the woods. You heard the call, recognized the fragmentation, and saw the iceberg beneath your life. You understood that you came in whole, and the world taught you to fragment.

In Part Two, you learned to see the breadcrumbs. You developed your witness—that observing presence that can see without being consumed. You recognized the signals from your authentic self, understood how your filters shaped what you could perceive.

In Part Three, you mapped the territory. You met your cast of characters—the protectors, the performers, the parts that developed to keep you safe. You traced your stories and patterns, encountered your resistance, and explored your hiding places.

In Part Four, you followed the trail. You learned to rewrite your Life Code, discovered the power of choice, moved through fear without waiting for it to disappear, and released the fallacy of perfection.

In Part Five, you came home. You recognized yourself. You welcomed back the exiled parts. You discovered what it means to live from home, to express your purpose, to let your wholeness ripple outward.

The longing that brought you here—hiraeth—has been fulfilled. But fulfillment, it turns out, is not the same as completion. Because the journey continues.

Home Isn't a Destination—It's a Way of Traveling

Here's what the journey has taught you that nothing else could: home isn't somewhere you arrive and stay forever.

Home is a way of traveling. An orientation. A relationship with yourself that you carry wherever you go.

You can be at home in chaos, when everything falls apart, or while facing the unknown. Home isn't about external circumstances, but internal alignment: being in right relationship with yourself—connected to your wholeness, anchored in your witness, aware of your patterns, living from your authentic self.

This is the great gift of the journey: you now know how to find your way back. The path isn't mysterious anymore. You've walked it. You know the landmarks. You recognize the breadcrumbs. You've done this before, and you can do it again.

Home is portable now. It goes with you. Not as a destination you might lose, but as an orientation you carry with you. Not as a place you could be exiled from, but as a way of being that remains available no matter where life takes you.

When You Wander Again (And You Will)

Let me tell you something important: you will wander again.

Not because you failed. Not because you didn't do the work. Not because this journey wasn't real or didn't transform something fundamental in you.

You will wander again because you are human. Because life is dynamic. Because growth happens in cycles, not straight lines. Because the universe has a way of presenting new challenges precisely calibrated to wherever you are.

New challenges will arise that you can't currently imagine. Old patterns will resurface when you least expect them—often in new disguises that take time to recognize. Circumstances will shift and shake what felt solid. Loss will visit. Change will demand adaptation. Life will do what life does.

This isn't a failure. This is the nature of being alive.

The difference now is this: when you wander, you'll know you're wandering. The witness you developed won't disappear just because you forget to use it. You'll catch yourself sooner. You'll recognize the signs—the familiar tightness, the return of old characters, the patterns you thought you'd outgrown making an unexpected appearance.

And you'll know the way back. Not because someone tells you, but because you've walked it yourself. The breadcrumbs are yours. The path is familiar. The skills are embodied.

Three years after finishing a coaching engagement, a client I'll call Helen called me. She'd moved across the country for a relationship that had since ended, taken a job she'd thought would be the answer, and found herself, two years in, sitting in an unfamiliar city feeling lost in a way that felt very old.

"I thought I'd gone backward," she said. "All that work, and here I am again."

I asked her to describe "here."

She thought about it. "Disconnected. Going through the motions. Not sure what I want."

I asked her how long she'd been feeling this way before she called.

"About three weeks."

Three weeks. Last time, before this work, she'd stayed there nearly three years before she could name it.

She caught it in three weeks. She knew what it was. She called it by its right name. She knew, on some level, what had caused it and what direction home was. She didn't need to start over — she needed to return. And the path was familiar because she'd walked it before.

"You didn't go backward," I told her. "You wandered. There's a difference."

She was quiet. Then: "I know how to get back now, don't I?"

It wasn't a question. She already knew the answer. The witness was still there. The breadcrumbs were still readable. Home hadn't moved. She'd just stepped away from it for a bit — and this time, she'd noticed.

That's what the work does. It doesn't stop the wandering. It changes how wandering happens—and how returning feels.

Wandering is part of the journey. Returning is the practice. And every return deepens your relationship with home.

Becoming Your Own Witness for Life

In Chapter 4, you met the witness—that observing presence within you that can watch your experience without being consumed by it. That capacity to step back, to notice, to see patterns while they're happening rather than only in hindsight.

That witness doesn't retire now that the book is ending. That witness is yours for life.

You are now your own witness. Your own coach. Your own guide. This was always the goal—not to make you dependent on a book, a program, an expert, but to awaken the capacity that was always within you. The answers were never outside you. The wisdom was never somewhere else. It was here all along, waiting for you to develop the eyes to see it.

You can observe your patterns without judgment now. You can notice when you've slipped into old code. You can ask yourself the questions that matter: *What's really going on here? What am I avoiding? What is this breadcrumb trying to show me? What would the witness say about this?*

The human witness—someone who sees you, a coach, a trusted friend, a community—will always be valuable. We are relational beings. We need each other. But you are no longer waiting to be witnessed to feel real. You no longer need external validation to trust what you know. You can witness yourself.

And when you witness yourself with compassion, seeing clearly without condemning, noticing without judging, you become the home you were seeking.

The Breadcrumbs Never Stop

Here's something beautiful: the breadcrumbs don't stop just because you've come home.

Your authentic self keeps leaving signals. Keeps pointing. Keeps inviting you deeper.

There are layers you haven't touched yet. Dimensions you haven't fully explored. Depths you can't yet imagine. The journey home was real and complete—and it was also just the beginning. Like peeling an onion, each layer reveals another. Like climbing a mountain, each summit reveals higher peaks.

The breadcrumbs that led you home will now lead you further—into greater expression of who you are, into deeper understanding of your purpose, into expanded capacity to contribute what only you can contribute.

What made you come alive at the beginning of this journey may evolve. The longings that called you here may transform into new longings. The purpose you've glimpsed may deepen and mature. New callings will whisper. New invitations will appear.

Pay attention. The same skills you used to find your way home are the skills you'll use to keep growing for the rest of your life. The witness watches. The breadcrumbs appear. The authentic self signals.

The trail continues. The breadcrumbs never stop. The journey deepens.

Life as School—We Learn Until We Move On

There's an ancient idea, found in wisdom traditions across the world: life is a school. We're here to learn.

Not to accumulate credentials or check boxes. Not to prove ourselves or earn approval. But to grow in consciousness, in love, in wisdom, in capacity to contribute. Every experience is a curriculum. Every challenge is a lesson. Every relationship is a teacher wearing a human face.

The curriculum is your life. The specific, particular, unrepeatable life that is yours. No one else is enrolled in exactly your course. No one else is learning exactly your lessons. The challenges that show up for you are precisely the ones you need—even when, especially when, they're not the ones you would have chosen.

You've been learning all along, whether or not you knew it. Every struggle contained a teaching. Every failure offered growth. Every heartbreak cracked you open to something you couldn't have received any other way.

And here's what this journey has shown you: you can learn consciously now. You don't have to wait for life to force growth upon you. You don't have to be broken open against your will. You can choose to grow. You can seek the lessons. You can welcome the curriculum.

We learn until we move on. Not just until retirement, until comfort, until we've "arrived" at some imagined finish line. We learn as long as we're breathing. The moment you stop learning, you stop living—even if your heart is still beating.

Stay curious. Stay humble. Stay teachable. The best students of life know that every day offers new lessons, no matter how much they've already learned. The wisest among us are the most willing to admit what they don't know.

The Dimensions Await—Deeper Territory to Explore

Throughout this journey, we've touched on six dimensions of your being: biological, neurological, psychological, cultural, relational, and spiritual.

We've explored how your Life Code operates across all of them. How breadcrumbs show up in each. How coming home means integration across all dimensions. We've mapped the territory, identified the patterns, and understood the framework.

But here's what I want you to know: each of these dimensions contains worlds unto itself. We've mapped the territory, yes—but there are depths we've only glimpsed.

The biological dimension alone—the wisdom of the body, the nervous system's intelligence, the cellular memory, the somatic expression of everything you've experienced—could be a lifetime's exploration. What would it mean to truly live in partnership with your body? To decode its signals with fluency? To heal at the level of the cells?

The neurological dimension—rewiring patterns, understanding the brain's remarkable plasticity, mastering the relationship between thought and experience—opens endless doors. What would full neurological freedom look like? What patterns still run that you haven't yet seen?

The psychological dimension—the inner characters, the shadow work, the continuing integration of all you are—never truly completes. There are always deeper layers to meet, to understand, to welcome home.

The cultural dimension—examining the codes you inherited, consciously choosing your values, and creating culture rather than just consuming it—is ongoing work. How do you want to participate in the collective story? What do you want to contribute to the culture that will shape those who come after you?

The relational dimension—deepening intimacy, transforming how you connect, healing generational patterns, showing up whole in your relationships—has infinite depth. What would your relationships look like if you brought even more of your authentic self to them?

The spiritual dimension—your connection to something larger, your sense of meaning and purpose, your place in the cosmic story—expands forever. The mystery deepens the more you explore it.

This book has given you the foundation. The framework. The core skills. But the exploration is just beginning. Consider this an invitation: wherever your curiosity calls you, go deeper. There is more to discover. There is always more.

The Book of Me—Never Finished

You've been building something throughout this journey: your Mind Map, your trail markers, your reflections and insights, your Book of Me.

That book isn't finished. It can't be. Because you aren't finished.

The Book of Me is a living document. You'll return to it. Add to it. Revise it as you grow. What you've written is the first edition. There will be more.

As you change, your understanding of your past will change. Experiences that seemed random will reveal their purpose. Patterns you couldn't see will become visible. The story you tell about yourself will deepen and mature.

As you grow, new territory will open. You'll discover aspects of yourself you didn't know existed. You'll integrate parts you haven't yet met. The map will expand because you will expand.

Keep your Book of Me close. Return to it in times of wandering. Let it remind you of what you've learned, of what you've discovered, who you really are beneath the forgetting.

And keep writing. The story isn't over. It's being written with every choice you make, every day you live, every moment you choose to show up as yourself.

What You Now Carry

As you close this book, you carry something you didn't have when you opened it.

You carry the knowledge that you were never broken—only fragmented, only wandered away from yourself. The wholeness was always there, waiting. You didn't have to become someone new. You had to remember who you always were.

You carry the ability to recognize your own breadcrumbs—those signals from your authentic self that point the way home. The unexpected tears, the quiet longings, the inexplicable joys, the recurring dreams. You know what they mean now. You know how to read them.

You carry a witness—an observing presence that can see your patterns, your stories, your characters without being consumed by them. A capacity to step back, to notice, to choose.

You carry a new relationship with your Life Code—knowing it can be examined, understood, and rewritten. You are no longer a prisoner of programming you didn't choose. You are the programmer now.

You carry the understanding that choice is always available—that between stimulus and response, there is a gap, and in that gap lies your freedom. You can choose. You can always choose.

You carry the permission to be imperfect—to learn through mistakes, to grow through falling, to be gloriously, messily human. Perfection was never the goal. Wholeness was. And wholeness includes everything.

You carry your purpose—or at least the breadcrumbs that point toward it, the through-line you're beginning to live. You know why you're here, even if that knowing continues to deepen.

You carry home—not as a destination but as an orientation, a way of being, a portable wholeness that goes with you wherever you go.

These are yours now. No one can take them from you. They are part of you—integrated, embodied, alive.

A Blessing for the Continuing Journey

And so we come to the end that isn't an end.

You came here searching. You leave here found—and still searching, because that's what it means to be alive.

You came here fragmented. You leave here whole—and still integrating, because wholeness isn't a finish line but an ongoing practice.

You came here longing. You leave your home—and still journeying, because home is a way of traveling.

May you trust the breadcrumbs, especially when the path is unclear.

May you be gentle with yourself when you wander, knowing the way back is always available.

May you witness yourself with the compassion you would offer your dearest friend.

May you live your purpose boldly, knowing that quiet purpose is no less significant than loud.

May you remember that you are learning until your last breath—and that every lesson is a gift, even the hard ones.

May you know, in your bones, that you were never broken. You were always whole. You just forgot for a while.

And may you leave breadcrumbs for others—not by teaching them what to do, but by being fully yourself, fully home, fully alive. Your wholeness gives others permission. Your journey lights the way.

The journey continues.

Welcome home. And godspeed.

The Ongoing Trail

Your Mind Map layer for this chapter is "The Ongoing Trail." This is where you leave breadcrumbs for your future self.

Someday, maybe soon, maybe years from now—you will need reminding. You will have wandered and forgotten what you know. You will be lost in the woods again, wondering how you got there.

What do you want to remember when that day comes?

What have you learned that you never want to forget?

What reminders would help you find your way back?

Write them down. This is your gift to the you who will need them someday.

Leave breadcrumbs for your future self. Truths you've discovered. Reminders of what works. Messages of compassion for the person who will have forgotten.

Because you will need them. And when you do, they'll be there—breadcrumbs you left for yourself, waiting to guide you home again.

The trail continues. And now you're leaving markers for the journey ahead.

Pause and Reflect

One final time, take a moment to sit with these questions. Let them work on you.

As you look back on this journey, what has shifted in you? What do you understand now that you didn't when you began?

When you imagine wandering again in the future, what will help you recognize it? What will help you return?

What breadcrumbs would you leave for your future self—reminders for the moments when you forget what you've learned?

Of the six dimensions (biological, neurological, psychological, cultural, relational, spiritual), which calls *you to go deeper? What wants more exploration?*

How will you continue learning for the rest of your life? What does it mean to approach life as a school?

What blessing would you offer yourself as you continue the journey?

The Breadcrumb

Each chapter closes with a single breadcrumb—a key insight to carry forward on your journey. This is the last one. Make it count.

The journey doesn't end—it transforms. You've come home, but home isn't a destination; it's a way of traveling, an orientation you carry wherever you go. You will wander again—not because you failed, but because you're human. The difference now is that you'll recognize it sooner and know the way back. You are your own witness now, your own coach, your own guide. The capacity was always within you; this journey awakened it. The breadcrumbs never stop—your authentic self will keep leaving signals, inviting you deeper into expression, purpose, and contribution. Life is a school, and we learn until we move on. Stay curious, humble, and teachable. The dimensions we've touched contain worlds unto themselves—depths you've only glimpsed, waiting for deeper exploration. Your Book of Me isn't finished; it's a living document that grows as you do. What you carry now—the knowledge of your wholeness, the ability to see breadcrumbs, the witness, the understanding of choice, the permission to be imperfect, your purpose, your portable home—no one can take from you. Leave breadcrumbs for your future self. Leave breadcrumbs for others by being your true self. The journey continues. Welcome home. Namaste.

Going Deeper: Your Digital Companion

The questions above are meant to stir something in you—to complete the inner conversation you've been having throughout this book. Take time to honor them fully.

In your digital companion, you'll find the following exercises for Chapter 18:

The Journey Reflection — Looking back at all five parts of your journey: what you learned, what shifted, what you now carry

Wandering and Returning Plan — Identifying your early warning signs and creating your personal path back home

Breadcrumbs for My Future Self — Writing reminders, truths, and guidance for the moments when you'll forget

Dimensional Depth Exploration — Identifying which dimensions call you to go deeper and creating intentions for continued exploration

The Life as School Curriculum — Reflecting on what life has been teaching you and what lessons are currently in progress

The Blessing — Writing your own blessing for your continuing journey

Mindset Mind Map Completion: The Ongoing Trail — Finalizing your Book of Me, First Edition, and leaving breadcrumbs for future editions

---

Thank you for trusting this journey. Thank you for showing up, chapter after chapter, doing the work, asking the questions, following the breadcrumbs.

This book will be here whenever you need it. Return to any chapter, any question, any breadcrumb. The trail is always available. The path home never closes.

And know this: there is more to explore. The dimensions we've touched here—biological, neurological, psychological, cultural, relational, spiritual—each contains depths we've only begun to map. Future explorations await. The journey continues in ways neither of us can yet imagine.

For now, carry what you've learned. Live what you've discovered. Be who you've remembered yourself to be.

The book ends here. The journey doesn't. I'll see you on the trail.

Chapter Nineteen

The Author and Resources

Continuing the Journey

About the Author

Wanda Taylor is a professional coach with forty years of experience walking alongside people who are successful on the outside and lost on the inside. She was designated as a Master Certified Coach (MCC) from the International Coaching Federation in 2004 — and is a National Board Certified Health and Wellness Coach (NBC-HWC) with advanced training from Duke University Health. Her certifications span life, executive, corporate, and health and wellness coaching, as well as hypnosis.

Wanda is the founder and CEO of Bay Centre Coaching Group LLC, a multidisciplinary coaching practice she established in 2004. She previously co-founded Bay Centre Inc., a school psychology and mental health practice, which she co-led for thirty-five years.

Breadcrumbs: Finding Your Way Home is her legacy work.

She lives and practices in Pensacola, Florida.

Connect with Wanda and the Breadcrumbs community at:

SKOOL: breadcrumbs.community: https://www.skool.com/breadcrumbs/about

Resources and Continuing the Journey

The work you've done in these pages is real. And it doesn't have to end here.

The Digital Companion

Each chapter of this book references the Digital Companion — a private, self-paced platform that holds all 167 exercises, 131 journaling prompts, and 117 downloadable tools from the Breadcrumbs journey, organized chapter by chapter.

The Digital Companion is hosted on Journal Engine, a platform chosen specifically for its privacy options. Your reflections are yours alone — you control who sees them. You can keep your journal entirely private, share selected entries with a personal coach, or open them to the Breadcrumbs community. Even I cannot see what you write if you choose to keep your entries private. This is your space.

Your purchase of this book includes **one full year of free access** to the Digital Companion.

Access your Digital Companion at:

https://journalengineportal.com/login

The Breadcrumbs Community

The Breadcrumbs community lives at SKOOL:breadcrumbs.community -- a gathering place for fellow trail walkers to share, support, and witness each other's journeys. A free membership gives you full access to the community space.

For those who want to go deeper, premium membership includes access to the full Breadcrumbs courses -- video teachings, audio Trail Talks, and bonus exercises that walk alongside the book chapter by chapter. Premium members also enjoy ongoing access to the Digital Companion for as long as their membership is active, plus special events, new resources, and an intimate community of people doing the real work of coming home to themselves.

The course and premium membership are never required. The book is complete in itself. But if you feel the pull toward more — trust it. That's a breadcrumb.

Join us at: SKOOL: https://www.skool.com/breadcrumbs/about

Personal Coaching

For those who want a guide for the journey, one-on-one and group coaching options are available through Bay Centre Coaching Group LLC. Details and booking information can be found at www.baycentrecoachinggroup.com or www.breadcrumbspublishing.com

The trail doesn't end here. It simply continues.

www.ingramcontent.com/pod-product-compliance
Lightning Source LLC
LaVergne TN
LVHW010640110826
845149LV00014B/2898